ABDUCTED

True Stories of Humans Kidnapped by Aliens

Book Titles by Betsey Lewis

The Galactic Knowing
Alaska's Deadly Triangle
Prophecy Now
Signals from Heaven
Lizzie Extraterrestrials Worldwide
Prophecy 2022 and Beyond
Stargates
Extraterrestrial Encounters of The Extraordinary Kind
Star Beings
Déjà vu
Ancient Serpent Gods
Mystic Revelations of Seven
Mystic Revelations of Thirteen
Earth Energy: Return to Ancient Wisdom
Communicating with the Other Side
Angels, Aliens, and Prophecy II

More books by Betsey on Amazon

Spiritual Books for Children
Alexander Phoenix
The Story of Rainbow Eyes
A Worm Named Sherm

ABDUCTED

True Stories of Humans
Kidnapped by Aliens

Betsey Lewis

ABDUCTED: True Stories of Humans Kidnapped by Aliens
Copyright © 2024 Betsey Lewis (Updated May 20, 2024)
ISBN: 979-8878120852

Cover design by Betsey Lewis

ABDUCTED

Dedicated to Dr. Ardy "Sixkiller" Clarke, who courageously traveled the Western U.S., Hawaii, and Central America to interview indigenous people about their strange encounters with Star People. Her information is invaluable in understanding the aliens visiting Earth and their agendas.

TABLE OF CONTENTS

"The universe is a pretty big place. If it's just us, seems like an awful waste of space." Carl Sagan (1934-1996) — Author, Astronomer, Science Communicator

CHAPTER ONE

THE ABDUCTIONS BEGIN

In the past six decades of ufology, an incredible amount of disinformation has been written about unidentified flying objects and abductions by extraterrestrials. Photo-shopped videos have inundated the internet and YouTube, information so contradictory it's impossible to separate fact from fiction anymore. One of the most convincing alien abduction cases, now a classic in the annals of ufology, took place on a lonely New Hampshire Road on September 19, 1961. Betty and Barney Hill, an interracial couple, had been on vacation in Niagara Falls and Montreal, Quebec, Canada, and were on their way home to Lancaster, New Hampshire around 10:30 p.m. when Betty noticed a bright light in the sky that moved below the moon and the planet Jupiter. At first, she believed she was watching a meteor falling, but the light moved upward like a plane. Betty watched as the light moved erratically as it grew bigger and brighter while urging Barney to stop the car for a closer look. Barney stopped at a scenic picnic area just south of Twin Mountains to walk their dog. Worried about possible bears, Barney grabbed a pistol from the trunk of the car. Betty watched the light through binoculars, now an odd-shaped craft flashing multi-colored lights, traveling in front of the moon. It dawned on Betty that she might be watching a flying saucer, especially after her sister had confided she had seen one a year earlier, but Barney believed he was watching a commercial airline. Soon he changed his mind when the craft began descending in their direction. Back in the car, he drove toward a mountainous stretch of road, feeling strange and fearful.

As the Hills drove along the isolated road, they continued to observe the strange sky object. Barney and Betty watched the craft's erratic movements and sensed the thing was playing a game of cat and mouse with them. Suddenly the craft descended rapidly toward them causing Barney to stop in the middle of the highway. The huge craft hovered approximately 100 feet above the Hill's 1957 Chevrolet Bel Air. Barney stepped out of the car carrying his pistol and moved closer to the object. He put the binoculars to his eyes and leapt back in shock; eight to eleven humanoid figures stood in the craft's window staring at him. All of the figures moved back except one that communicated to Barney telepathically, "stay where you are and keep looking."

Red lights on what appeared to be batwings telescoped out from the sides of the craft and a long structure descended from it. Barney tore the binoculars away from his eyes and ran back to his car, terrified, and told Betty, "They're going to capture us!" Next Barney remembered driving away at high speed, telling Betty to look for the object. She rolled down the window and looked up, but saw only darkness above them, even though it was a bright, starry night. Soon they heard beeping and buzzing sounds, which seemed to bounce off the trunk of their car, and at the same time, they felt dazed as if they had entered an altered state of consciousness. Oddly, they had traveled 35 miles south but only had hazy memories of the road. They recalled making a sudden unplanned turn, encountering a roadblock, and observing a fiery orb in the road.

Next, the Hills were home by dawn feeling disoriented. Their watches had stopped working, and Barney noted that the leather straps on his binoculars were torn, although he couldn't recall what happened. Then he noticed his best dress shoes were scuffed on top as if he'd been dragged over the ground. Betty and Barney quickly showered to remove any contamination from the encounter, and Barney felt compelled to exam his genitals and found nothing unusual. They could only recall fragments of their encounter, including the moon-shaped craft sitting on the road. After sleeping from their ordeal, Betty noted her dress was torn at the hem and the zipper and lining were covered in a pinkish powder.

Later, Betty and Barney found shiny, concentric circles on their car trunk that had not been there earlier. Barney, concerned, passed a compass over the circles and found that the needle whirled rapidly, but slowed when they moved it away from the circles.

On September 21, Betty telephoned Pease Air Force Base to report their strange encounter, withholding some of the details for fear of ridicule. The next day Major Paul Henderson telephoned the Hills to learn more details about their unearthly encounter and determined in a report dated September 26 that Betty and Barney had mistaken the object for the planet Jupiter (the report was later changed to "optical condition, inversion" and insufficient data"). The report was forwarded to Project Blue Book, the U.S. Air Force's UFO research project, where Dr. J. Allen Hynek, an astronomer, professor, and ufologist, acted as their scientific advisor until 1969.

Betty wasn't about to let the investigation end with the Air Force's ridiculous explanation for their encounter. She read the book, *Flying Saucers: Top Secret* (1960), by retired Marine Corps Major Donald E. Keyhoe who was Director of the National Investigations Committee on Aerial Phenomena (NICAP), a civilian UFO research group, and wrote to him about their incident in New Hampshire. Keyhoe passed Betty's letter on to Walter N. Webb, a Boston astronomer and NICAP member.

Webb's first meeting with the Hills was on October 21, 1961. During a six-hour interview, the Hills provided Webb with their conscious memories of the incident, but much of their memory was still blocked. Webb stated that "they were telling the truth and the incident probably happened exactly as reported except for some minor uncertainties and technicalities that must be tolerated in any such observations where human judgment is involved (i.e. exact time and length of visibility, apparent sizes of object and occupants, distance and height of the object, etc.)."

Nearly two weeks after the Hills' UFO encounter, Betty began having lucid dreams for five successive nights. They abruptly stopped after the fifth night and never returned, but they were so detailed and real, that she couldn't put them out of her head. She mentioned them to Barney, but he didn't seem interested, so Betty never mentioned the dreams again. By November 1961, Betty was jotting down her nightmarish dreams and the beings who occupied the craft. They were five feet to five feet four inches tall with matching uniforms, military-like caps, black hair, long noses, bluish lips, and ears but had a grayish cast to their skin.

In the dreams, Betty recalled humanoid-looking beings walking up a ramp into a disc-shaped metallic craft. Once inside, Betty and Barney were separated by the beings while Betty protested. Betty said one of the leader-like beings said that if she and Barney were examined together, it would take much longer to conduct the examinations. In the examining room, a new being, "the examiner," spoke to Betty in English, using a calm voice to quiet her fears; however, the examiner's English was difficult at times to understand.

The examiner told Betty that the test would determine the differences between humans and his species. Betty was then put through a thorough medical examination, which included scrapings from her leg and fingernail trimmings. These tests seemed benign until a long needle was inserted into Betty's navel, causing her excruciating pain. She later felt the test was to determine if she was pregnant. The leader noted Betty's pain and waved his hand over her eyes and the pain vanished instantly. After the testing from the examiner, Betty had a conversation with the leader about a strange book covered in rows of symbols which he said she could take with her. Curious, Betty asked the leader where he was from, and he proceeded to pull down an instructional map dotted with stars. The leader then asked Betty if she knew where her planet was located on the map, but nothing on the map looked familiar to her. The leader then said, "If you don't know where you are, how can I tell you where I'm from."

In another dream of Betty's, the beings escorted her and Barney from the ship as the other beings on the ship forbade her to take the book, stating that they did not want her to even remember the experience. But Betty, being obstinate, said they couldn't erase the memories from her mind, that one day she'd recall the whole encounter.

The leader alien told Betty that they could resume their drive home after the craft departed.

On November 25, 1961, the Hills were interviewed by NICAP members. One discovery stood out about the drive home; the drive should have taken about four hours, but instead took seven hours. Betty and Barney had no explanation for the missing time. The Hills couldn't recall the missing time between Indian Head and Ashland, 35 miles, but both Betty and Barney recalled a fiery orb sitting on the ground.

Betsey Lewis

Dr. Benjamin Simon conducted hypnosis sessions from January 4, 1964, through June 6, 1964, regressing Betty and Barney separately, so that they didn't repeat each other's recollections. Barney was hypnotized first and seemed to have extreme anxiety reliving the encounter. Barney said that due to his intense fear, he kept his eyes closed during much of the abduction and examination, but his descriptions were similar to Betty's recollection of the beings from her conscious memory. What stood out about the hypnosis session was Barney's intense fear of their eyes that seemed to pierce into him. He kept saying under hypnosis, "Oh, those eyes. They're there in my brain. All I see are these eyes . . . I'm not even afraid that they're not connected to a body. They're just there. They're just up close to me, pressing against my eyes."

Barney, like Betty, recalled being dragged aboard the disc-shaped craft and separated from Betty. He believed that's how the tops of his shoes were badly scuffed. Next, Barney was taken into a room by three beings and told to lie on a small rectangular exam table as a cup-like device was placed over his genitals. Barney sensed they had extracted semen. The beings then scraped his skin, peered in his ears and mouth, and inserted a tube in his anus. (Author Whitley Strieber also experienced this during his abduction examination). Barney believed they were counting his vertebrae.

Betty's session was similar to her five dreams, however, there were a few differences. Under hypnosis, the beings were different in appearance than her dreams and the technology on the craft was different. Betty supplied more details under hypnosis not covered in her dreams and exhibited considerable emotional pain during her capture and examination. Dr. Simon ended one session early because Betty was crying and in considerable distress. At one point Dr. Simon suggested Betty recall the three-dimensional, holographic star map the leader had shown her and sketch it as best she could. Although Betty recalled many stars on the

14

map, she drew only those that stood out. Her map consisted of twelve prominent stars connected by lines and three lesser ones that formed a distinctive triangle. She said the leader explained the stars were connected by solid lines to form "trade routes," whereas dashed lines were to less-traveled stars.

Oddly, Dr. Simon concluded from the hypnotic session with Betty and Barney Hill that their encounter was pure fantasy even though they both had physical body markings and other strange markings on their car and the scuff marks on the tops of Barney's shoes as if he was dragged. But Barney and Betty disagreed with Dr. Simon's conclusions, believing they had been abducted by extraterrestrials. The Hills went back to their regular lives, discussing their encounter only with friends, family, and a few UFO researchers, but the Hills never sought publicity. By 1966, author John G. Fuller had interviewed the Hills and Dr. Simon and wrote about their encounter in his famous book, *The Interrupted Journey*, which became a huge success and was later made into a television movie starring James Earl Jones as Barney.

That wasn't the end of the Hill story. In 1968, an elementary school teacher and amateur astronomer Marjorie Fish of Ohio, read Fuller's *Interrupted Journey* and was fascinated by Betty's "star map." She wondered if she could find the star system the UFO beings came from, and constructed a 3-dimensional star map, assuming that one of the fifteen stars represents the Earth's sun. Her map consisted of thread and beads, basing stellar distances on those published in the 1969 Gliese Star Catalog. Fish spent hours, days, and several years studying the information and the only fit that seemed plausible was the double star system of Zeta Reticuli. She hypothesized the UFO might have come from a planet orbiting Zeta Reticuli.

Interestingly enough, the distance information needed to match the three stars forming the triangle Betty recalled was not available until the Gliese Catalog came out in 1969.

The Fish map hypothesis was sent to Terence Dickinson, editor of Astronomy Magazine, who did not endorse her conclusions as well as several astronomers. Dr. David Saunders, a statistician who had been on the Condon UFO study, argued the unusual alignment of key sun-like stars in a plane centered around Zeta Reticuli (first described by Fish) was "statistically improbable to have happened by chance from a random group of stars in our immediate neighborhood".

The debate over the Hills' encounter continues to this day.

On February 25, 1969, Barney died of a cerebral hemorrhage, and Betty died of cancer on October 17, 2004. The Hills' inexplicable encounter left us with more questions than answers and is one of the best in ufology history. I, for one, believe the Hills encountered alien beings that night on a lonely New Hampshire Road. Unfortunately, there's no empirical evidence to prove the Hills had a close encounter with aliens, and so we are left to trust our intuitive feelings on the incident and the type of people Betty and Barney Hill appeared to be — unassuming people who never sought publicity.

CHAPTER TWO

TRAVIS WALTON'S ABDUCTION

Travis Walton is another high-profile abduction case that took place in Northern Arizona on November 5, 1975. Walton, a logger, working with a logging crew in the Apache-Sitgreaves National Forest, was returning home to Snowflake with his crew around 6 p.m. that evening when they spotted a strange bright light coming over the hilltop. As they drove closer, they spotted a silvery disc, approximately 8 feet high and 20 feet in diameter, hovering above a clearing. Rogers, the driver of the truck, slowed to a stop, and Travis leapt out and ran toward the disc, according to the story. The other men shouted for Walton to return to the truck, but Travis didn't listen and walked under the craft. At that point, the craft made a loud spinning noise and began to wobble from side to side as Walton walked away, and that's when they said a blue-green beam of light shot out from the craft and hit Travis.

Travis lifted slowly into the air, his arms and legs outstretched caught in the beam of light.

The crew assumed Travis was dead, and drove off quickly, fearing the disc was chasing them. After going down the dirt road nearly a quarter of a mile, Rogers stopped and the crew decided to go back to the site to find Travis. When they returned, the disc and Travis were gone. They searched for him for a half hour and then returned home. Police were called in, and by the morning of November 6, many officials and volunteers were searching the site area where Travis had vanished. After an extensive search by many people, they found no trace of him, and police were beginning to suspect foul play by Travis' crew.

Soon Travis Walton's case spread internationally, and new reporters, ufologists, and the curious began traveling to the little town of Snowflake.

During the Walton case, many baffling statements came out about Travis Walton and his crew, which may or may not have been linked to Travis' sudden disappearance. This only fueled the critics who suspected an elaborate hoax was taking place. One statement that bothered those investigating the case was by Travis's brother, Duane, who claimed he had witnessed a UFO similar to the one seen by the logging crew. He further stated that he and Travis had both decided that if they ever witnessed a UFO again, they'd get as close as possible. Duane even suggested his brother would not be harmed by aliens because "they don't harm people". Travis later stated he never had any "keen" interest in UFOs, but a taped statement from his brother stated to the contrary.

Meanwhile, police officers made repeated visits to the home of Mary Walton Kellett, Travis' mother, who had a small ranch at Bear Creek, 10 miles from Snowflake. Many felt that Mary was acting very nervous and suspicious as if she was "hiding something or someone". Soon Snowflake's town Marshal Sanford Flake (real name) announced the entire event was a prank orchestrated by Duane and Travis. Some of the crew took a polygraph test when questioned if they had any knowledge of harm being done to Travis or if they knew where Travis' body was buried. They all passed the test. However, no one thought to ask if they were involved in a prank.

Five days later on Monday, November 10, Grant Neff, Travis' brother-in-law, received a call at his home in Taylor, Arizona, not far from Snowflake, from a weak voice saying, "This is Travis. I'm at a phone booth at the Heber gas station, and I need help. Come and get me." Neff believed it was a prank caller. But the caller persisted, screaming, "It's me, Grant . . . I'm hurt, and I need help badly. You come and get me." Finally, Grant was convinced that it was Travis, so he and Duane drove to the gas station in Heber, where they found Travis collapsed in a telephone booth. He was wearing the same light clothing as when he'd disappeared, not enough to keep him warm in the frigid temperature of 20 degrees Fahrenheit nighttime temperature. He appeared thinner and facial hair had grown on his face.

On the drive back to Snowflake, Travis acted strange, apparently frightened and shaken by his experience, mumbling about terrifying eyes. Travis believed he'd been missing for a few hours, not days. Duane, Travis' brother, decided not to contact authorities out of concern for his brother's fragile condition. But by not notifying authorities, Duane would face charges with the police that he was an accomplice to Travis' cover-up.

To add to the mystery, the police followed a tip from a telephone company employee that someone had called the Neff family from a pay phone at the Heber gas station. Two deputies were dispatched to the telephone booth to dust for fingerprints, but none of the prints seemed to belong to Travis Walton. This fueled more fire for the skeptics who already believed the entire incident was a prank; while others countered that the fingerprint examination was carried out in the dark with flashlights. Meanwhile, Travis bathed and tried to eat, but couldn't keep any food down.

There seemed to be a series of missteps with Travis' return and subsequent examinations. First, Travis was driven to Phoenix by his brother Duane for a medical examination to meet Dr. Lester Steward, who turned out to be a hypnotherapist, not a medical doctor. According to Steward, Travis spent 2 hours in his office, but Travis and Duane said only 45 minutes, another strange twist to the story. Finally, Travis met with two medical doctors who discovered a small red spot at the crease of Travis' right elbow not near a vein. Also, Travis' urine test revealed a lack of ketones, which was unusual. Because of Travis' loss of weight after five days of having little or no food as he stated, his body should have started breaking down fats to survive, and this should have shown very high levels of ketone in his urine.

During that time ufologist William Spaulding had announced to the media that he and Dr. Steward had questioned Travis for two hours and had uncovered inconsistencies in Travis' account that would "blow this story out". It came out that Travis and a friend's younger brother had committed check fraud a few years earlier by altering payroll checks. This was Travis' only brush with the law, and he received only two years' probation.

Philip Klass was one of Travis' biggest skeptics, investigating the case thoroughly, which was recounted in his 1983 book, *UFOs: The Public Deceived.* Klass discovered that some of Travis' family were obsessed with UFOs and talked often of being abducted before Travis' encounter. Further investigation revealed Travis had watched the television movie, *The UFO Incident,* starring James Earl Jones and Estelle Parsons on the Betty and Barney Hill's UFO abduction case, three weeks before Travis vanished on November 5, 1975. Another revealing element was no one in Walton's family seemed upset about his disappearance, and Duane claimed his younger brother Travis was "simply lost in space". What was Travis' motive if the story was hoaxed? According to Klass, Walton's 27-year-old boss was seriously behind schedule on his logging contract, and the UFO encounter may have provided a way to get out of the contract. It should be noted here that Klass had his own detractors, claiming he'd do anything for publicity.

This is Travis's description of the incident: as his memory returned while on board the UFO, he found himself surrounded by three beings with large bald heads, and enormous brown eyes devoid of the white part of the eye that humans have. They all wore orange jumpsuits while Travis was on a table and in pain, weak, and having trouble breathing, yet he managed to jump to his feet, shout at the creatures, and grab a glass-like cylinder off a shelf. He tried to break it, but the object wouldn't break. The creatures soon left the room.

Some critics find this part of the story questionable. How could Travis find the strength to get off the table and fight the aliens?

Travis left the "exam room" and ventured along a hallway to a spherical room with cupped-shaped chairs. He sat in one of the chairs as lights began to come on and stars projected on a round planetarium ceiling. He pushed a lever and stars rotated around him slowly, and when he released the lever the stars remained stationary. Next, he walked towards a rounded door, searching for another door. He heard a sound and turned to see a tall human figure wearing blue coveralls with a glass-like helmet. He later noted the man's eyes were gold and larger than normal. As they walked, Travis asked questions, but the being didn't answer until he found himself in an aircraft hangar with a similar disc-shaped craft inside, but twice the size. More human-like beings appeared: a woman and two men resembling the first man, but without helmets.

Travis was led to a small table, and once seated on it, the woman placed an oxygen-type mask over his mouth and nose, and he passed out. The next thing he remembered was waking up outside the gas station in Heber, Arizona as the disc-shaped craft hovered over him and then shot off in the sky.

I have never met Travis Walton; however, I did have a brief phone conversation with him at his northern Arizona home in 1993 when I was investigating alien abductions for a screenwriter in Los Angeles. Travis was polite to me but he seemed displeased with the way the aliens were portrayed in the 1993 movie, *Fire in the Sky*, produced by Tracy Torme, actor/singer Mel Torme's son.

The movie was based loosely on Travis' book, depicting the gray aliens as malevolent beings, contrary to Walton's account. Still, much of Travis' story disturbed me. Why didn't anyone in the town of Heber report a massive disc-shaped UFO hovering above the telephone booth the night Walton was deposited there? Surely someone would have reported it to the police, yet no one did. Why didn't the aliens communicate with him in some way? Not even telepathy was used which most abductees report.

In Walton's book, *Fire in the Sky*, he seemed more concerned that people doubted him than in focusing on what occurred during his alien contact. Another element that disturbed me about his case, and please correct me if I'm wrong; Travis never exhibited any physical markings on his body as most abductees receive during an examination, such as a scoop mark, recurring nose bleeds, or the classic implant in their hand, nose or other body parts. Walton did return from his ordeal thinner than he was before the incident, dehydrated, and having facial hair, which meant he was somewhere for five days. Most abductees have been abducted since childhood, but Walton never discloses any such recall, and most abductees are examined and returned after an hour or two.

Since Travis Walton's story became headline news, he has greatly profited from his book, UFO conferences, media interviews, and a movie, unlike Betty and Barney Hill who never sought publicity, or Betty and Bob Luca who seldom gave interviews. It seems the real UFO abductees are reticent about their encounters, fearful of ridicule and loss of their job and reputation, and don't seek self-aggrandizement.

Recently I watched a documentary on Travis Walton's abduction where his logger co-workers were interviewed. During the interview, the co-workers mentioned a man posing as a forest agent appeared with a Geiger counter to measure radiation in the area a couple of days later. One of his friends confronted the "Geiger counter man," who was mentioned in the credits of the movie but was cut from the final production. The man said he only found "background radiation," but when Walton's friend put a hard hat that had been worn during the encounter under the Geiger counter, "it jumped off the scale," Walton said.

All the men in the current interview appeared to be traumatized by the event. Truth or fiction — the verdict is still out.

Betsey Lewis

CHAPTER THREE

WHITLEY STRIEBER'S COMMUNION

On December 26, 1985, at a secluded cabin in upstate New York, novelist Whitley Strieber went skiing with his wife and son, ate Christmas dinner leftovers, and went to bed early. Six hours later, he found himself suddenly awake and forever changed. Thus begins the most astonishing true-life odyssey ever recorded — one man's riveting account of his extraordinary experiences with visitors from "elsewhere".

But Whitley discovered that wasn't the first time he encountered the "Visitors". It began when he was a child. Two years later in 1987, Whitley penned the New York best-selling book, *Communion*, that became a movie in 1989, starring Christopher Walken as Whitley. The movie didn't do as well. After Strieber's story swept the globe, he received hundreds of thousands of letters from readers who had similar encounters, convincing Strieber that we are not alone.

Little did Strieber know his journey into the unknown was far from over. Over the decades, rare interviews under hypnosis detail how beings subjected him to disturbing experiments, recurring encounters, and visions from beyond the grave. A rare video shows a surgeon attempting to remove an *alien device implanted* behind Strieber's ear.

For the first time in nearly 40 years, Strieber agreed to return to the cabin and the stone circle that marks the spot of his first abduction, while investigative journalist Melissa Tittl and UFO researcher Jeff Belanger conduct a paranormal investigation. They wondered if the property was a portal to an alien world, or was there something about Strieber himself that remained a beacon to the visitors? Ultimately, Strieber and the team attempt to crack the mystery that still swirls today. Why are these entities visiting us? Do they come with a warning? And what does this world have to do with the next?

Whitley wrote this: "I am Whitley Strieber, author of the book *Communion*, which detailed my close encounter of the third kind. It happened in December of 1985 and was a complete shock to me. I was not interested in UFOs and had no idea that anything like this could happen. I also had no idea what had happened, except that it was strange and quite difficult. As memories returned, I became more and more concerned about my mental health.

" After weeks of tormenting myself over whether or not I had a brain tumor or was going insane, taking all sorts of medical tests, I was left to conclude that what I remembered from the night of December 26 had really happened. I had been taken to a small, round room, raped using a device that induced an erection, had semen removed from my body, experienced the terror of a needle being pushed into my head, and left badly traumatized and confused. I suppose that animals being tagged in the wild experience similar stress.

"Initially, it didn't occur to me that this was an accurate memory of a real event. I thought it was some sort of hallucination. But the pain from the rape soon caused me to go to the doctor, who told me that I had an injury in the wall of my rectum. In other words, I had been raped.

"I was in no way prepared for this. It still didn't occur to me that what I remembered seeing — beings with huge black eyes and other, smaller ones in dark blue coveralls — could be what was actually there.

"At the time I was a well-known novelist, mostly for the horror-thrillers *Wolfen* and *Hunger*, but also for more serious books like *Warday*, written with co-author James Kunetka, which was a warning about the danger of limited nuclear war.

"My brother had given me a book for Christmas called *Science and the UFOs* by Jenny Randles. I would normally have ignored it, but I was at my wits end about my experience. I had, after all, seen what appeared to be aliens and this book covered the subject. It turned out to contain a description of an experience very like mine, and a reference to a researcher who happened to live a few blocks from me, Budd Hopkins.

"Meeting Budd and some of the close encounter witnesses he knew set me on what has become a lifelong quest to understand this strange experience. Even now, I cannot say for certain that there is a relationship between close encounters and UAPs. As I point out in my new book *Them*, in all the years that the close encounter experience has been reported, there is not one independent witness to the abduction and no reliable video either of the abductors or an abduction in progress.

"What is this really? The short answer is that it is certainly something. It cannot be identified as any known form of mental issue.

"It is not just about abductions, such as the one I experienced. The variety of encounters being reported is astonishing. When people make up stories, they are generally based on other stories. But, judging from the hundreds of thousands of letters I received after publishing Communion, thousands of which my wife Anne collected and cataloged, that is not the case here. (The letters are now housed in the Archives of the Impossible at Rice University in Texas.)

"In *Them*, I analyze 11 of the letters. Most of them involve multiple witness events, and this is common. (But nobody ever seems to have a camera...) They are literally beyond strange. For example, one encounter involves an entire family seeing and trying to communicate with bizarre creatures in the trees around their house. Another involves two different witnesses observing an extraordinary event beside the Grand Central Parkway in Queens that nobody but them appears to have seen. (One of these witnesses was a PhD psychologist who also had what is known as exquisite vision, better than 20/20.)

"This could all be some sort of contact with what we might think of as aliens. But I suspect that it is going to turn out to be far stranger than a conventional story of beings coming from another planet. What form will that take? Will we ever conclusively relate the contact phenomenon to the UAP phenomenon? All interesting and compelling unknowns.

"And that is why I call these entities "visitors" rather than 'aliens.' They come and go, never staying in any contact situation for very long. Aside from trauma and some enigmatic injuries, they leave no evidence behind. They may or may not be aliens. As I have speculated in *A New World* and developed in *Them*, they may even be in some way human.

"Perhaps, hidden in the relationship between us and them, there is an answer to another question: who is this species we call "human" that is so radically different from every other species on Earth, and why do we see the world as we do?

"During this time of increasing evidence that there is somebody else here besides us, presumably with motives, needs, and hopes of their own, it is important to remember how deep the mystery actually is. And it is not only a mystery about our visitors, it is one about us.

"Yes, I wonder who they are. But I also have another question: who are we?"

CHAPTER FOUR

THE HEWINS ABDUCTION CASE

ET Abductees Audrey Hewins and her sister Debbie Hewins were both abducted by gray and reptilian aliens since childhood. This is their frightening story.

What perhaps makes the alien abduction claims of Audrey and Debbie Hewins all the more intriguing is that the abductees are identical twin sisters. Furthermore, the encounters were multiple and took place over many years since they were very young. Before they even realized what to make of the strange incidents invading their lives, the two girls would often plead with their parents not to send them to their room at bedtime due to the "bald men" who terrorized them in the middle of the night. They would further describe these men to their parents as having large heads and huge, black eyes.

Of course, twins have fascinated humanity at large since the beginning of time. This is very much still the case in our contemporary era, with many scientific studies undertaken on all manner of aspects of twins' lives, including potential supernatural abilities, as well as unique telepathic bonding. Indeed, if we are interested in twins and their unique existence, then why wouldn't visitors from other worlds who are already seemingly looking to study humanity? Whether that is the case or not is open to debate. The case is certainly thought-provoking.

Strange "Bald Men" Appearing in The Middle of The Night
There have been several written accounts of the Hewins sisters' case over the years of the Internet. However, one of the most detailed can be found in the book *The Alien Abduction Files* by Kathleen Marsden, who dedicates an entire chapter to the affair. As well as the details about "bald men" with large heads and large eyes mentioned above, Marsden documents how the two young girls began to keep notebooks of their encounters from the age of five. Initially, the pages were filled with sketches of the strange men. However, when they learned to write they began to keep much more detailed notes.

According to the diaries, these strange "bald men" would often appear in a brilliant blue light and a fog that glowed unnaturally. Furthermore, there was often a strange sound "like a swarm of bees" that often accompanied their presence.

For all of their notes, however, these initial encounters compared to their later accounts were rather vague and disjointed. However, on one occasion the twins had the sudden realization that they were above their house, and it was at this point that they also both realized they were dealing with entities that were not merely strange men, but from another world.

While most of the time the two sisters were abducted

together, one particularly harrowing incident happened to Audrey when she was seemingly on her own. Her first memory of this encounter was of realizing she was alone inside a strange room, apparently a room inside the aliens' vehicle. However, as soon as she came to this realization, her surroundings appeared to melt away. Suddenly, it appeared to her as though she were simply standing in space. Even stranger, she was looking down at Earth.

These experiences, though, were about to take a much more drastic turn.

Missing Time

It was when they were 11 or 12 years old when some of the more detailed, and harrowing encounters unfolded – encounters that the two girls would recall and record much more clearly. And these encounters were much more than mere visitations but quickly progressed to abductions.

The two girls recorded that these apparent alien entities would undertake "all kinds of experiments" on them, experiments that took place onboard the creatures' spacecraft. Whenever they would wake from these experiences, their memories of these encounters, while disjointed and hazy, were more prominent.

They also had specific windows of "missing time", which made the girls contemplate the notion that their alien abductors could target specific memories of the encounters to ensure the girls could not remember them. This is an interesting detail that has been suggested by several other researchers into alien abduction cases.

Although the encounters were undoubtedly bizarre, the girls, by and large, took them in their stride, even accepting the events as just being something that was a part of their lives. However, as the years progressed, they began to encounter other strange entities – specifically, reptilian entities.

Encounters With Reptilians

If we return our attention to the work of Kathleen Marsden for a moment, the encounters with entities from other worlds continued — even when the two sisters had moved from their home state of Ohio to Massachusetts. These entities were unlike the gray, bald, large-eyed "men".

These were lizard-like humanoids that would appear in the girls' bedroom — essentially, reptilians. While they would perform all manner of experiments on the girls, on at least one occasion, both sisters claimed they were taken to an underground location and raped by a large, reptilian humanoid. And while this claim might sound preposterous to some, it is a claim that has been made many times by many people all around the world.

Audrey would state to Marsden that these reptilian entities "have no sympathy (and) no feelings at all". They would continue that launched "vicious attacks" against her and her sister, and when they are near you can "feel their energy" as though they are "sucking the energy from you". Once more, this is an interesting detail. Many people who claim to have had experiences with reptilian entities, or to have researched them, have put forward that these creatures feed on energy, particularly negative energy. It is certainly worth taking note of.

She would further describe that these reptilian entities were at least six feet tall and often had a "sci-fi-type demon voice". They also wore a strange cape that was tied with a string that had a metallic quality to it.

The Bizarre Encounters of January 2007

Marsden also detailed several accounts from years later when the two women were adults. One of these happened to Audrey on the evening of 3rd January 2007. She explained to Marsden that she had an increasing feeling of anxiety, largely because she could sense that something was going to happen, and these curious entities were set to return. She would elaborate to Marsden that the feeling was like a "magnetic sensation – like I'm attracting something". She admitted it was hard for her to explain fully what she felt like, it was a feeling that she had known since she was a young child, and it was one she had always associated with the "bald men" who visited her and her sister in the night.

Then, her memory became hazy somewhat. She did recall, however, waking on a table with the feeling that something was "scraping my left ovary". As soon as this realization came, she blacked out, most likely, she suspected, due to something being administered by her abductors.

Marsden also notes that, based on Audrey's notes, these visitations often occur either just after or just before the full moon. The January 2007 incident occurred the day before the moon was at its fullest. Audrey herself explained this—it happens to be the time she would be ovulating, which she suspects is "the best time for (her abductors) performing their reproductive experiments" on her. Once more, this notion is something that has been put forward by other UFO investigators.

Taken From Her Bedroom
Audrey would inform Marsden of another more recent encounter a short time after the above events. On this occasion, she suddenly found herself awake in her bedroom. It was late – the middle of the night – and she had a strange "tingling" sensation running through her body. A few moments later, she felt her muscles going into a strange spasm. Within moments, her entire body was paralyzed, and she was unable to move. The only part of her body that she could move was her eyes.

She would continue that her room suddenly "filled with pale bluish light" that announced the arrival of the reptilian entities. She recalled that the "light shimmered and moved like a pool reflection on the ceiling". She forced herself to keep her eyes open so she could see her potential abductors.

She continued that there was a tall iguana-like reptilian humanoid suddenly standing in the light with two smaller entities on each side of him. She further described this entity as wearing a black cape and with "almond-shaped black eyes and (a) ridge over his brow" that was "much like an iguana or a Neanderthal might have". This creature appeared to be giving the two smaller entities instructions, which they duly carried out.

As they approached, Audrey found that she could suddenly move, and she immediately reached out toward one of the creatures, grabbing it by its throat. As this was happening, she could hear several voices in her head, almost as if she could telepathically hear the strange creatures talking to each other. At one point she heard one of the voices state that they should "watch out for the mother".

The struggle between her and her potential captors continued. She managed to temporarily free herself from their grasp and ran to her bedroom door. When she opened it, however, there were more of the smaller, gray creatures standing in the hallway outside her room. Before she could contemplate anything else, a sudden burning sensation took over her body. Then, she lost consciousness.

Floating In a Strange Fluid
The next thing he recalled was "hovering in the center of her room" and "passing through the mirror on a dresser". Before she knew what was happening, she was outside of her house, floating in the air, and looking up at the night sky. She could also see amber and blue lights coming from above her, and when she looked down, she noticed her home getting steadily smaller.

Her next memory was of being inside the spacecraft in a strange room. Even worse, she was inside some kind of cocoon-shaped device and surrounded by a strange, thick gel. Strangely, despite this gel surrounding her, she could still breathe with no difficulties. After several moments, she realized that she was "floating in a viscous, pale, greenish-gray fluid" in a room with around half a dozen other devices containing other people. She further noted how the room was seemingly round and contained three separate doorways.

She continued to look around, noticing that there were many of the gray-skinned bald creatures moving around the room and into the respective doorways. They appeared to be pushing hospital-like tables from one place to another, all of which appeared to contain people.

It was at this point that she realized a group of these strange creatures had noticed she was awake. Within moments, although she didn't understand how they had forced her to lose consciousness once more.

Further Experiments And Procedures
Her next memory is of waking up on a metal table in a large round room. She was completely naked and could see several different strange entities around her – as if she were in the presence of several different races of aliens, just one of whom was seemingly human-like with blond hair and blue eyes that appeared to be glowing. She also noticed the reptilian entity that often appeared in her room.

After gathering her thoughts, she suddenly attempted to leap from the table and run for the doorway. However, she simply fell to the floor. Her next memory was of hovering around a foot from the ground. In front of her was a bizarre-looking creature that had a "worm-like body" and a "parasite-type mouth".

She would recall that she reached out for the creature, seemingly injuring it temporarily before it scurried off away from her. A moment later, she found herself floating up and being positioned back on the table, laying her on her front. She then told Marsden how a "big machine came down and attached to the back of my spine". She then noticed a "burning sensation" run up and down her back.

She asked them what the purpose of the machine was, and she was told that they were "altering or activating her DNA" which would lead to some kind of enlightenment. Before she could contemplate this strange goings-on any further, she was suddenly turned around, so she lay on her back. Then things turned even more harrowing. A claw-like device came down from above and completely removed her eye. As it held her eyeball aloft, a needle-like device inserted something into her eye socket before replacing the eye in place. She recalled that she didn't feel any pain during this bizarre procedure, but that she did feel a strange fear. Her eye, incidentally, would be irritated for days after.

Information "Lying Dormant" Waiting to Be "Activated"
From there, she was taken into a room that resembled some kind of strange classroom. She could see multiple desks, all lined up facing a strange chalkboard. In each of the desks was another person, facing forward. She was seated at one of the desks. She watched as a human-looking person walked to the front of the room, seemingly a teacher, and addressed them.

This teacher-like entity told them that everything they needed to know was "lying dormant in them" and would "activate" when needed in due time. According to Audrey's memory, she asked what the point of all of them learning this knowledge was, if none of them could remember it after the respective encounters. She was simply told that everything they needed was inside their mind and, once more, that it would automatically activate when required. This is an interesting detail, suggesting that multiple people are being programmed in some way and that this programming will activate and become live at some later, unknown (to us) date. This suggests a very purposeful and real end goal to these strange extraterrestrial encounters.

The next thing she realized; she was waking up in her bedroom with no idea how she had gotten there. To the best of her knowledge, the encounters continue still today. She did begin to notice strange black, unmarked helicopters flying around her house regularly. This itself perhaps suggests that there could very well be some kind of behind-the-scenes, dark agency government organization that also plays a part in these strange affairs.

Further Suggestions of An Alien-Human Hybridization Program?

The bizarre and sometimes harrowing encounters experienced by Audrey and Debbie are without a doubt some of the most intriguing on record, not least as they are twin sisters who have seemingly experienced a lifetime of alien abductions and, in turn, invasive and strange procedures and experiments.

The fact that they are women should not be played down here. Many UFO and alien abduction researchers have pointed out before that a larger proportion of alien abductees particularly repeat abductees are female. Furthermore, these abductions almost always begin in childhood and appear to stop only once the respective woman has reached the stage in their life when they can no longer conceive. This would suggest that there is indeed an aspect of studying human reproduction.

In my case (author), I had two childhood UFO experiences in Idaho, and believe that I was spared later abductions for their hybrid experiments because I began taking birth control pills at nineteen after having my daughter.

Going a stage further, the idea of some kind of hybridization program being at the heart of these alien abductions can also not be discounted. Indeed, as bizarre as it sounds, many researchers have arrived at just such conclusions – that aliens are abducting human beings for some kind of project that will see the creation of alien-human hybrids. And the reasons for this remain unknown. And while that notion might sound truly bizarre to some, it is one that we should perhaps not discount without further investigation. After all, if there is any truth to such notions, then the fate of humanity could reside in our understanding of such ideas. Article by Markus Lowth on UFO Insight

CHAPTER FIVE

THE CURIOUS CASE OF CHRIS BLEDSOE

On September 7, 2023, I interviewed an extraordinary man named Chris Bledsoe on Stargate Radio. Chris has the uncanny ability to summon orbs and otherworldly beings at his home in Fayetteville, North Carolina. The people of Fayetteville have witnessed the orb phenomena and so has the History Channel's Beyond Skinwalker Ranch investigative team when they visited his home. They discovered by monitoring his brain waves that Chris goes into a meditative state and contacts the orb beings and they appear in the sky or the nearby woods.

After the events of 9-11-2001, Chris lost his business and was in financial ruin and suffering from a debilitating chronic disease by 2007. His world was crashing down on him. He was on the verge of the unthinkable — suicide.

That same year, fishing along the banks of the Cape Fear River with three co-workers, and his teenage son, Chris walked away from the campsite and in desperation cried out to God for help. Suddenly, a UFO appeared. When he walked back to his friends, he found them dismayed and terrified by the UFO orbs chasing them and how Chris vanished for four hours. Meanwhile, Chris was stunned that he was gone that long. His son Chris Jr. was hysterical after an orb held him down during the four hours.

After that night things began to change — Chris was healed of his Crohn's Disease and his financial situation began to improve.

The first time he met the Lady of Light was in 2012. At first, he experienced an angry bull charging at him, and he was the matador. It galloped as if it were itself an aspect of the wind. Just as he thought he was going to meet his end, the bull jumped over him, knocking him on his back. He saw stars and branches beyond its translucent body as he fell backward.

Lady of Light and Bull painted by Doug Auld.

Chris rolled over on his stomach so he could try to stand

up and run. He pushed himself up from the ground to his hands and knees and saw a woman floating in a circle of light. Poised still and silent, she gazed down at him. He then rose to his knees and spent a minute trying to take in what was happening before him.

Chris found himself kneeling within the circle of light emanating from the Lady. She was about the height of Chris's chin and was barefoot. She wore a gleaming robe that was simple and featureless and hung down to her ankles. To Chris, the robe appeared to be like an ancient priestess's attire from Roman times, plus long sleeves drooping past her wrists and an unadorned collar. She had blonde hair and the most dazzling blue eyes he had ever seen. He realized that she was only four and a half feet or five feet tall at the most. Her eyes radiated a sense of calm.

She spoke to Chris in his mind. "You know why I'm here."

As she spoke, Chris was in a trance-like state and said missing time and the beings who captured him were all tools she had used. They were guardians she sent to do her bidding. She vowed that if Chris continued his mission, she would protect his family and him, she would allow the orbs to be photographed and would allow him to show these phenomena to witnesses outside of his family. If he promised to continue talking about the things he witnessed, she'd never leave his side.

For long portions of her disclosure, she raised her pointer finger to her lips as though she were telling Chris to keep a secret or be quiet. He didn't understand what she was saying. Later she told Chris that he would understand when the time was right.

Before the Lady had entered his life, he had been given a bizarre round creature without a head. Later, the Lady told him it was an icon of humanity: directionless, senseless, without a head or tail, in dire need of protection and guidance.

The Lady warned him that there were forces at work to

cast the phenomena in a negative light and that if this view won out, humanity would be set on a path to ruin. Chris's work was to prevent this dangerous deception from taking root. She did not explain why, but that he was chosen to tell humanity of the phenomena's benevolence.

"A new knowledge must arrive. Mankind must awaken to it." The Lady of Light's final words were, "This is your burden. You must bear it."

The orbs continued to visit Chris, but the Lady didn't reappear until Easter 2013. Chris was transported by an Orb to a desert area that reminded him of Southern Utah. He landed in a canyon carved deep into the land. The orb bubble popped open revealing three beings like the first time he encountered the Lady of Light with their bodies glowing ivory-yellow like the moon.

Finally, the Lady was there in Light as the canyon gleamed around her bluish-white aura. Her dress was a brilliant white as she sat on a massive stone-carved throne in a recess in the canyon wall. When Chris and the beings approached the front of the throne, the beings gave her a slight bow and turned to walk away, leaving him alone. She stood up from the massive stone throne and hovered over the carved-out canyon floor, never touching the ground. Just forty feet away and twenty feet above him she spoke a parable that took a long time for Chris to decipher.

When the red star of Regulus aligns just before dawn in the gaze of the Sphinx, a new knowledge shall come into the world.

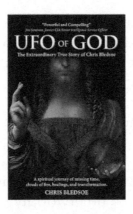

Later Chris was told by an astrologer that Regulus, the brightest star in the constellation Leo, will align with the Sphinx in 2026 close to Easter. The ancient Egyptians saw it in 2372 BCE. According to another astrologer, the Egyptians would have seen Regulus align at midnight in the midheaven on a particular night when it aligned perfectly. This alignment happens once every 25,722 years.

Chris believes The Lady was telling us something wonderful will happen near Easter in the year 2026 that will change humanity from the old ways to a new age.

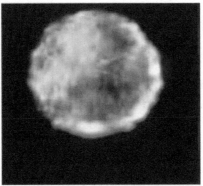

Bledsoe has captured over 2,000 videos of orbs flying over his home in the last two years. Pictured is an up-close image of an orb taken in 2012. It was hovering three feet off the ground when he snapped it 15 feet away

Chris was warned about COVID-19 in 2019 by a tall,

majestic figure with broad shoulders. A Jesus figure perhaps, but Chris didn't say in the book. He was told by the being, "We will allow you to film us more and share with witnesses. Share the truth. Difficult times ahead."

Chris sensed the warning meant famine, plague, and unrest would befall humanity soon. Was the entity's warning about Armageddon? Without knowing for sure, Chris didn't want to alarm people if he misinterpreted the message.

I believe Chris is an honest man, telling the truth about his bizarre encounters with otherworldly beings, but was it real or holographic? I have many questions: why was Chris healed of Crohn's Disease, and from the pain of rheumatoid arthritis and other health issues? Why is he required to suffer as the Lady seemed to indicate? I find this disheartening if these entities claim to have our best interest but want us to suffer for it.

What if what Chris witnessed was mind-control used by the CIA from 1953 through the late 1970s, or perhaps a hallucinogenic drug? If the orbs and the Lady of Light are extraterrestrials, they might be colluding with the U.S. secret military and Chris is an experiment to further their Project Blue Beam.

Do you remember Project Blue Beam from the 1990s, a conspiracy theory that a military/government project existed whose purpose was to create an artificial Second Coming? As per the alleged theory, the New World Order's purpose is to abolish all Christian and traditional religions to replace them with a one-world religion and to abolish the family unit today and replace them with individuals all working for the glory of the new One World Government.

Already Christian religion is vanishing as we move closer to a New World Order of Communism.

Much about Chris's story reminds me of the three children of Fatima, Portugal who witnessed a similar Marian entity with orbs or inside of orbs while tending sheep in the town of Fatima on May 13, 1917, at solar noon on the 13th day for five more months through October 13, 1917, when the Lady produced miracles as promised. She appeared in an orb-like Chris's Lady of Light, and she healed many in Fatima. On October 13, 1917, she made the sun spin wildly and appear to fall toward Earth to the horror of thousands gathered that day.

It had rained hard that day and the people were soaked, standing in mud, waiting for the miracle. At solar noon, the rain ceased, and the clouds were pulled apart, revealing what one reliable witness claimed was a disc with a sharp rim and clear edge, luminous and lucent. It was smokey silver in color. The sun does not have a silver color, not that anyone has ever observed. The odd thing was that not one astronomer noticed anything usual with the sun on October 13, 1917. Only those gathered within a five-mile radius witnessed the miracle of the sun. What the people described wasn't the sun, but possibly a huge UFO Mother Ship.

The Lady told the children that the two youngest, Francisco, nine, and Jacinta, six, would suffer greatly and die soon, but Lucia dos Santos, nine, would live a long life. The two youngest, Francisco and Jacinta, died from the Spanish Flu raging worldwide at that time. Lucia dos Santos became a cloistered nun and joined the Carmelite order and died on February 13, 2005, in Coimbra, Portugal.

What were the odds of Lucia dying on the 13th day of February, the day of the month the Lady always appeared?

Some say Chris is dealing with demonic forces. They aren't demonic, but they might not be benevolent. Perhaps they use life-like holographic images to deceive us and make us believe they are religious figures seen through the ages. Why was Chris taken to Utah or a desert canyon somewhere in the world, and why not to another planet or space? Why the theatrics?

Another mystery about Chris Bledsoe — why didn't he use the beautiful painting of The Lady of Light instead of Leonardo da Vinci's painting *Salvator Mundi* of Jesus on the cover of his book, *UFO of God*? There isn't any mention of Jesus in his book. The Lady of Light appeared to be more benevolent than the foreboding *Salvator Mundi* on his cover. It was a peculiar pick by Chris.

Certain extraterrestrials like to deceive humans and use mind control. Thousands of people claim they have been abducted and told the world is going to end and they are chosen for a special mission, but the mission is never revealed, and the world never ends. Many abductees have claimed the aliens controlled their thoughts and bodies. Often abductees feel violated, not only by the experiments conducted on them but also by tampering with their thoughts.

On September 20, 2023, Earth Mysteries Investigator Linda Moulton Howe said on her Earthfiles YouTube channel that a whistleblower knows the JSOC (Joint Special Operations Command) and the Zodiac Special Forces are interacting with "advanced biological AI beings" on Earth at or near Fort Liberty that just happens to be located 11.4 miles north of Fayetteville, North Carolina where Chris Bledsoe resides. Coincidence? Maybe not!

Chris wrote in his book that NASA conducted experiments on his brain to undercover how he communicates with the orb intelligences. Are Chris's entities involved with JSOC and Zodiac Special Forces in northwestern North Carolina not far from Chris's home?

The Map on the next page shows how close Chris lives in Fayetteville, North Carolina to Fort Liberty and Pope Field Military Bases.

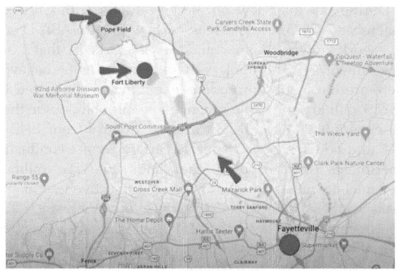

Map of Fort Liberty and Pope Field in North Carolina

Could these special forces be linked to Chris's encounters, and was he programmed during his first encounters in 2007 while on a camping trip when he went missing for over four hours? There is much more going on with Chris's experiences with the orbs and the Lady of Light that might involve the U.S. military. I do not believe that the entities that Bledsoe came in contact with (and is still in contact with) are of Source, the Creator, God, or the fundamental force of creation. It appears to me that whatever these entities are, they are putting a lot of effort into convincing humans they are sent by God when it is far more likely that they are simply creatures from another place or dimension who want human beings to worship them as God for unknown reasons — such as control of the planet? There are many species and beings in our Cosmos, but they are not gods or spiritual just because they have advanced sciences and technology.

Unfortunately, I believe that ultimately Chris Bledsoe is one of the thousands of victims of shadow forces. What Bledsoe and others take from his experiences appears naïve and dangerous.

During my interview on Stargate Radio with Chris on September 7, 2023, Chris discussed how great NASA is and his work with them, and I remarked that our Government/NASA is not as magnanimous as he believes. There are too many horrendous experiments conducted by the U.S. military and Government on people oblivious to their evil experiments like MK Ultra Mind Control from 1942 to 1944, and how the U.S. Chemical Warfare Service conducted experiments that exposed thousands of U.S. military personnel to mustard gas, to test the effectiveness of gas masks and protective clothing. In Vietnam. The experiments involved at least 254 chemical substances, but focused mainly on mid-spectrum incapacitants, such as LSD, THC derivatives, benzodiazepines, and BZ.

NASA has kept the truth for us about what giant structures on the Moon and Mars, and what the astronauts have seen. How can we believe anything they tell us?

The military shot accident victims up with plutonium, tested nerve gas on sailors and tried LSD hallucinogenic on soldiers. The military continues to push the envelope in seeking new warfare techniques based on cutting-edge science and technology.

Why would my remark upset Bledsoe? Either he is naïve, or he has been mind-controlled into believing he was taken to a remote location in southern Utah and introduced to a Marian-looking woman who sat on a throne as ETs bowed to her. What kind of experiments did they conduct on him?

I believe that Bledsoe is a good, honest man who has been used by governmental types steeped in secrecy for control and other experiments. I've read many true stories by abductees that tell of horrendous experiments on them, not just ordinary people but military too. It's time our politicians uncover the truth about UAPs and beings that reside deep underground and in our oceans that our military has known about for decades and continued to work with them.

NASA recently released a report stating that they found

no evidence that UFOs are extraterrestrial. Do they mean that UFOs are controlled by earthly beings? Why in the world would NASA bother experimenting on Chris's brain if he's not in contact with aliens or otherworldly beings?

A curious observation made by Chris Bledsoe was the insignia that aliens wore on their suits was similar to President Trump's Space Force emblem. Are Chris's beings time travelers or just deceptive aliens?

The Space Force symbol is on a dark blue disc, between two constellations in white, a light blue globe grid-lined in silver surmounted by a silver delta both encircled diagonally by a white orbit ring, all beneath a white Northern star in the upper left portion of the disc and above the Roman numerals "MMXIX" (year 2019) arching in white.

CHAPTER SIX

RENDLESHAM FOREST INCIDENT

One of Great Britain's most mysterious UFO incidents happened at Rendlesham Forest in Suffolk on three consecutive nights in late December 1980, involving credible witnesses. The area is a dense forest of pine trees with a prominent lighthouse and other buildings on the island. It was rumored that the National Security Agency (NSA) was operating a covert intelligence unit in the area at the time of the incident. On the night of December 26, 1980, Gordon Levitt, who lived on the edge of the forest, was out in his garden with his dog when he noticed a peculiar object flying toward him. He described it as an upturned mushroom with a greenish-white glow. The craft moved silently over Levitt and his dog toward the twin NATO air bases of RAF

Woodbridge and RAF Bentwaters. The next morning, Levitt's dog was ill, cowering in his kennel as if frightened. Several days later, the dog's condition worsened, and it died.

U.S. Air Force patrolmen John Burroughs and Budd Parker were on night duty when they spotted what looked like a plane about to crash, but soon realized it was hovering and going to land in the forest. The craft also displayed pulsating-colored lights. Burroughs called the sighting into the base at 2 a.m., knowing aircraft shouldn't be flying at that time of night and in that vicinity. Soon security patrol sergeant Jim Penniston was on his way in a jeep, driven by Herman Kavanasac. Arriving at the scene, the men believed a plane crashed and was engulfed in flames, but after further evaluation, they determined the craft had landed not crashed. Budd Park stayed behind while Penniston, Kavanasac, and Burroughs walked into the forest. As they tried to radio back to the base, their radios began to encounter static. Kavanasac was ordered to stay back near the road to relay messages to the main base while Penniston and Burroughs walked deeper into the trees. At that point, the men encountered crackling like a thunderstorm and reported their hair stood on end and their skin tingled.

Penniston described it as a conical object about the size of a small car, floating on beams of light (others reported seeing thin legs) only 30 centimeters above the ground. It had a strange, misty aura, and on its side were black marks that could have been writing. As the men tried to get closer to the object, they found they couldn't. They described the experience as surreal as if walking in thick syrup or tar and never reaching their destination. Suddenly, there was a flash of light, and the craft soared up into the air.

The next morning, they returned to the area and found many trees had their tops broken and three holes in a triangular formation were found in the frozen soil. An A-10 plane flew over the site at dawn, picking up large amounts of infra-red radiation in the forest. A security cordon was set up around the perimeter of the woods to prevent any curious airmen or local villagers from getting in the way. An hour earlier a security patrol had spotted strange lights floating in the sky above the forest, but these lights had quickly disappeared. Several soil and tree bark samples were taken at the site.

That following night the UFO returned and was spotted at 1:48 a.m. by a group of men who had ventured into the forest, including John Burroughs and Sergeant Adrian Bustinza. This time the light was described as a pillar of yellowish mist split in the middle like a rainbow prism. A group of men led by Deputy Base Commander Charles Halt (later promoted to Lt. Col.) followed the light through the woods, crossing a farmer's field and stumbling through a small brook. They chased it for more than an hour and then it suddenly shot skywards. Halt reported, "Now we observe what appears to be a beam coming down towards the ground – this is unreal." By then Halt decided to return to base with his tired, wet men.

Reports continued of strange lights above the Woodbridge base, flashing laser-like beams down on the security area of the base. Hundreds of personnel were said to have witnessed the lights that night. It's interesting to note that there were rumors of nuclear weapons housed at RAF Bentwaters but denied by the base and the British government at the time. Ten years later, the British government admitted that nuclear weapons were stored at that facility.

James Penniston noticed raised glyphs on the craft, like Egyptian hieroglyphs, and said the craft felt warm when he touched it. Soon after the incident, Penniston began receiving reoccurring random numbers of ones and zeros. The numbers puzzled him, and he sensed they meant something, but what, he wasn't sure. He cataloged them in a notebook and put them aside. Three decades later the binary code continued to haunt him until October 2010, he gave the notebook of numbers to a computer programmer. What the programmer deciphered from the code were the cryptic words, *"Exploration of humanity for planetary advancement."* The set of numbers also included a set of coordinates pointing to a "lost" island off the coast of Ireland called Hy Brasil. According to Celtic myth, the people that lived there were highly advanced and did not want to mix or even befriend those on the mainland, Ireland, or Iceland because they believed they were barbarians.

What can we take from the message? Who is exploring humanity for planetary advancement and why?

Rendlesham UFO Insignia on Craft

CHAPTER SEVEN

ALIENS AND OZ

The next story goes beyond the outer limits of alien abductions. Betty Andreasson who later married Bob Luca recalled alien beings abducting her since her childhood in the 1940s to the present day, which was documented in six books by the distinguished author and researcher, Raymond E. Fowler. Betty's story is one of the best-documented accounts of an encounter with beings from another dimension or universe with strange religious overtones. It's as if the aliens plucked out Betty's deep-seated religious beliefs and other elements in her life from her subconscious thoughts and made those experiences into a three-dimensional movie. She entered her own *Wizard of Oz*.

In 1967, Betty and members of her family suffered disturbing memories of an experience that happened in her home in South Ashburnham, Massachusetts. Betty

Andreasson was working in her kitchen while her seven children and her mother, and father were in the living room. Shortly after 6:30 p.m., the lights in the house briefly blinked. Immediately thereafter, a reddish-colored light beamed through the kitchen window. The sudden darkness in the house set the kids' nerves on edge, and Betty ran to comfort them. Her father rushed into the kitchen to peer out the window and found the source of the unusual light. To his shock, he saw five small humanoid beings hopping toward the house!

Betty tried to interest the UFO community in her story, but it wasn't until a team of investigators headed by Raymond E. Fowler that her story began to be taken seriously.

Originally Betty had written to Dr. Allen Hynek about her encounters, who filed her letter away for two years until a Massachusetts volunteer group of researchers contacted CUFOS and requested any abduction cases to study. Dr. Hynek forwarded Betty's letter to the group, and from there, Betty began regressive hypnosis with Dr. Edlestein. Soon the subliminal hypnosis unleashed a flurry of memories. Betty was having scary flashbacks. During that time, she was given a lie detector test and psychiatric tests and passed with flying colors. Later the publication of *The Andreasson Affair* by Raymond E. Fowler, Betty and her new husband Bob were hounded by television, newspaper/magazine interviews. All the attention frightened Betty who was naturally shy.

In some of Betty's experiences, she recalled floating in a giant blue sphere similar to the *Wizard of Oz* movie where Glinda, the good witch of the North, floats down in a bubble to Dorothy after she landed in Oz. Betty watched a transparent bubble approach, which carried her away like Oz's good witch. In another episode, the little gray 3-4 foot aliens gave Betty glass-like shoes and she's taken to a Crystal Forest and a Crystal Lake, where everything she touched turned to color. Betty underwent what appeared to be a mystery school initiation. She was made to wear "white raiment"' and to enter a womb-like device to be "born anew." During a 1950 abduction, one of Betty's eyes was temporarily removed and a probe was placed inside her head. She was taken to a place called "home" to meet the *One* through a glass door like Dorothy entered to meet the *Wizard of Oz*. Both Betty and Dorothy wore glass shoes and were told they were "going home." In another instance, Betty found herself in an *Alice in Wonderland*-type Garden and running as Alice ran during her encounter with the Queen.

Much of Betty's hypnotic sessions were filled with extreme trauma. One of the strangest segments of Betty's encounter took place with the Elders, tall human-looking beings with pale skin, white hair, and pale blue eyes, who wore white robes. She was taken to a place where strange creatures were in tubes. She was told that's where they conducted *biobics*, the name of a process where eyeballs are grown for the Watchers, the small gray beings. The Elders explained that sometimes the natural eyes of the Watcher became burnt by too much light because their eyes were open all the time. It was necessary to replace them. The Elders further explained the Grays are servants to them, and they are the ambassadors of the "master of rings, cycles, and orbs."

Betty later described the gray beings wearing a type of coverall, blue in color, with a wide belt. An insignia of a bird (Phoenix?) was on their sleeves. The hands only had three fingers, and they wore boots. The creatures did not move human-like but floated as they went.

During Betty's abduction, she was privy to a mystical ceremony involving three tall Elders as they stood over a round, circular design with lines marking it as if it was a pie cut into six pieces. Betty watched in wonder and awe as the three elders stood with their hands outstretched, touching each other's hands forming a triangle, and bowing their heads. Suddenly a ring of light formed in the middle of the Elders and light poured out of their foreheads, making a perfect triangle. At this point three more Elders joined the three in the ceremony, each placing their right arm over the next one. Then they began to chant a long "Oh" sound and a ring of light materialized around them.

Two V-shaped beams of light burst from their foreheads and formed a six-pointed star with a smaller light in its center. The two triangles formed what appeared to be the Star of David with a circle of light in the middle and the light that emitted from the Elders' foreheads quickly vanished as the Elders raised their hands and continued to chant. The outer ring surrounding them moved upward and shrank to that of the inner ring. Together, the rings orbited around each other in every direction before forming a large basket-ball-sized orb of lavender-purple light, which floated in the middle of the group.

It's interesting to note here that many people have reported OBEs (out-of-body experiences) and NDEs (near-death experiences) while in the presence of tall male beings in white robes.

So much of Betty's experiences with these beings seem metaphorical or symbolic. Another example of this was when Betty was instantly beamed by a flash of brilliant light in a hospital room by an Elder. In many instances, Betty found that the beings could manipulate space, time, and physical objects, and she had a sense of astral projection in her astral body. Betty was shown a hospital scene where she watched an elderly man lying in a bed, accompanied by a black woman with her head bowed. Next, she watched "black things" trying to pull the man out of bed, and a white light pulling in the opposite direction. There seemed to be a spiritual tug-of-war going on between the black entities and the light entities.

Betty described the black things as faceless with a head, long arms, and skinny body fighting for the old man's soul. Suddenly the Elder, who had accompanied Betty to the hospital bed, tossed a tiny marble light at the black things and they vanished.

After reading this I flashed back to the 1990 and the hit movie *Ghost*, where black, formless demons grabbed the antagonist villain and disappeared into the night. Could the aliens be monitoring and downloading our moves to frighten and control us? It's as if the aliens have studied us so thoroughly, and know how to push our emotional buttons to manipulate us. They can read our deepest fears, our passions, our loves, our fears, and joys, and use these elements to control us. They know us from the inside out—literally!

The Elders communicated to her their love for Jesus and that he would be coming back soon, perhaps for Betty's well-being only. In 1967 Betty was brought before what appeared to be a holographic display of death and rebirth of the legendary Phoenix bird rising from its own ashes, perhaps symbolizing humanity's ability to rise from the ashes of its destruction. The bird was huge. The beings then led her to a giant door, where a being lived called "The One." He imparted some great, secret knowledge to her that she was not allowed to recall under hypnosis.

It seems many abductees or contactees are given Earth-shattering images and messages that remain stored in a secret area of their mind. Why the secrecy? Why the games? Some believe Betty was abducted by demons or fallen angels, but what are fallen angels—aliens perhaps? Betty was told that they are carrying on genetic experiments on humans because the human race will become sterile by pollution and bacteria and the other terrible things on Earth. They are creating hybrids so the human form will not be lost, . . ."the fetuses become them." This again could revert to the continued cattle mutilations taking place worldwide.

Raymond Fowler suggested that UFO abductions and animal mutilations may be research and experimentation by breeders or alien-type veterinarians checking up on the health of animals and humans for the future progeny they are creating to inhabit Earth. Humans own animals, some are treated with love and kindness, while others are abused, which might be how different alien species regard us as lower animals.

In some instances, there are reports where aliens teach the abductee in a school of some kind. Perhaps when we sleep we are being taught on a higher level of existence by the Watchers (Guardians, as I refer to them). I can relate to recurring dreams of classes and schools over the years, but I've never been able to recall the lessons. Other abductees recall they were taught an alien language and how to use sophisticated instruments.

I wonder if humans can return in future incarnations as aliens. Could these aliens be preparing some of us for the next soul journey in an alien body?

Betty's husband, Bob Luca was hypnotized, revealing more about the spiritual body and the alien's agenda. He stated that the body was a shell, and the essence we call the soul is what goes on and on. The real us! Our existence on this Earthly plane is one step in many learning steps. It is a never-ending process. When Bob was asked about the future, he said it is not known by us, but at times we are given warnings and information by the Elders, those who watch over us and make decisions and help us if they deem so. On occasion, people are given glimpses of the future, such as a tsunami or earthquake. When one or two people are given such a future warning, it may be for their benefit only, so that their soul can complete their life cycle. Accidents do happen, but those who have a destiny to fulfill will survive a disaster.

Bob went on to say that we are all constantly monitored. "Nothing we do in life escapes them [The Watchers/Guardians]. Every thought, every deed, every word both good and bad, is recorded from the time we are born until we die. The cosmos is a giant recorder. It is determined from these records how quickly we advance to the next step—by what teachings, and hardships we must experience for soul growth. When we think life is unfair and a child dies young, the child has advanced and can go on to the next classroom. People who are sick or injured are being tested as well as the people who love, care, or know that sick person. All reactions are being recorded. Life is like a cup of tea — if the cup is broken, the tea seeks another container, and so does the soul."

This reminded me of the Akashic Records which contain all knowledge of human experience and all experiences as well as the history of the cosmos encoded or written in the very fabric of existence. A universal computer!

Bob was then asked about evil — why does it exist? He replied, "Those who create evil serve a purpose to help the righteous advance. It's all part of the life cycle. Everyone on this plane of existence can do evil, but those who don't — those who stop evil, those who overcome evil, advance, and gain tremendously in the next realm. Everything in our reality is either positive or negative; light and darkness, hot and cold, evil and good, hate and love. It's not that we need evil for good, we need evil for choices."

The hypnotist continued to question Bob on good and evil, and Bob gave a surprising answer by saying, "We are headed for some very distressing times before we evolve on this planet. As the population grows there will be those who have and those who have not. There will be greed, starvation, and much anger and dissension."

When asked if there will always be evil, Bob said, "There will come a time when evil will be wiped out, but not for a long time. We have a long way to go!" As a whole, we are advancing technologically, but our spiritual growth is lagging far behind. When asked how animals fit into spiritual evolution, Bob said, man will be surprised to find how animals fit in. Those who harm animals will find their actions have been recorded. All of the Creator's creation is sacred, from the lowliest to the most magnificent. Animals do not evolve as human beings, but they do have a spirit." Lastly, Bob said the Creator can't be explained, "It would be like explaining space or the universe, which is impossible."

As I mentioned earlier, if Bob's information from the ETs on the evolution of animals and they're reverence for them is correct, then how could aliens mutilate our cattle, horses, and other animals? It appears not aliens are spiritually evolved. Certainly, more is going on regarding the mutilations than we can imagine. That's why I find it hard to believe an advanced being would mutilate animals for the last 50 years.

Although both Betty and Bob's story is beyond belief, it's interesting to note that Betty agreed to polygraph tests and passed all of them, and her psychological tests proved she was normal.

Raymond Fowler during the time he was investigating Betty and Bob Luca was urged by his Evangelical Christian family to stop researching the Luca case, fearing he was entering into demonic territory. However, his book *UFO Testament: Anatomy of an Abductee* tells of his personal experiences with alien beings.

For a brief time, Fowler's grandchildren were banned from visiting him, but things have been resolved. In 2010, author and UFO abductee Whitley Streiber interviewed Raymond Fowler on his *Unknown Country* Radio Show. Fowler talked about what may have been his encounters with alien beings through the years, and how he made several discoveries of scoop marks on his shin bone, remarkably like the scoop marks Betty Luca discovered on her arm and leg. Raymond sought a doctor's opinion on the marks found on his leg, and the doctor confirmed it was a punch biopsy, and wondered when he had this procedure done. Fowler also sensed something had been inserted into his nose after waking up on several occasions with blood on his pillow. The doctor suspected there was a calcium deposit in his nose and wanted to remove it, but Fowler's family forbade it, and the surgery was never performed.

If we don't open our minds and release our ancestral fears, how will we ever grow and advance beyond superstitions, control, greed, hatred, anger, and jealousy? Raymond Fowler investigated Betty Andreasson Luca and learned she is one of the most pious people you could ever meet, yet his family feared the devil was tempting him and Betty.

The only way we learn is from study, investigation, and analysis. It's time to release the dogmas that we hold onto so tenaciously. If humans had never ventured beyond territorial walls believing the Earth was flat, where would we be today? It takes courageous people like paranormal researchers like Raymond Fowler, the late Dr. John Mack and Budd Hopkins, Dr. Barbara Lamb, and Ann Druffel who dared to go where others feared to go.

If the majority of publicized UFO/abductee stories in the news were thoroughly investigated, I'm sure a large percentage of those stories would be proven fake. Such fictional stories hurt true investigative work by serious investigators like Dr. John Mack, Dr. James E. McDonald, Jim Marrs, Budd Hopkins, Dr. J. Allen Hynek, Ann Druffel, Stanton Friedman, Raymond Fowler, Linda Moulton Howe, and many other outstanding ufologists.

The biggest question of all is can we trust what the aliens tell us?

Betsey Lewis

CHAPTER EIGHT

ETs IN COLORADO

Katie (Griboski) Paige is Colorado MUFON's State Director. She is a STAR Investigator for MUFON and is the team lead/administrator for MUFON's MARRS Team. She's the host of MUFON What's Up Radio Broadcast on KGRADB and is the author of *Letters of Love & Light - Four Decades of UFO Encounters, Experiences & Sightings Shared with Ufologist R. Leo Sprinkle Ph.D.*

Katie has also been on the Travel Channel's UFO Witness, Gaia's Beyond Belief, the History Channel's Ancient Aliens, and Ron James's Film Accidental Truth and History Channel's Beyond Skinwalker.

Not only has she investigated hauntings and UFO events, but she has also experienced paranormal activity since childhood which she believes is connected to extraterrestrials in Colorado.

Across North America, there are a handful of locations where multiple, seemingly paranormal events are concentrated, including a ranching area in Elbert County, Colorado which is just southeast of Denver. The animal mutilation mystery first came to national prominence in the mid-70s after hundreds of cattle (and a few horses) were discovered all over the state, many of them carved up with surgical precision. One of the areas that was hard hit by mystery mutilators was Elbert County, where ranchers endured a multi-year onslaught of weirdness. Author Katie Griboski's family owned the ranch at the epicenter of the paranormal events.

"We experienced some really scary frightening things out on that Ranch," Griboski told Mystery Wire. "Strange boxes, helicopters, menacing people, paranormal activity, circles on the ground. They mutilation not only of horse but of sheep. There was a sheep, a horse, and many hundreds of cattle almost occurring daily," Katie said.

Griboski's new book, *Letters of Love and Light: Four Decades of UFO Sightings and Encounters Shared with Dr. Leo Sprinkle PhD*, is a compilation of UFO witness statements given to Dr. Leo Sprinkle. Griboski said, "I went to research the ranch, 82 boxes were at the Heritage Center in Laramie, boxes and boxes of this pioneer's work. Handwritten letters from people all around the world from the '60s '70s '80s '90s."

"Well, at heart I'm a researcher. I love to go to the archives. I love to go through documents. I experienced some things as a young girl on a ranch in Colorado. In UFO folklore it was known as Clearview Colorado. Sometimes people refer to it as the Rocky Mountain Ranch. However, it's in Elbert County, Colorado. My sister and I spent a handful of time out there. It's kind of a long, convoluted story. My mom worked for United Airlines, divorced my father in '73, and met a gentleman in '75. So, he and his wife were separated at the time, she had a new love interest. They had three sons, and they owned the ranch property. They had three sons; they owned the ranch property. The two younger sons and the father lived with us during the week to commute to the United Airlines computer center. And the two younger boys went to a bigger High School in Colorado, Cherry Creek High School. The oldest son stayed on the ranch.

"Every Sunday night, we'd hear of you know, at the time 1975 to 1978 it was high cattle mutilation time, Linda Moulton Howe did a lot of investigative work out there. I don't claim to be a cattle mutilation expert like Chuck Zukowski's wheelhouse and Christopher O'Brien's wheelhouse, but we experienced some really scary frightening things out on that Ranch, which I just gave the presentation on here today. Strange boxes, helicopters, menacing people, paranormal activity, circles on the ground. Mutilations of horses and sheep. There was a sheep, a horse, and many hundreds of cattle almost occurring daily. My passion is research and interviewing these folks.

"I know, people will ask me like, why research something that happened over 40 years ago, giving away my age? But the answer to that is, it's personal to me. Number one. Number two, the activity still occurring. As I've learned at this conference, other ranches encounter strange boxes, strange noises, and Sasquatch creatures. White Sasquatch exist, they called them 'white fuzzies' out there at the time. We haven't solved what this is yet. We had confirmation and things through NORAD and the Colorado Bureau of Investigation was involved. And if you know, Elbert County just is not too far from, you know, Colorado Springs Air Force Academy and Camp Carson and that.

"It's just been a passion. I started investigating this back in 2012. I joined MUFON. Came in as a field investigator and worked my way up the ranks and did my due diligence with cases and I just love interviewing people and asking those questions because even Project Bluebook, they were really focused on nuts and bolts craft, you know, we saw sphere, we saw this, we felt that. And now you can go back all these years later and say well, wait a minute, what about the high strangeness stuff? Did you have paranormal stuff going on in your house? Have you seen these weird blue orbs or the orange orbs? You know, that's what I enjoy doing?"

Duncan Phenix
With the ranch? We'll talk about that real quick. It's been compared to Skinwalker Ranch, which seems everybody knows these days, it has its own TV show, right? Would you rank it as that sort of?

Katie Griboski
Well, it's interesting, and I started the presentation. What I want people to understand is, that when I was a kid, we were threatened not to talk about this by disembodied electrical voices. Your friends will remain silent concerning us. Okay, we've allowed you to remain. It was terrifying stuff. And I grew up, I mean, I always had memories of these things that occurred. I witnessed one of these disappearing boxes, but I never knew it was reported. I never knew anybody knew anything about it. And so, one day in 2013, I came across a book, "Hunt for the Skinwalker" by George Knapp and Colm Kelleher. And I'm reading the book not knowing anything about Skinwalker Ranch. I'm just thinking it had the word ranch on it. And I come to their chapter, other hotspots. And in there they talk about the Colorado ranch. There are several pages in that book talking about our family's ranch. And of course, the names and the location were changed, but I knew because of the weird dynamic of the family, like that's it. And so it was through George's book that I learned that Dr. Leo Sprinkle. John Derr and Peter Van Arsdale were the initial investigators out there on the property. I called my state director at the time because he needed to get in touch with Leo Sprinkle. Got in touch with him. He wrote me a letter back really quickly, a handwritten letter. He doesn't do computers or internet or anything confirming that yes, this is

the blank ranch in Elbert County, and I was out there (the) next week, looking through all the original files. And then John Schuessler bestowed upon me the original briefing document from back in the day. It was chock full of interesting information, and it's just been a rabbit hole that I've jumped in. And I can't get out of it now.

On Dr. Leo Sprinkle though, one night in a dream, what happened, I went to research the ranch, 82 boxes are at the Heritage Center in Laramie, boxes and boxes of this pioneer's work. Handwritten letters from people all around the world from the '60s '70s '80s '90s. And for three and a half years, I put together *Letters of Love and Light, Four Decades of UFO Sightings and Encounters Shared with Dr. Leo Sprinkle PhD*.

These are all the juicy parts of letters that I organized into chapters, I even found a pre-snowflake Arizona, Travis Walton abduction from 1937, which is really interesting. And I've got to know Leo well. And to do this book, one thing this book did for me is make me very humble very fast. Because when you're looking at the lifetime work of a pioneer like Dr. Sprinkle, you realize that we're just reinventing the wheel. You know, when I'm like, Oh, I'm really on to something with these crystals, and this frequency, and vibration. They were talking about that in the 60s, you know. So, for me, it's a mission of just trying to find little bits of new information that we can share. And, you know, I like to hide away in dusty boxes, but at some point, you come out and you share it. That's where I am right now on my path is sharing.

Duncan

And as you hinted at, you do you have some information that you're researching right now goes back a few years. Tell us about that.

Katie Griboski

This is a case that came to me a couple of years ago. Brigadier General Arthur Exon. And there was rumored that one of the

Roswell bodies from '47 was taken to a mortuary outfit in Denver is the exact quote. And as fate would have it, some weird synchronicities happen. I received this case from the morticians... her father was best friends with the mortician Lou. Lou just recently passed away, I was glad I got a camera out there and interviewed him. Out of California, I was assigned the case and got to meet Lou and his wife and hear about the caper that he pulled off. He was a mortician at a mortuary in Denver. And in the basement was a room where they stored the chairs and in the corner was a vault and it had sat there for years and years and years and years. And he never really thought there was a body and there was like a body wouldn't be sitting there. And they were told never to touch it. It was actually on hold from a judge. Okay, so there was a court-ordered hold on this body for years. And I've been researching now because, in this field, I'm trying to get all my ducks in a row and documents because this is quite a story. He pulled this caper; he opened the vault and in the vault was a child-size casket. He opened it up, this body is soaked in seven layers of formaldehyde cloth, peeled back the layers of cloth, and all the visceral in the body was removed.

The genitals are completely cut out. Little orifices for ears, almost no mouth, very heavy brow, not as big-eyed as some of the ETs but smaller. So, he didn't connect it to ET at the time. He wasn't into any of that. He thought hydrocephalic child, but it was very unusual because my first question was why don't you take pictures? Why didn't you ... it was an alien Roswell body. He didn't connect that at the time. He felt he violated this little being, right? This little malformed child was put back, closed up and he didn't think about it again and it just sat there.

He just happened to be in Roswell, New Mexico, talked to Ramey or somebody, heard about the rumor that there was maybe one of the bodies held in a mortuary up in Denver. I started investigating the judge trying to find any document I could because if you're holding something legally there has to be paperwork on there. The problem is you need to file a number or name. What do you name it? So, I've been going to the Eisenhower Archives. Of course, Eisenhower's have a strong Denver connection with Mamie being from Denver. But the judge, what I learned about him, 33-degree Mason, the lodge is actually not too far from Fitzsimmons and Lowery at the time. Pieces are starting to fall into place around this case. My mother was in an independent living facility, and they asked me to come do a little presentation on UFOs 101. I did that, I'm like okay, sure, do UFOs 101. And I was talking to the nice folks in the home about this Roswell body case, and the judge and one of the ladies goes, "Sherm? His widow is on the fifth floor. You want me to go get her?" I'm like, you've got to be kidding me. And I've done two interviews with the judge's wife and learned about the Eisenhower connection. I think I know where the little body is, not ready to say it yet, sorry people. But yeah, because I need to have my ducks in a row for that. The ranch phenomenon (is) very interesting. I have two kinds of love or interests that I'm really pursuing heavily. And of course, COVID cut all that down with archives, everything was shut down. I'm anxious to get back on the horse and pursue that. Talked a lot to Bob Wood about it actually, at one of the symposiums.

Duncan Phenix
Are you working with anyone else on this?

Katie Griboski
No, but I would love to have a team. I mean, I've been kind of going both the ranch phenomenon, I have my close friends that, you know, absolutely helped me and supported me. But this kind of research in this kind of work takes teams. And I haven't had that. But I'm certainly open to that. I'm all about sharing information, especially meeting Dwayne, Trey, and James here about the other ranches. I'm all about like, here,

here's what I got. Let's figure this out, you know, especially with these weird boxes.

Duncan Phenix

What is your take on the current situation of not only Skinwalker getting so much attention, with the Navy videos, and the national news media paying attention taking this topic as a whole seriously?

Katie Griboski

I think it's fascinating and shocking—my personal belief. Well, there you ask the kind of two questions. So why are the ranches becoming more popular and out front? Well, we got to owe that to George Knapp and Skinwalker Ranch, of course, and the show, and it's being pushed out there. All of a sudden, not only are we learning of all these other metro and these other locations, not just in the United States, but around the world. So that's great. And there's nothing more important than connecting these places together and going and what I mean the high magnetism, they're very highly magnetized areas. What's that about? The Navy videos with Lou Elizondo, and I feel that they're trying to get ahead of something, like they know, something's coming. I've talked to so many people that have this sense of like, something's on the horizon, right, that some big something. And I think for decades, we've had a slow drip. I think they're trying to get ahead of something and prepare the public for whatever this news is going to be. I don't think we're going to learn anything explosive all at once. But there's nothing bad about this coming to the forefront. Because before, you know, even just two years ago, when they said, what do you do, Katie? Because I was a graphic designer and I have my degree in Visual Communications. And I stopped all that to do this full time—to write the book. And they're like, really, why? And now with all this coming out, almost every day, there's something on the news. I'm like, yeah, you see, you know, so that's kind of nice.

Betsey Lewis

CHAPTER NINE

THE MOJAVE INCIDENT

In one of the strangest and least publicized UFO encounters, author Ron Felber chronicled the abduction of a young middle-class couple from Southern California in his book, *Searchers: A True Story of Alien Abduction* ©1994, and republished the book in 2015 under the title *Mojave Incident*.

For Steve and Dawn Hess, their journey into high strangeness began on the weekend of October 21, 1989, in the high Mojave Desert. It was both a sightseeing trip and a hunting trip. Driving late at night in their 1987 Ford pickup complete with a camper shell, they landed in a washed-out section of road because of the poor visibility from foggy conditions.

Dawn recounted how their three-year-old son was acting oddly. Before leaving home, their son said something about a "spaceman."

That evening they arrived at the Midhills campsite to find it filled and nowhere to camp. Steve made the decision to drive on near Woods Mountain. Five hundred yards across the desert basin stood Tabletop Mountain. They were in the desert alone, feeling nervous about their decision to stay there. By 9:13 p.m. an eerie quiet crept over their camp.

Steve thought about returning to the Midhills campsite, but it was getting late, and the rough terrain gave him second thoughts. As they sat outside under the stars beside their campfire, they noticed nine objects shining so intensely above the mountain they created daylight around them. Dawn and Steve tried to analyze what they were seeing — stars, balloons, experimental craft from Nellis Air Force Base. Soon the nine craft had repositioned themselves on the horizon over the crest of the mountain range in the form of a large 'M'. Although they were both frightened, they became paralyzed in fear when hundreds of shiny objects flashing signals to one another filled the entire nighttime sky.

Dawn believed the Russians were invading the Mojave Desert as Steve tried to reassure her that wasn't possible. He instructed her to get into the truck while he doused the campfire so they wouldn't be seen. He grabbed his 12-gauge Ithaca shotgun, 7mm Browning rifle, and dozens of rounds of ammo and told Dawn to get into the camper shell. Soon hundreds and hundreds of glowing objects were raining down on them in the blackened sky, hitting the desert basin, and then bolting forward toward their camper.

The white objects had all landed now and thousands of pairs of red eyes glowing in the dark surrounded them. There were a few typical-looking grays, and accompanying them were three-foot creatures with heads the size of a cat's, translucent torsos, and thin limbs. Steve wanted to shoot them, but Dawn kept saying, "Don't do anything to harm them. You have no chance. If you harm them you'll get us killed."

By 10:55 p.m., an enormous spacecraft descended out of the dense clouds and hovered one hundred yards above the desert floor. They estimated it was as big as a football field in diameter and shaped like a disk with an elevated dome that rose from the center. It was encircled by brilliant white lights flashing in what appeared to be coordinated, coded rhythms. It seemed as if the white light in the form of a triangle from the ship was moving slowly across the desert as if scanning for something. Then a rumbling began as if it was digging in the ground.

At that point, Dawn began to pray to God and Jesus for help and forgiveness. Steve recalled his UFO encounter as a boy of fifteen; this wasn't the first time he'd seen them, and neither was it for Dawn.

Suddenly Dawn had an epiphany, realizing the area they were in was a part of the Paiute legend, seen in their petroglyphs dating back six hundred years ago. The Native Americans considered this part of the desert sacred; a place where the deities came to show themselves to tribal priests. One of the most famous ancient petroglyphs is known as the "Mojave Twins," a huge ground drawing that can be recognized from planes passing high over the desert, similar to the Nazca drawings. Dawn realized the beings outside their camper were exactly like the "Mojave Twins".

Photo of one of The Mojave Twins geoglyph near Blythe, CA

As the hours ticked by Steve and Dawn found themselves in a will of minds with the aliens, seemingly a one-sided psychological game. It was as if the aliens were studying them and their emotional responses to their lives — past and present. At times Steve flashed back to possible encounters with the aliens throughout his life.

Inside the camper shell, the truck was rocked by the aliens, but the aliens had not come in to get them — not yet anyway. Then an illuminated figure raised its three-digit fingers in Dawn's direction, and a fleck of light the size of a cigarette butt passed from its fingertip through the window and into her abdomen. Dawn screamed, trying to get at the thing that was now inside her.

Both Steve and Dawn felt as if they were being lifted and separated from Earth. Suddenly a smoke-white, swirling form descended from the sky, a (female) being so radiant it could have been called an "angel." She wore a lucid robe and her presence seemed peaceful. The woman spoke and said, "It's all right. I'm here now to protect you. Be at peace. It's almost over."

Here again, is another example of an angelic being accompanied by aliens. Was the angelic woman a holographic image used to calm Dawn or was this a real angelic messenger sent to help her?

Dawn was Mormon and perhaps her religious beliefs were downloaded from her subconscious memories.

By morning's light, the aliens had vanished, and the desert appeared normal again. Two years later, on November 21, 1991, Steve and Dawn agreed to be regressed through hypnosis to that frightening night in 1989. Unknown to them at the time, hypnosis revealed the couple had been taken on board a craft and examined since the desert encounter. Steve revealed their presence on Earth has been more advanced, and they hope humans might be able to encounter them without mass hysteria by making contact with select people to help raise consciousness and communicate that there are intelligent beings and a whole existence that parallels our world.

When asked where the beings come from, Steve replied, "They may have been here all the time. Existing spiritually, then becoming physical."

"And why do they want to make contact?" Steve was asked.

"To deliver a message that the world needs to be as one. That's if there's war or massive destruction, they will intervene."

Dawn felt they wanted to make contact with the population. She believed they were like specimens to be observed and studied for their reactions to them so they would know how to approach us in the future. They need to understand humans. Dawn said there are many different kinds of beings visiting Earth, including different hybrids. Then Dawn shocked the author and the others gathered in the room during the regressions when she said, "They are sent on missions from the One Supreme. There's One Supreme Being that controls all of them. He sends missions here. They're not here on their own accord." Dawn further stated the aliens were neutral and unemotional.

When asked what the One Supreme Being wants, Dawn replied, "For all the galaxies to live harmoniously together."

The Hesses have never sought publicity for their story. Dawn and Steve's story is similar to Betty Andreasson Luca's story when she met the One. Both women have devout religious beliefs and both cases were given positive reinforcement that they (the ETs) are here on a benevolent mission and only have our best interest at heart.

Steve and Dawn Hess appeared on the SYFY Channel's *Paranormal Witness* television show, where Dawn revealed that because she became pregnant during this encounter her daughter might have alien DNA. She was convinced her baby would be a hybrid human/alien. Another strange aspect of this story is Hess's daughter was born with RH-0 negative blood, which might be a sign of alien DNA.

CHAPTER TEN

NATIVE AMERICAN ENCOUNTERS

In Dr. Ardy Sixkiller Clarke's book, *Encounters with Star People,* she was told a story about Black Elk and a special stone he carried with him all his life after a UFO encounter. The story goes that Black Elk was visiting his cousin Benjamin. He was in the sweat lodge, when according to Benjamin's family; a circular craft came out of the sky and hovered over it. Suddenly a stone penetrated the closed door and landed between Black Elk's feet. He picked up the stone but had to complete the sweat lodge ceremony before he could leave. By the time he was able to leave the lodge, the spacecraft was gone. Another holy man on the reservation remembered Black Elk and how he always carried the rock and how he still used the sacred pipe. He said that when he lit his sacred pipe,

Black Elk would laugh and call his pipe an antenna for contacting the Star People.

Dr. Clarke's source said, "Black Elk believed the Star People came to Earth hundreds of thousands of years ago from Sirius and the Pleiades. He called them the answers of the people."

Much of his writings come off as arcane and symbolic, but in the following passage from *Black Elk, The Sacred Ways of a Lakota* by Wallace Black Elk and William Lyon, the Sioux shaman does not mince words, having said, "So when I went to vision quest, that disk came from above. The scientists call that a...Unidentified Flying Object, but that's a joke, see? Because they are not trained, they lost contact with the wisdom, power, and gift. So that disk landed on top of me. It was concave, and there was another one on top of that. It was silent, but it lit and luminesced like neon lights. Even the sacred robes there were luminesced, and those tobacco ties lying there lit up like little light bulbs. Then these little people came, but each little group spoke a different language. They could read minds, and I could read their minds. I could read them. So, there was silent communication. You could read it, like when you read silent symbols in a book. So, we were able to communicate...They are human, so I welcomed them. I said, "Welcome, Welcome..."

One of the most prominent Sioux Indians of all time, a historic figure, a cousin of Crazy Horse, tells us that he met ETs who arrived in a luminous disk. Others, such as the modern-day new age figure Standing Elk (also known as Chief Golden Light Eagle), widely featured on YouTube and a regular at Star Knowledge Conference proffer a blend of "wisdom teachings" purportedly emanating from "Star People," of the "Star Nations," who include everyone from White Buffalo Calf Woman to Buddha, the Egyptian god Thoth, and Krishna. Dressed in chiefly regalia, he speaks of karma and the energy of the fifth, sixth, seventh, eighth, and ninth dimensional frequencies, attracting both white conferees and native skepticism, all the while offering spiritual teachings that, while embracing Star Beings, veers significantly from the sensibilities of many of his own people, many of whom are Christian and therefore reject his spiritual panoply, and others who are merely suspicious.

Dr. Ardy Sixkiller Clarke, a former Assistant Professor of Education Leadership at Montana State University, whose native heritage is Cherokee and Choctaw, talked about Native American UFO and alien encounters on my Rainbow Visions Network. She claimed to have had encounters with Star People when she was a child. When she was quite young, she came upon a man and woman not of this world, who told her they were "her ancestors." This incident (not conveyed in her book) occurred late at night, Clarke said, as she made her way to an outdoor privy, continued for hours, and involved advanced technology, a craft that she entered. She went on to say that her contact with the man and woman was not an isolated event but continued later in her life.

Clarke's books are filled with similar accounts, some of which describe benevolent visitors, others that aren't so benevolent that abduct people against their will. The names of the indigenous people she interviewed were changed to protect their true identity.

One account, given by Native American hunters in Idaho, just outside Yellowstone, describes a large craft settling down in a valley and discarding a bison carcass that the hunters found the next day, surgically mutilated.

The initial account in the book is told by a tribal police official and his wife, a school teacher, Tim and Sarah, whose names were changed to address their concerns about job security, according to Clarke. While driving in Eastern Montana, on their way to Billings, Tim pulled over, having spotted dead cattle by the roadside, and then saw a light emanating from an object resembling a "large cylindrical propane tank" the length of a football field. The object, the couple told Clarke at a restaurant off I-90, circled to the other side of the road then settled above Tim's pickup truck, emanating a blinding light. The next thing they knew, the couple reported, according to Clarke, was that they found themselves inside their truck but on the other side of the road, and the cattle carcasses were gone. Later that night, arriving at a hotel in Billings, they could not account for four hours of lost time.

When asked about the reception such stories, and her book, receive among the public and in academic circles, MSU in particular, Clarke told me that among Native Americans, traditional legends about Star People provide a more accepting context than among whites, and that her mother for example readily accepted the account she told her as a child — yet she was instructed not to speak of it to others because they would not understand.

Clarke said there has been no reaction from MSU or academia, about her books, but that she has heard from people all over the world since the publication of her books. Although retired, Clarke retains the position of Professor Emeritus at MSU. She continues to work extensively with indigenous peoples and has been adopted and given traditional names by the Blackfeet, Northern Cheyenne, and Lakota. The stories she has gathered are from indigenous people in the Western and Southwest United States and in Central America.

Uncle Beau's Story
Ardy Sixkiller Clarke interviewed an elder named Uncle Beau in *Encounters with Star People*. "The old ones tell stories about the people from the stars who lived underground up near Tanana [Alaska], he told Clarke. She listened to the 84-year-old elder talk about the Star People and asked what he had seen. "You would not believe some of the things I've seen," he replied, as he sat on a tree stump that served as a stool. There are many stories the old ones told about the Star People

who lived among them and went underground near Tanana. The Inupiat believe they came to Earth on a spaceship."

Clarke asked if he had seen any spaceships and he replied, "Plenty of times. I was born here in the Athabascan territory. I was here before Alaska became a state and my people lived here for thousands of years before any white man ever came here. There were spacecraft visiting Alaska when it was called Aláxsxaq, and they will be visiting long after there is no more Alaska."

"Where have you seen UFOs?" Clarke asked.

"On the road between Nenana and Denali," he said. There is a deserted stretch of highway, and they land up there. The Air Force knows of their existence. I'm sure of that. Everyone up this way has seen them, but they don't talk about it. The military doesn't like it if you talk about UFOs. A lot of people from town work at the airbase, so we are quiet about it. But privately, we know that they come here."

Uncle Beau also related a story about his niece's sons who used to work at the base. He arrived one morning to find the base closed. They told the workers to go home. When he reported to work the following day, one of his friends who was stationed there told him that a UFO had landed the previous night. He said there was a place up there where the UFOs go underground. The place was guarded day and night. No one was allowed near the site; however, his friend had a high-security clearance.

Uncle Beau added this cryptic message, "I don't think a lot of what they do up there makes sense. It is supposed to be a place for training troops how to survive in Arctic weather. Why does the military need that kind of training? When are they going to fight a war in the Arctic? I think it is a place where the aliens and the military collaborate and where the aliens can go underground freely without us regular people seeing them. I don't know what they are doing together, but I think that is how they use the place. My nephew's friend said the aliens look like us. So maybe they are the ancestor."

Mary Winston's Story

"Yes. We knew of the Star People from our grandparents. The stories were passed down thousands of years. We were brought here by the Star People who lived at the top of the world."

"What do you mean, at the top of the world?" Clarke asked.

"They live under the North Pole. That is the 'top of the world.' They brought us here to live on the Earth and they live inside it, at the top of the world. Our home planet was becoming overpopulated, and they needed a new place for us. Thousands were chosen to live in this new world, but most of them starved. Earth was different from our home planet. The food was different. We had to learn new ways to build shelters. So, my ancestors were like pioneers from another world."

Mary discussed her grandfather's meetings with the Star people and said, "The people at the top of the world are looking for another planet for the people. He said they believe that one day all the snows will melt and there will no longer be the frozen land. It will change our lives too much. We will not be able to survive. New people will come and take our land. They will homestead at the encouragement of the government. I hope I do not live to see that day." She paused for a moment and added, "When I cross over, they will come for me. After we are buried, they come and take our body and our spirit home to the stars."

Clark then asked, "Do you mean that if I dug up your grave a week after you were buried, I would find nothing but an empty casket?"

"That's what I mean," she replied. Mary has since passed and has probably joined the Star People in the Stars.

In Clarke's book *Sky People,* she interviewed Eduardo, a young waiter, living in Guatemala who had seen and interacted with UFOs through the years. He related a story when he was headed home from work on a very clear night

ABDUCTED

after the bar had closed. Suddenly he saw a craft come from the West. It was a large orange thing, shaped like a bicycle wheel. It moved around and around. He felt hypnotized by it.

Suddenly a bright light came down from the bottom of the craft. It was a beautiful sight and he had a sense of calm. He no longer felt tired. Voices told him to be calm. The blue light changed to a white light which frightened him. At first, he thought it was going away, but it just hovered as he ran toward his mother's house. He heard their voices. He couldn't move and was paralyzed.

Eduardo felt he was seeing a Jesus miracle because there were many 'Jesus miracles' in his country.

Clarke asked what happened after the light changed to white.

"I was taken on board their craft. They showed me around and told me that they loved the Maya people. I was chosen because of my Maya heritage. They said that the knowledge from the stars has always been hidden in the Maya hieroglyphs, but they have never been deciphered correctly. So, they have decided to choose a Maya man to teach the knowledge to the world."

"Do you think you are that man?" Eduardo's friend Mateo asked.

"They said I was a messenger. They said the Earth is changing and that a new world will come soon. They said there will be wars and Earth shaking. People will starve because the Earth will burn. We are living in the fourth world, but a fifth world is coming. It is too late to stop it. I am supposed to tell the people to get ready. The four horsemen will come first. They will ride on white, red, black, and yellow horses, symbolizing the four corners of the world and the colors of the people of the world. When these horsemen appear, the fourth world will end, and the fifth world will begin."

Clark and Eduardo's friend Mateo thought he was confusing Biblical revelations with aliens. "Did the aliens tell you about the four horsemen?" Clarke asked.

"Yes. And other things," Eduardo replied.

Eduardo couldn't remember the other things; his memory was a little fuzzy, adding that he didn't want anyone to know about this. He described the beings as smaller, about four feet tall. They were dressed in white suits and wore masks with helmets, like motorcycle helmets on their heads. They hid their faces behind large goggles. He admitted being frightened of them.

There are strange hand paintings discovered in rock art and on ancient building sites throughout the world. Scientists have not been able to answer what they represented, but a Maya elder explained the significance of them.

Mateo introduced Clarke to Yoc, a Maya elder, who looked younger than his eighty years. Yoc told them they are the space people, the Sky Gods, the Star People, the extraterrestrials or aliens — whatever you like to call them. They are the ones who left their handprints. There are many different Star People. They come from many different places. Only one group is connected to the Maya. Some of the Star People are from this solar system, but not all. There is a confederation and that thousands of spacecraft visit Earth on any given day. At this moment, there are hundreds of spaceships circling the Earth. Our governments do not have the technology to see them. They tell me that their people live all over Earth watching and helping man."

Yoc went on to tell them that he is in contact with the Star People who live among us. "They help scientists to improve the lives of people. They help leaders who work for peace. They perform many tasks as I understand," he said. "They come in sixteen-year cycles. They left in 2000; they will return in 2016. Then will stay sixteen years and leave again. It takes sixteen years to travel to Earth."

According to Yoc, aliens have a lifespan of 800 years. He said they told him that we are the only warring planet in the solar system. There are other planets that war, but they are not in this solar system. They told him that there are planets where the inhabitants still live in the Dark Ages and do not even know about the wheel. There are planets where the inhabitants never age and there is a planet that is so far advanced to others that the beings there can assume almost any form they choose simply by using their mind. They say there are planets with cities inside of crystals that shine like the moon at night because the planets have no other night source of light.

Yoc's description of a crystal city reminded me of Betty Andreasson Luca's description of the place she was taken by the gray aliens where she visited crystal lakes and buildings described in Fowler's book *The Watchers.*

Clarke met another young Maya man named Benito who was a driver/guide at the San Cristobal Hotel. His father called them 'the people who guided us here.' They were our teachers at one time; they taught people about the universe — today they just come to warn about the dangers of radiation, pollution, and the destruction of the climate and collect medicines.

Benito said, "We call them the *Tuhohani,* the people from the stars."

Clarke asked him if he thought the Earth would be destroyed.

"This is the fourth world, Señora. It has been destroyed before. Each time, people were careless with the Earth. There is a reason why we are here. We were placed on this planet to look after it. We have been allowed to evolve as a people, but we have not been able to perform the task given to us. A day is coming when we must answer for our disregard of our mission. On that day, the Earth will be turned upside down."

When asked how he knew this, Benito said, "They tell me. The Mayan language is the language of the *Tuhohani.* That's what they speak too. They warn us that we must prepare for the future."

Asked what they looked like, he answered, "They look like us for the most part, although some are taller and fairer. They speak our language, but they only communicate with the healers."

"When the Earth is destroyed, do you believe that is the end of the planet?"

He answered, "There will be a fifth world. The fourth world will be cleansed and those who survive will have another chance. The *Tuhohani* will be here to help those survivors begin a new world. This will be our last chance to make things right with the Earth and to fulfill our tasks."

Benito believes that the Maya will survive because they are the caretakers of Earth.

Leland's Story

Dr. Clarke included another bizarre story involving clone humans, which begs the question if true—why are aliens creating clones that resemble living humans? Several sources claim that human-looking alien beings have integrated into human society and currently live in major cities. Further study of us seems out of the question because they have been experimenting on us for eons. If they planned a takeover of the Earth, it would seem more feasible that they would have done it before we developed nuclear weapons. Or are they the ones responsible for the chaos and escalating tensions throughout the world?

Clarke met Leland, an artist known for his Native American handcrafted drums, in the summer of 2000. She traveled to meet him at his cabin, located on a rutted dirt road near the Nebraska border, to pick up a drum for one of her colleagues at the University.

Leland was tall, which is a common trait for Northern Plains Indian men, and already his age was showing with his swollen arthritic fingers. He had a "bum knee" as he explained to Clarke that he had worked in Nebraska breaking horses. He had worked many jobs through the years including cowhand, a garbage collector, a ditch digger, a bronco buster, construction, a rancher, and a warrior. He also claimed his grandfather fought in the Little Big Horn battle on July 25 and July 26, 1876, where 268 men died, including General George Custer.

It didn't take long before Leland said, "There ain't many who speak Indian anymore. I have seen many things too. Things that most people could not imagine."

Clarke's interest was piqued at that point and asked what he meant. That's when he began by asking if she believed in people who live on other planets and visit Earth.

Then he began to pour out what he had experienced. "They are not the Star People; the old ones taught us about. The Earth is being invaded. I believe my ranch is a drop-off center."

Clarke asked him what he meant by the "drop-off center."

"That is where they drop them off," he said. "They come at night. They hover over the field. They lower automobiles to the ground. They're filled with people. The craft goes away and when the car returns the next night, only the driver returns. They take the car and driver on board their spacecraft and then they're gone again." He then added, "I think they take them to bus terminals, airports, or cities. Anyplace where they can live unseen."

Clarke asked if these people would stand out and Leland answered that they would have to take them someplace where a stranger could fit in. In the cities, no one would know. "They look like humans, but they're not humans. A few years ago, six to be exact, a craft came in, hovered in that field, and lowered a car to the ground." He pointed to a vacant area almost directly across from his cabin. "The car drove toward the highway, but before they reached it, they had a flat tire. I was watching them from the window there," he said, pointing to the kitchen window. "The lights were off in the house, but

I could see as clear as day. It was a full moon, not a cloud in the sky. The driver got out and walked around the car. He looked at the cabin and then slowly moved toward it. I saw him at the door, but he just stood outside without knocking. It was like he either didn't know what to do or he was thinking about it. He avoided looking at me, so I never got a good look at his face, but he had a short, thick neck. Almost no neck. Like his headset directly on his shoulders. Maybe that's why he struggled with the necktie. He just stood there. I got a feeling he wanted me to follow him." The man didn't say a word to Leland.

"He turned and walked toward the car and I followed. There were three men and two women waiting in the car. None of them spoke. When I got to the car, he pointed to the flat tire. I took the keys out of the ignition and looked in the trunk. I found a tire iron and a spare and took it around to the front. I explained the tire had to be changed."

"Did he understand you?" Clarke questioned.

"He understood, but when I told him the passengers would have to get out of the car, so I could jack it up, he appeared confused. I walked around and opened the door and motioned for them to get out. They all filed out on the opposite side and stood in a huddle behind the car. They didn't come near me."

Leland told Clarke that he fixed the tire and motioned for the passengers to get back in the car. As he started to go back home, the driver gave him ten silver dollars — real silver dollars! He sold nine of them to a pawnshop for a hundred dollars and kept one silver dollar, showing Clarke.

He explained, "It's my lucky silver dollar. It reminds me that I touched an alien and lived to tell about it." Again, he continued to tell Clarke why he thought they were non-human. "Well, they came in a spacecraft for one thing. They weren't friendly. None of them spoke to me. They acted strange like they were scared or didn't belong here. The women were wearing those high heels and had trouble walking in them as if they had never worn them before."

Leland said the aliens had not visited in four months. The cars they had were big black cars, like Chevys or Buick, but he wasn't sure of the make of the cars — most likely American-made (or were they alien-made?).

When asked why he had not reported the bizarre incidents to tribal people, he felt that they'd take him away for being insane. Soon they walked out to a field where he pointed to their tire tracks. "That's where the spacecraft hangs in the sky, a car drops down like it's on an invisible elevator. It [the car] travels along the path to the main highway."

Leland then pointed to a barren circle. "Nothing grows there. That's where the craft hovers above the ground. They've killed all the grass."

Author's comment: Oddly, Clarke never thought to photograph the barren circle and include it in her book.

Finally, Clarke asked Leland why he thought the visitors were coming to Earth. He shook his head and looked off toward the sky. "Maybe Mother Earth is a better planet. Maybe they are coming here to learn our ways. Or maybe they are the Christopher Columbus of this time and they're just waiting to take away from the white man what he took from us."

Clarke wasn't sure if he really meant that or was just making light of them.

Over the two years, Clarke wrote that she visited Leland every chance she got. His story always remained the same. Two months before his death, she stopped to see him and met his friend Walter. The aliens had returned.

Clarke never saw Leland again, but Walter gave her Leland's prized silver dollar, saying he thought Leland would have wanted her to have it. Why didn't Dr. Clarke have the silver dollar analyzed to find out if it was minted in the United States?

Clarke had met two Native Americans who claimed to have either encountered a twin clone or seen aliens dropping off cloned humans. Our government knows what is going on and the alien's ultimate agenda, yet they allow it, probably because they want greater technology in exchange for the aliens experimenting on us. Are they biological robots here to monitor humans? Is a planned invasion about to happen? With everything going on in the world, I suspect that a great number of soulless human-looking beings are among us, and here to stir up global events.

Another Star People story came from another Maya elder, who was eighty years old and lived in the Guatemalan jungle. He talked about the Shining Ones or Space People. They are the ones who left their handprints. He told Clarke that there are many types of Star People. They come from many different places. Only one group is connected to the Maya. Some of the Star People are from this solar system, but not all. There are sixty-seven solar systems in a confederation and thousands of spacecraft visit Earth on any given day. At this moment, there are hundreds of spaceships circling the Earth, and their people live all over the Earth watching and helping humans. Our governments do not have the technology to see them. Although the Star People left Earth in 2000, he believed they would return in 2016 and would stay for sixteen years and then leave again."

Clarke asked why they are known as the Shining People and the elder replied, "In their true state, they are balls of light. It is only when they assume a human form that you see them. Otherwise, you are blinded by them. Many people never know they have met them. They see balls of light, not realizing that they are actually living forms."

Addie and Tansy's Story and Their Horses
This story comes from Dr. Ardy Clarke's 2019 *Space Age Indians: Their Encounters with the Blue Men, Reptilians, and other Star People.*

Addie and Tansy are friends and grew up together on the reservation (the location was not revealed in the book). Their parents owned adjoining ranches. The girls entered the rodeo circuit and were state and regional barrel racing and calf-roping champions. Besides their rodeo pursuits, they enjoyed horseback riding and camping, writing music, surfing the internet, and staying in touch with friends and relatives on social media. They often took their horses for three-day weekends into the nearby hills. Something unimaginable happened on one such trip.

Addie met with Dr. Clarke and pointed out the general area where her favorite camping spot was over the nearby butts in a low valley surrounded by hills. She and Tansy would pitch a tent under the trees and spend their time surfing the net, making videos on our cell phones, writing music, and going on long rides. They always took enough food to feed an army.

Both girls were high school juniors and could have passed for twins. They were both about five feet seven and trim. They told Ardy that working the ranch and lifting hay bales kept them strong and in shape. Addie had her dark braided hair, worn to her waist, and Tansy's thick black hair was pulled in a ponytail. Although they were beautiful, they didn't seem to be aware of it. Their joy for life, their humor, and their love for the horses, their families, and each other would have made any parent proud.

The girls admitted they weren't competitive with each other—just everyone else.

"Addie, your mother told me that the two of you had an encounter with Star People on one of your camping trips recently. Can you tell me about that?" Dr. Clarke asked.

Addie responded, "It was more than an encounter. It was a kidnapping if you know what I mean."

"Our kidnapping happened last year," Tansy said.

At the time of the encounter, the girls were fifteen years old. Addie continued, "It was a Friday afternoon when we packed our horses for the trip. Some clouds were moving in from the west, but we decided to go anyway. We'd camped out in the rain, and we weren't going to let a few clouds keep us from our weekly campout."

"It was going to be our last camping trip until Thanksgiving weekend," said Tansy. "School was going to start the following week. She paused for a stick of gum and offered one to Addie and Dr. Clarke.

When the girls arrived at their special spot, they hurried to put up the tent and put all their food and belongings inside. They started a fire and planned to heat up chili made by Addie's mother. Addie took a deep breath and said, "It was several hours later. As the evening grew dark—it gets dark about seven now, the clouds became more threatening, and when the first clap of thunder came, followed by lightning, we checked on the horses and decided to get inside the tent."

Tansy said it was a downpour and only lasted a few minutes. After the storm, the girls crawled out of the tent to check on the horses and then tried to save their fire.

"Once we got the fire going again, we decided to take the horses to the pond for a drink," said Addie. "We got the flashlights, mounted the horses bareback, and headed to the water. We no sooner headed toward the pond than a bright light came down from the sky and shined directly on top of us." Addie looked to Tansy, reaching for her hand for comfort. "The horses became frightened and started to run toward the pond. It was all we could do to hold on."

Tansy continued the story. "Whenever we went, I looked upward trying to figure out where the light was coming from and it blinded me.

Addie took over. "Suddenly, I had the strangest feeling. Everything went silent. There were no animal sounds, no tree sounds, not even the sound of the horses drinking. It was like everything on Earth, at least in our little spot, stood still. I didn't even have a chance to mention it to Tansy when all of a sudden, we were airborne.

Tansy described that she and Addie and the horses were rising in the air as they hung on for dear life. The horses went limp. Tansy hugged her horse Juniper around the neck and clung to him. She was dizzy and was afraid she'd fall off. Addie's horse Starwood was lifeless too, thinking he was dead. Then she thought the four of them were dead. She began screaming as loud as she could, but there was no one to hear me, not even Tansy, who appeared as lifeless as Juniper.

"The next thing we knew, we were in a huge, strange room," said Tansy. "We clung to our horses' necks, and when we sat up, we saw several short, skinny little people approaching us. There were the strangest people I had ever seen."

Addie added that they were bald with huge black eyes, and they were not wearing any clothes. They had the strangest skin, kind of rubbery looking. Their coloring was strange. Then she screamed and passed out because when she came to Tansy and I were on tables in another room. Her first thought was of her horse Starwood, and where he was. She thought they had done something with him. Addie yelled at them, but they just stood there staring at her.

Dr. Clarke asked what happened next, and Addie replied, "That's when these tall men came into the room. They looked like humans, and I yelled at them and demanded to know where we were. I wanted to know about Starwood."

What struck Tansy was they looked like pale, hungry humans who had been locked up somewhere without any sunlight. Their hair was very thin. They had long faces, and their skin was so white, she thought they were ghosts. (alien/human hybrids have been described like Tansy's description). "They were dressed in funny white suits with a blue band around their arms. One of them approached us and told us that the horses were okay and that we would be okay."

Addie thought they looked like women but thought they were men — but she wasn't sure. They were very dainty.

They girls didn't speak to them out loud, but sensed the horses were okay. The man's manner calmed the girls, almost as if he was a friend.

Next, the beings took blood samples, a strange of our hair, and scraped our skin. "But they inserted something into us. I don't' know how to describe it. It was a glass tube or a glass needle of some kind. I'd never seen an instrument like that. It was a long object. I screamed when I saw it, but one of the tall ones said it would not hurt," said Tansy.

Addie believed they were doctors who inserted the instrument into her navel. As if prompted, both girls pulled up their t-shirts and displayed a round, red mark about the size of a dime. Dr. Clarke examined it and they were identical in size, shape, and placement, reminding her of a blood-blister that she had as a child.

"It's been years, and the marks remain. It didn't hurt," Tansy said. They said it wouldn't hurt and it didn't. It's a constant reminder."

"They marked us forever," said Addie. "After that, they said we were too young and that we should come with them. Those little freaky guys came, held us by the arm, and took us to our horses."

Suddenly, they were back on Earth, sitting on their horses as though nothing ever happened. The horses drank from the pond, a clap of thunder filled the night, and they looked up and saw the outline of a huge round object lift upward and disappear in a flash of lightning. They stayed up all night talking about the strange event.

Tansy had a theory, "I think our age saved us. They said we were too young for childbearing."

Addie jumped in, "I think they discovered we were virgins, and they stopped their tests on us."

"Why else would we be too young?" Tansy questioned. "They said they were looking for breeders. We were too young to be good breeders. I think they were looking for females to breed — just like we breed horses. It makes me sick to think they breed people. Maybe they planned to make us pregnant. When they discovered we were just girls, they let us go. I hope they don't come back when we get older."

"If they do, we'll kick their butts," Addie included. They looked at each other and fist-bumped and laughed joyously.

Tansy said she got the same message that they were too young. "We were not good specimens. That is it. But I think Addie is right. They had other plans for us but decided it was not right because of our youth."

Dr. Clarke asked if the aliens used the word specimens.

"That's the term he used," said Tansy. "He looked me in the eyes and said I was not a good specimen. While I was in their presence, it meant nothing to me, but afterward, I was angry to think they considered me, a human being, as a specimen like I think of a frog in our biology class. The teacher called the frog a "specimen" in our biology class."

Dr. Clarke said, "I have never heard of anyone being abducted with their horses."

"Well, there is another thing about our horses," said Tansy. It's like a miracle. You're going to think we're crazy but it's like our horses are younger. We hoped they would perform with us through college, but both of us were already training a backup for Juniper and Starwood."

"The most amazing thing happened," said Addie. "At first, we noticed changes in their ability to run and their general response to our cues as riders. But the most amazing thing was their energy levels. They had more stamina and more agility. Their response to our bodies and to our directions was amazing. It's like they could read our minds. Do you think Star Men could do something to our horses to make them mind-readers?"

Dr. Clarke shook here head, "I'm not sure."

"And why would they do it?" Addie asked, looking at Dr. Clarke for an answer.

"Well, I think they did something to them," Tansy said. "They're like super-horses. They've gained a lot of attention on the rodeo circuit. Several judges have labeled them the best barrel racing and roping horses in the country. This past year, we've been offered thousands of dollars for stud services. I don't know what those Sar People did, but we know the changes in Starwood and Juniper have something to do with them."

Addie said they had not bred their stallions. "Our dads and grandpas think we'd better keep their newfound abilities under wraps. They want to be the first to breed them. We're just looking for the right mares."

The girls agreed that they hoped the special abilities their horses now had would be transferred to their offspring. Tansy remarked that they were good horses, but not super horses. "They were as good as they could be. They helped us win a lot of competitions and hopefully, they'll get us college scholarships, but they were not the best in the world. I think now they are the best in the world."

"They told us the horses were excellent specimens," Addie said, "but I was apprehensive. I didn't like the word specimens. To me, my Starwood was not a specimen. He was part of the family. I worried they were doing tests on them like they were doing to us."

"That's a strange response. Did they elaborate on what they meant by *excellent specimen*?"

"Nothing," Tansy said. "It's obvious they did something. The horses are different, in temperament, but it's like they're super horses. You're going to think I'm crazy, but I always talked to Juniper. I raised him from a colt, and when I was little, I called him and Addie my best friends. As I grew up, I knew he didn't understand all my chatter, but I still talked to him like he was my best friend. But now it's different. It's like he understands what I say."

Dr. Clarke then asked if Tansy could give her an example of her horse's new behavior.

"Sure. Last week the wild daises were in full bloom in that field." Dr. Clarke followed her finger as she pointed to a large meadow. "I decided I would pick a bouquet for Mom. She loves wild daisies. She says they are better than roses. So, I told Juniper I wanted to pick some daisies for Mom, and he looked at me and immediately trotted off toward the meadow. I stood and watched him. I was like he knew what I was talking about. When I hesitated in following him, he sauntered further toward the field, then stopped and looked back as though he was waiting for me to follow him. He did this several times before I joined him in the meadow."

Addie chimed her about her experience with Starwood. "Similar things have happened to me. One morning I told Starwood I wanted to pick some wild strawberries for breakfast, and he headed directly for the strawberry field without any direction from me. The trip to the wild strawberries was not a ride across the fields. It required descending several ravines to reach them in a low-lying gulch. He knew exactly where I wanted to go with no direction from me. It's like he led me; I didn't lead him."

"I wish I knew what the Star Men did to them," Tansy said. "It could change veterinary science. You know, we're Space Age Indians. We have grown up in a world where travel to Mars will happen in our lifetime. What they did to our horses is something out of science fiction, and it has changed our lives forever. The Star Men have given us a glimpse of what the future holds for us in the space age."

After the interview, Dr. Ardy Clarke met the girl's horses who raced around the corral like young colts. Starwood's pinto coloring was beautiful; Juniper was a gorgeous palomino. When the spotted the girls, they raced toward them. Dr. Clarke sensed the horses appeared to understand their youthful owners before they even uttered a word.

Dr. Clarke stayed in touch with the girls for a while. Both planned to study animal husbandry and veterinary science when they graduated from high school. Both were accepted to the university in a junior enrichment program. Since their abduction, they have not wavered I their belief that the Star Men changed the direction of their lives and turned their horses into super animals. They eventually bred Starwood and Juniper with champion mares their father purchased from a Texas breeder. Dr. Clarke wondered if the birth of the colts would share the special evolved traits of their fathers, and if that is the case, what would that mean for the future of horses?

CHAPTER ELEVEN

THE BENEVOLENT BLUE MEN

The following Blue Men stories were investigated by Dr. Ardy Sixkiller Clarke in her book, *Space Age Indians.*

Dr. Clarke traveled to Hawaii to meet with a former interviewee and connect with some colleagues involved in the Native Hawaiian Charter School Movement. While she was there, she learned that an old friend had been admitted to the Veteran's Hospital on the island. Ira, who identified himself as a Dakota Sioux and the best tracker in the Vietnam War, had lived on the island since he left the military. The first time he was in Hawaii was when he was on R & R while in Vietnam and fell in love with the islands. He decided to stay.

Ira, who was named for a Pima Indian Marine who was

immortalized as one of the six marines in the famous photo of the flag raising on Iwo Jima, had suffered for years from COPD emphysema.

Ira positioned his pillows as Dr. Clarke hugged and kissed him, as he began his story. He told her that seven of his comrades were American Indian veterans all living in Hawaii, and they were all in the same squad in Vietnam. He considered them the best trackers and that was the reason they were detailed to the Recon Unit. The men entered the hospital room and Ira introduced them. They had gone through drug addiction, alcoholism, and PTSD.

"To the space age Indians and brotherhood," Wilson said, as he poured another round of Jack Daniels and the group toasted each other.

"Who are the space age Indians?" asked Dr. Clarke.

"We are!" they replied in unison.

When the bottle of Jack Daniels was half-empty, the conversation turned to Dr. Clarke's books. Chester, another Vietnam comrade began, "This encounter is the reason we call our group the Space Age Indians.

"I'll start at the beginning," Ira said as he paused, removing his oxygen mask, and coughed. After a moment, he continued, "We were a part of a Recon Unit located about twenty miles south of the DMZ. We set up a bivouac in a jungle area that had a few steep hills. One night, we went on a reconnaissance mission into a small valley to the east of our encampment to check out some reported activity. Chester was in command. He was our sergeant." Ira looked at his barrel-chested friend who sat on the bed next to him.

Chester intervened as Ira struggled to speak. "I sent Ira ahead to scout out the situation. He was the best damn scout in the Marine Corps and kept the rest of us alive." All six men nodded in agreement. "I counted on him to keep us safe. When Ira returned, he reported sighting a small bad of VC [Viet Cong] on the north hill about two klicks from our position."

Percy took over the conversation and mentioned the strange blue light, and then Ira took over. "I didn't know what it was. A huge blue ball hung in the sky about three times the size of the full moon. It was slowly making its way across the sky. I watched it approach the earth, closer and closer, until it rested on the hill across from the VC camp. I heard the excited voices of the VC as it came to rest, but not speaking their language I wasn't sure what they were saying. But I understand that they seemed in wonder of it as I was. Shortly, after that, I headed back to the base to report."

"When Ira reported the blue light, I discounted it as an anomaly," Chester said. "There were strange things that happened in the jungle at night, but I couldn't shake the feeling that something about this night was different. There were no sounds around us and that made all of us uneasy."

Mathias stepped in and said, "Usually at night, the jungle reeked with noises and sounds that were sometimes deafening. Despite the unusual situation, Chester ordered us to follow him into the night where the enemy encampment was located. We were no more than a half a klick away from the VC, when a barrage of gunshots pierced the night. Strange thing though, the VC were not firing at us but were directing their fire at the valley below."

"We hunkered down and had a ring-side seat into what appeared to be a one-sided battle," Ira said. "The VC fired with abandon at flittering blue reflections moving about in the valley below. We counted three glimmering lights but couldn't make out any forms, although the images appeared to be moving upright and in a methodic fashion. Again and again, the blue images ignored their assault. Finally, a beam of light landed squarely in the middle of the enemy. There was a lightning flash and a thunderous boom and we never heard a weapon fired again."

"Did you think the blue entities had taken out the VC encampment?" Dr. Ardy Clarke asked.

"We didn't know," Chester continued. "I ordered the men

to stay hidden and wait out the night and observe. After the explosion on the hillside where the VC were located, we heard no further sounds or firing. While I assumed their encampment had been destroyed, I wanted to approach the camp in daylight. At the same time, Ira was keeping tabs on the blue entities who were roaming the valley floor. Not more than ten minutes passed when Ira alerted me that the blue images had changed direction and were headed toward our position."

Ira jumped into the conversation again. "By the time I recognized the forms to be human-like but encased in this shimmering blue light, Chester ordered us to retreat further into the jungle and away from the direct path of the beings. I returned to lead the team to a safer position when I came face to face with one of them. We both stood and stared at one another. He was a tall being, probably nine feet tall and muscular. I was frozen. I dropped my rifle to the ground and at the same time, he lowered his arm. I knew he wasn't my enemy. I called out to my companions to lower their guns and the seven of us stood in amazement at this giant, shining blue creature that stood before us.

"It was difficult to make out any features since the shining light that surrounded him morphed his face. Seconds passed and two other humanoid figures joined him. They stood silently, as though assessing us, then walked past us and disappeared into the jungle."

Dr. Clarke then asked how he knew they were not their enemies, and Ira said that he sensed it. "I never heard a voice. I just knew." He looked to the other men, and they all nodded in agreement.

"Moments later, we saw the blue ball that Ira originally saw," Chester said. "It lifted off the hillside and disappeared into the sky."

Next, Addison said, "We knew we had just encountered star men."

"But that's not the end of the story," Ira said, as he began to cough uncontrollably. When Dr. Clarke reached for the nurse's button, Ira held up his hand, and as if by a miracle his coughing stopped. "This story should be told. I've met other vets who have encountered the blue men, and none of us have ever told our story. I think it's time."

Everyone agreed.

Chester began to talk about their trip into the valley. "We were still stunned by what we had seen, and every one of us seemed lost in our thoughts. As Ira headed out in front of us, occasionally returning to assure us the area was clear of VC, we reached the valley floor and began the ascent up the hillside where the enemy encampment had been located.

"Do you remember the smell?" Ira asked. His friends agreed. "It wasn't the smell of gunpowder. It was an overwhelming smell of hot metal and jungle rot. A cloud of smoke hung over the area, making our eyes sting and our noses run. We gagged and covered our faces."

Ira started coughing again. Dr. Clarke handed him a glass of water, and Ira reached behind him, pulled out the Jack Daniels bottle, and topped it off the water. "Just what I needed."

Chester filled everyone's shot glasses and continued the story. "The strangest thing about the whole site was there were no bodies. The weapons were there, but some melted, others hung from trees as though flung into the sky. Clustered around the machine gun post were three circles of darkened earth. As we moved around, we found seven more. It was like the enemy soldiers had evaporated and all that was left were discolored circles."

"Dust to dust. As we said, we're not the only ones who saw the blue men. There are other stories out of Vietnam about the blue men. We never reported our experiences. We agreed among ourselves to remain silent. The brass would've never believed us anyway," Ira said.

"Or they'd think we were on the wacky-tabacky," said Wilson, who claimed to be the best-looking member of the group. "But I swear on a stack of Bibles, this happened, and it is true."

"Not only blue men were encountered on several occasions by other squads," said Chester. "I am going to give you the name and address of a friend in another unit who met reptile men in the jungle. His story should be told as well." Dr. Clarke then handed Chester her notebook, and he wrote the name. She decided her next stop would be in Oklahoma to meet Sherman, the friend of a friend who had a story to tell.

"I know of another vet who encountered the Blue Men," said Addison. "He told me they saved his life. Let me have your notebook and I'll give you another name. You guys remember Ute. We called him Ute because he is a full-blood Ute from Colorado, I think. His real name was Alphonse. We felt Ute suited him better. Anyway, he lives on the Big Island and grows coffee. I'll call him and tell him about you. He's a good guy. Unlike us, he married a beautiful Hawaiian girl and had lots of little Utes. If you go see him, I know he will talk to you."

"You know, your story is quite unique," Dr. Clark said.

"Bizarre is what it is. But it's true. We were all witnesses to the event," Ira said. Everyone then swore it was true.

"To me, there was irony in the encounter," Chester said. "Here we were, the seven of us in this godforsaken part of the world fighting to stay alive while NASA was basking in the glory of putting a man on the moon (1969). That's another reason the name for our group, Space Age Indians, is appropriate. We know more about space than NASA. We have touched space. We know there's life out there; something NASA is still trying to discover."

"And we know something else too," Ira interjected. "Man will never be allowed to move beyond this planet in his present warmongering mentality. When we encounter an indigenous space race and say, 'We come in peace,' this time we better mean it."

Dr. Ardy Clarke closed with this comment: *Before leaving*

the hospital that afternoon, I took the names and email addresses of all of Ira's friends and promised I would keep in touch. At the desk, I spoke with the VA administrator and asked to be notified if Ira's condition changed. I signed a form stating that I would be responsible for taking care of his last arrangements. The next morning as I stepped out of the shower in my hotel room, the phone rang. Ira had passed away in his sleep. He had died exactly seventy-two years on the date of his birth. We had a memorial service on the beach for Ira — his six friends and me. I chose the site of our farewell in the same location where I first met Ira. A Native Hawaiian chant offered up by one of Ira's Native Hawaiian friends pierced the stillness. At midnight we took a dip in the ocean and toasted Ira with shots of Jack Daniels.

On my way home, I carried an urn with Ira's ashes. I planned to take it to North Dakota when the snows melt and spread his ashes on Strawberry Hill, a place where the wild strawberries grow. Deer, antelope, prairie chickens, and rabbits stop by throughout the year. It is a fitting place for the only man to propose to me on a beach in Waikiki.

Ute's Story

Before leaving Hawaii, Dr. Ardy Clarke took a short plane trip to the Big Island to meet Ute, the man Addison had mentioned at the hospital while visiting Ira. She rented a car and drove to the Hilo Hawaiian Hotel off Banyan Drive. The next morning, she drove to meet Uta, who lived fifteen miles from the town of Hilo.

As Addison stated, Ute was a full-blood Ute and a Vietnam veteran. He could have passed for a number of different ethnic groups found on the Hawaiian Islands. He greeted Dr. Clarke warmly as they walked on a slippery hillside. They sat on a wooden bench and looked out over his property. Ute said it was his favorite place on the island and a place where he liked "to talk story," a common expression in the islands in which people tell stories from the heart.

"I was eighteen when Uncle Sam sent me to 'Nam," Ute

began. "Just a boy right out of high school. Uncle Sam had a long arm and could find you anywhere in those days. I didn't want to go, and I thought of going to Canada. I had this dream that I would never see Colorado again or my Dad. There was just Dad and me in those days. I had a sister, but she died of pneumonia when she was twelve. My dad died while I was in 'Nam. I didn't find out about it until six weeks later. By that time, the tribe had already buried him. I never went home then, and I haven't been back since."

Dr. Clarke said her readers would like to know his story and that she would disguise his identity and the place where he lived so that no one will ever find him. Dr. Clarke also promised she'd never print his story without his permission.

Ute began his story. "Uncle Sam lied to Americans during the war. I was part of several units sent to Cambodia. The Cambodians, who claimed neutrality during the war, were not neutral. They allowed the Viet Cong to establish bases and move back and forth across their borders. The year was 1970, and with Nixon's election in the U.S. was shifting its position of winning the war to one they called Vietnamization, which was to shore up the Vietnamese government and eliminate the border threat from Cambodia. Of course, we know how that turned out. Nixon claimed it was the South Vietnamese army that was invading Cambodia, but the truth was, we were right there with them."

"I heard that you have a story about the Blue Men. Can you tell me about it?" Dr. Clarke asked.

"Our plan was to invade a territory called Parrot's Beak. I don't know why it was called that. I never saw a parrot that day. The VC took us on in a full battle. Soldiers were falling all around me. It was probably an hour into the battle before I suddenly realized I was separated from my squad. I was alone." (Parrot's Beak is located 65 km north-west of Saigon).

"What do you mean, you were alone?"

"None of the men who entered into the invasion with me were standing. They were all dead, dying, or in retreat. I remember finding a large tree. I sat down, my back leaning into it, and I cried. I know that my dream of never returning to Colorado has come true. I was going to die. There was no escape.

"I remember standing and throwing my weapon away. I had killed my last man. If I was going to die, I decided that I wasn't going to be the aggressor. I was going to die without a weapon."

Dr. Clarke asked, "How did you manage to get out of Parrot's Beak?"

"It was the Blue Men. They saved me. I fell to the ground in prayer. I asked Jesus to look upon me favorably. I asked him to forgive me for my sins and especially for killing the VC. As I prayed, a light engulfed me and the next thing I knew, I was floating upward through the sky."

"Were you aware that you were being taken away from the battle?"

Ute replied, "No. When the light fell upon me, I thought God had come for me and I was dead. I didn't understand I had been taken by the Blue Men. I woke in a clean, cool room. There were blue lights, a hazy mist, and I was no longer dirty, hot and sweaty. My combat fatigues were clean. I felt fresh and energized. I sat up from a metal table in the room, but I was still disoriented. I had no idea where I was or how I got there. I walked around the room, and I decided I was in heaven, maybe in a holding room, and God was going to judge my fate."

Dr. Clarke then asked when he realized that it was not God, but the Blue Men.

"I'm not sure how long I was in the room. I think time must be different in space. It could have been five minutes or five hours for all I know. But as time passed, a tall, blue spirit man entered. I say he was a blue man, but it was hard to make out his characteristics. His whole body shimmered. Later he explained to me that their bodies in their natural form were not solid, but they were beings of light. He said they could move back and forth between light and solid material, but it was tedious and for the most part, they did not take a solid form because people were alarmed by a solid blue man."

Dr. Clarke asked if the blue men told him why he was taken.

"To save me. They had been observing the battle and saw me prostrate on the ground, praying, and decided I was worth saving. I'm still waiting to find out what made me worthy when dozens of others died." Ute continued his story and how long he stayed with the blue beings.

"For several days earth time. When the invasion was over and the remaining troops were retreating, I was taken to a safe place where I could join other combat troops unnoticed. When we returned to base, I discovered I was the only one from my squad to survive. That was a tough thing to deal with. I was sent to R&R, and I ended up in Hawaii. I was on the beach in Waikiki one night when I met two Hawaiian girls. They were sisters. They took me home with them, and I met the rest of the family. It was the first time since I was drafted that I felt like I had a home. When I got out of the military, I returned to Hawaii and married the oldest one. We are still together and have six beautiful children. I am blessed. All because of the Blue Men."

"While you were on board their spacecraft, did you learn anything?" Dr. Clarke asked.

"I learned that their civilization is more than a million years older than ours. Once they live in a solid, material form, but over time they learned how to turn their bodies into energy without destroying their soul." Ute went on to explain he interrupted as their soul. "Well now, I am putting my own assumptions on them. I guess it was their soul. They were able to function as beings anyway, but maybe it was not their soul. Anyway, being able to become light beings allowed them to ease the population problem until they could find other worlds where their people could spread out and live."

Dr. Clarke asked, "Are you saying they told you their

planet was overpopulated?"

"Yes. So, once they found a way of turning them into light energy, their scientists, leaders, and people of knowledge became light entities. The workers stayed solid, material beings for a time. Today, the light beings and the solid beings live together peacefully. There is no intermarriage between them but they have a mutual respect for one another. The light beings never age. They can live forever, but they do occasionally become solid beings so they can experience the real world."

"Did they ever become solid in front of you?"

"Only one. He was my caretaker. He felt it would make me more comfortable. As I said, they were giant men. Eight feet tall or taller. Their skin was blue, which they attributed to the atmosphere on their planet. They had perfect human features otherwise. Their civilization has spread out to two other planets in their part of the universe. On one of the planets, the people ceased being blue over time. They have also recorded diminished growth in their offspring."

"Did they take you to their planet?"

"No, we stayed above the Earth. They had instruments to magnify different places on Earth. That's how they observe what's going on. They don't believe in aggression. They're a peaceful race, and then they use their advanced knowledge and skills to defend themselves peacefully."

(Remember in Ira's Blue Men story, he, and his comrades couldn't find any trace of the VC after the exchange of gunfire the next day. They found weapons melted at the VC encampment and there was a strong smell of smoke. If the Blue Men obliterated the VC, they certainly aren't as peaceful as they claim. Or perhaps they moved the VC to another place, but Ute was saved while his men died by the VC.

Dr. Clarke asked how they defend themselves.

"Mind control and by removing subjects to a different setting."

Dr. Clarke then asked if the Blue Men had any human

qualities.

"If you mean emotions, I didn't see much. It was obvious that they were compassionate in that they saved me, but I saw no such thing as laughter, joking, sadness, or happiness. They were stoic, all business." Ute went on to describe how they communicate. "In light form, they used telepathy — that was a new word for me — but I learned it was thinking thoughts and responding in thoughts. But when he was in solid form, my caretaker spoke as you and I spoke. He said that few of his people spoke as you and I spoke. Over time, evolution has changed them, and they no longer had to speak."

"What did you think about that," Dr. Clarke asked.

"I told him I wasn't sure I would like to live in a world where people could read my thoughts. He told me that it eliminated needless thinking. People learned only to think and speak when necessary. They learned to keep thoughts blank. When a child is born to a solid couple, they remove children at the age of two who demonstrate exceptional intelligence. They allow those children to live in a special colony."

Dr. Clarke questioned the word 'colony'.

"That's the word he used, but it seemed to mean in an area removed from others. There they are free to dream without their peers knowing their thoughts. These are the future scientists and people of knowledge. Eventually, they too become figures of life and help the others in developing new technologies."

"Can you think of anything else they told you?"

"One other thing. They still have babies like we do, but only the solid couples." Ute explained what happened to the other babies that don't meet their intellectual specifications. "He said they become workers."

"And who are the workers?" Dr. Clarke asked.

"They are the specials. They build the cities and help modernize the new planets. They are taken care of spiritually by the light people and according to him are very happy in their role."

"Has your encounter with the Blue Men changed your life in any way, other than the obvious?"

"They saved me, but then I wonder if it was my fate all along and I would have lived without their interference. The fact that I never returned home to Colorado does not mean they had anything to do with it. I fell in love, and the Big Island is my home until the big one blows and sinks it into the sea. But there is one thing: I am a walking example of a man who knows the truth about life in outer space. The Blue Men exist, just as you and I. They keep a watch on Earth and they tell me, if we choose to destroy ourselves, they will let it happen. But, in such a case, if I so choose, they will come for me and my family and take us to another place."

"Do you believe that?"

"I believe they have that much power. I'm not sure I will go with them. Earth is my home. I can't imagine that I would ever leave Mother Earth. She sustains me by allowing me to support my family, growing coffee in the rich soil on our small twenty-acre farm, and so far I can't think of any place else I would like to live."

Dr. Clarke asked Ute if he had anyone else that she might interview about 'Nam. Ute suggested several friends who encountered the Blue Men.

"Do you have any idea why so many Vietnam veterans saw UFOs during the war?"

"I've thought about that. I think if you could take a survey of Vietnam veterans, you'd find that probably as many as five out of ten saw UFOs or had direct encounters with aliens. While the stories vary and can seem outrageous at times, I believe their stories. It was a war of the elites fought by the poor. The rich got richer off of Vietnam. The poor got poorer. We came home drug-addicted, alcoholic, and mentally ill — all so the fat cats could count their money.

Mele's Blue Men Story

Again, this story comes from Dr. Ardy Sixkiller Clarke in her book *Space Age Indians*.

Mele, who admitted to being a drug addict while in Vietnam, underwent treatment when he was stationed in Hawaii after a two-year stint in Vietnam. He decided to make Hawaii his home once discharged from the military. A Chickasaw Indian by birth, Mele preferred the ethnic diversity of Hawaii over his home state, Georgia. While he also admitted to being involved in the production of marijuana on a small scale when he first left the military, he attributed his sobriety to his Japanese-Hawaiian wife who supported him while he earned a degree in astronomy. He welcomed my visit when I contacted him about telling his story.

Dr. Clarke drove from Hilo to Waimea over Saddle Road. While Waimea was the center of cattle ranching on the Hawaiian Islands, she met Mele at the 9,200-foot base camp of the astronomical observatory at Mauna Kea. Her home is at 6,000 feet in Montana, but she felt the elevation difference immediately. As she leaned against the rental car to catch her breath, she noticed a man approaching, wearing Bermuda shorts and a t-shirt with "Save Mauna Kea" on the front.

Mele explained that there's only thirty percent less oxygen at that altitude than at sea level. He had a small oxygen unit he carried with him at all times. Slowly they descended the volcano and arrived at the town of Waimea.

Mele began telling Dr. Clarke about his life. "I'm 71 now. I came here after 'Nam at twenty-one, so fifty years. A half-century. I love the islands and this park. While it's state-owned, it's leased by the Waimea Outdoor Circle for environmental research, education, and restoration. Their goal has been to remove invasive plant species and replace them with endemic and canoe plants [plants brought to Hawaii by Native Hawaiians in their canoes], along with the endangered and threatened plant species native to Hawaii. It's a place of restoration and anyone who served in Vietnam needs a place of restoration."

Dr. Clarke asked Mele about the Blue Men after Ute had told her that he had his own experiences in Vietnam.

"I haven't told this story since I was in 'Nam," he said. "Ute shared with me his encounter and I shared mine. We were brothers in arms in more ways than one. A lot of brothers saw the Blue Men in 'Nam. I've heard many stories. I believe they were a group of alien visitors who found the war abhorrent, and they were studying our behavior. Now I must tell you, that's my theory. I have no proof or evidence to support it."

Dr. Clarke asked about his incident with the Blue Men.

"Did you ever hear of Operation Ranch Hand? It was herbicidal warfare instituted by the military. I was in *Dak Son* area when they decided to drop their spray, Agent Orange." Mele paused to get his breath again as he and Dr. Clarke found a bench and sat down.

"Anyway, word came down about the spray. I was bent out of shape. I knew the brass knew we were in the area, and yet they indiscriminately decided to spray the region. I was looking for a place where I might find some safety when I came upon a cave. The opening was small, but I crawled inside anyway. As I was pushing myself along on my belly, I saw flashes of light further down the cave. I don't know why I did it, but I continued crawling on my belly toward the light. Even when I was doing it, I thought it was a stupid thing to do. It was just bright flashes like you see if someone was welding in the dark."

"How big was the cave?"

"At the entrance, it was small. I literally was on my belly, pushing myself along with my arms. But about thirty feet inside, the opening became larger and then larger again until I could stand. I'm five feet nine. As I got nearer the light, the flashes increased. I was thinking I had found an opening to one of the VC tunnels. Instead, I was in for the surprise of my life."

"Weren't you afraid to explore the cave?"

"I was nineteen. Invincible. I didn't even think. I just wanted to find out what was going on. The cave was winding. In other words, there were a number of turns and bends, but when I came around the third bend, I saw them," Mele said and began to cough.

Dr. Clarke asked if he was okay and then offered a bottle of water to him.

"It amazes me what you women carry around with you. No wonder you're in better shape than us guys."

Mele continued his story. "I saw three tall entities. They were surrounded by a blinding blue light. At that time, it hadn't registered with me that they were aliens."

"When did you realize they were Star People?"

"I was trying to conceal myself so I could spy on them. I was still trying to determine who they were and what they were doing. My first thought was that they were wearing strange suits. Then I felt a hand on my should and I almost died of a heart attack — when I turned around, I came face to face with a blue man. Before I could react, he took me by the arm and guided me into an enlarged area. I swear, you could have put a jumbo jet inside the area. It was huge, and in the middle sat a spacecraft."

"Can you describe them?"

"They were big, at least eight feet tall. They were muscular, big muscles on their arms like they were body builders. They made me know they didn't believe in war and weren't there to hurt me or anyone else. While they did not take sides, they felt the pain of both sides. They asked me why I was fighting the other men, and I told them I didn't know except that my government told me to fight."

"How did they react to that?" Dr. Clarke asked.

"They told me that governments did not control a man's actions on their plane."

"How long did you stay with them?"

"Perhaps an hour in the cave. They offered to take me away with them. When I told them I couldn't go, they offered to remove me to safety. I took them up on that, and they took me on board and placed me in an area free of Agent Orange. It took me several days to find my squad. Everyone thought I was dead. I didn't tell them I was with the Blue Men who saved me from my own military."

"So do I understand that they took you onboard their spacecraft?"

"They not only took me onboard, but they also showed me Earth from space. They told me Earth was too beautiful to be destroyed by war and biological weapons and that I should do more to change it. I discounted their thoughts. I didn't believe I could make a difference."

"Have you changed your mind about that?"

"I believe we can make a change in our family or our neighborhoods, but I don't think anyone can change the minds of the Washington politicians or brass. They only care about themselves, not us."

"Did the encounter change your life?"

"I got a degree in astronomy. With its high elevation, dry environment, and stable airflow, Mauna Kea's summit is one of the best sites in the world for astronomical observation. Yes, I would say they changed my life. I search the universe for life. It's my hope one day I will see the Blue Men again. Before leaving the Blue Men, I asked them if I would see them again and they told me: 'Watch the skies. We are always there, watching and observing.' So that's what I do I watch the skies."

Follow-up: *Although Dr. Clarke returned to Hawaii almost every year, She has not seen Mele again. She thinks of him occasionally when she watches the night skies over her home in Montana. Like him, she hopes someday to see the Blue Men.*

Sherman's Story: Saved from the Reptilians by the Blue Men by Dr. Ardy Sixkiller Clarke
Dr. Clarke arrived in Binger, Oklahoma on a cold, blustery day in

January. She was there to talk to a veteran with a story about reptilian creatures he encountered during his tour of duty in Vietnam. She drove to the Caddo Indian Government Office and inquired about Sherman with the receptionist, but she had no knowledge of him. After many dead ends, she located him at an elder center specializing in veterans suffering from terminal diseases in a city some eighty miles away. When she told Sherman that a marine in Hawaii had given her his name, a smile crossed his face as he recognized the name of his old friend, Chester.

"You will have to sit close to me, "Sherman said, "or your tape recorder might not pick up my voice. "I'm a victim of 'Nam in more ways than one. Not only was I nearly blinded, but I suffer from COPD."

While he settled himself in a leather recliner near the end table, Dr. Clarke set up her tape recorder. Sherman was a small man and stood more than five-feet-two inches tall and probably weighed no more than a hundred pounds. His wiry black hair, peppered with gray, reminded me of several elders I saw in the reception area of the Caddo Government Hall. He wore thick-rimmed glasses, which he admitted did not help much, so he had long ago given up reading, which was his favorite form of entertainment.

"I spend my days listening to the radio and books on tape. After the war, I suffered from PTSD. Because of this, I suffered from PTSD. Because of this, I never married. I'm the last of a long line of family warriors. It's for the best. If I'd lived a normal life, married, and had children, I'd probably have a son or grandson in Iraq and Afghanistan. Too many senseless wars, but that's not why you're here. You don't want to hear the life story of an old dying Indian man."

Dr. Clarke said she'd love to hear his story and she had all the time in the world.

"It's a good thing I never met you in my younger days. I might have broken my vow of bachelorhood," he said, chuckling loudly. "But first things, I have never told anyone this story, except for Chester. Perhaps its time the world knows about the reptile men.

"I joined the Marine Corps as soon as I was eighteen. I didn't wait for the draft. Being small, I guess I wanted to prove something to myself and maybe the world, that a small man could join the Marines. I graduated from Paris Island and was sent to 'Nam immediately. When I arrived in-country, I had no idea what was in store for me, but I found out the second day I was there." He paused, pushed the lever on his recliner and took two sips of water.

"I was in-country no more than forty-eight hours when word came to our unit that a tunnel had been located. If you don't know about the tunnels, it is something out of another world. The VC dug tens of thousands of miles of tunnels underneath the Cu Chi district northwest of Saigon. They used them to house troops, transport supplies, mount surprise attacks, and set booby traps. Whenever one was discovered, 'tunnel rats' would go into the tunnels to sabotage their underground network, kill any VC inside, set up explosives, and blow up the tunnels. A network of small access holes about two feet wide and three feet deep accessed their tunnel system."

Sherman was one of the tunnel rats. "As I said, on the second day I was there, I was taken to a place where South Vietnamese soldiers, who were on our side, trained Americans to navigate the tunnels. There were also Aussies and Kiwis in training. We were chosen, along with others, because of our size, which was similar to the stature of the Viet Cong, to become part of that program. Following the training, it was a matter of days before I was crawling on my hands and knees through these tunnels. I was given a flashlight, a pistol, and a knife. They were my only protection."

"Did you ever think of refusing to become a tunnel rat," Dr. Clarke asked.

"Refusing such a duty meant immediate court-martial,

and I did not want to spend the war in lock-up, but that idea never occurred to me. I loved the exhilaration of crawling through the tunnels and sabotaging the VC. I figured when I destroyed a tunnel, I saved dozens of American lives."

"What kind of men became tunnel rats?"

"We were an arrogant bunch. We stayed to ourselves to maintain our sanity. We were each other's support. We never took drugs and bragged about doing a job that no sane man would do. We frequently questioned the brass. We hated the second lieutenants. The college boys who knew nothing about war except what they had learned from textbooks."

"How did they feel about you?"

"I think they were afraid of us. Like I said, any man who would go into those tunnels had to be half-crazy. I think they saw us as a threat. Fragging was more common than most people know. Do you know about fragging?"

Dr. Clarke responded. "I think so. Wasn't fragging the deliberate killing of a fellow soldier?"

"Usually it was an NCO (noncommissioned officer) or a second lieutenant. As the war dragged on and it was common knowledge that we were losing, fragging became more frequent, and the officers more afraid." Sherman stopped momentarily as if revisiting the past. "We did some bad things in 'Nam," he said with regret in his voice.

The word fragging was a term coined in the Vietnam War when many of these murders were committed using fragmentation grenades. Fragging incidents in combat were usually attempts to remove leaders perceived to be incompetent and a threat to survival. Most fragging incidents, however, occurred in rear-echelon units and were committed by soldiers on drugs or because unit leaders were enforcing anti-drug policies.

Dr. Clarke then asked if he encountered the reptilians in one of the tunnels.

"I had just returned from R&R in Hawaii. After thirteen months in Vietnam, we were allowed to go on leave for seven days. I chose Hawaii, even thought it was generally the destination of married soldiers, because I was not interested in Southeast Asian prostitutes. I loved Hawaii. I should have moved there when some of my friends took up residence there. Chester invited me, but I stayed in the Oklahoma hills where I was born. If I had it to do over, I would be a Hawaiian. Don't you think I could pass for a Native?"

Dr. Clarke agreed.

"During my first thirteen months in 'Nam, I probably set charges and searched more than ten dozen tunnel openings. I never once encountered a VC, unlike some of my buddies. Several met their death in the tunnels. The day after I returned from R&R, a tunnel entrance was found. Reportedly, the brass believed that this was a key tunnel that linked villages and VC support bases all the way to the Cambodian border. Reportedly, there had been a number of strange activities going on in the area, and the brass thought it was a key entry point to the tunnel network."

"Did you go alone?"

"Two of us were sent in. Sheldon, an Aussie, and me. It was a multi-level tunnel, going four stories down. Once I skirted through the entryway on my stomach, I was in a small room high enough for me to stand. I signaled Sheldon who joined me in a few minutes. The room was furnished with a table that contained a variety of bomb-making materials and several containers filled with rounds of rifle shells. We also found some military rations and bags of rice stashed next to the wall. We set a charge and continued along the tunnel. We traveled through several underground sleeping chambers. There were hammocks made from US parachute nylon strung between bamboo poles. After that, we thought we had reached a dead end. We could not find any more trap doors. The walls seemed solid rock or packed clay dirt. We were getting ready to return topside when Sheldon leaned against a wall and fell through it. There we found a long narrow passageway. We crawled through a smooth tube-like tunnel. It was maybe twenty feet long."

"How far were you down at this point?"

"Maybe twenty feet underground. It was fourth level as I recall."

"And at this point, you had not encountered any Viet Cong, correct?"

"Correct. When I exited the narrow tunnel, I found myself in a well-lit room, larger than any I had encountered. I waited for Sheldon, who joined me within seconds. The sight, too, astounded him. Neither of us could locate the source of the light, but the room was as bright as daylight. The walls around the room were like smooth, polished stone. Off to the left of us, a stone door stood. It was larger than any normal door, which was confusing to us since the VC were small men. As we approached the door, looking for another tunnel, we heard noises coming from behind the door. We readied our weapons, planning to kill anything that came inside. That's when we saw the reptile men."

Dr. Clarke asked if they fired at them.

"I never got off a shot. They were frightening figures, especially for an Indian boy from Oklahoma. Sheldon whispered that we had to get out of this place, but it was too late. Just as we saw them, they saw us. They were not like humans. I would say they stood about eight feet tall and were a brownish-green color. They moved like lightning. Sheldon fired but the bullet hit the ceiling. Their bright yellow with black cat-like pupils were evil. As they attacked us, I noticed only three fingers on their hands that were more like claws than human hands. Their noses were slits, and their faces were flat. They actually looked like lizards.

"Although they stood upright on huge, bulbous legs, they had a huge tail which allowed them to move swiftly across the floor. They had a strange collar around their necks that appeared as part of their body. It reminded me of a turtle shell where the head could be retracted in time of sleep or threat."

"How did they react when they saw you?

"They hissed and gurgled among themselves. They

pounced on us, lifted us off the ground, and threw us against the wall. As they continued to hiss, they showered us with some kind of substance they ejected from their mouths. While I was lying on the floor, I saw them walk through another stone door and disappear. Sheldon and I picked up our rifles. Both of us were dizzy and had trouble seeing, but we made our way to the stone door where we saw the reptile men disappear before our eyes. After that, I lost consciousness. I'm not sure how long I lay there, but when I woke, I was outside the tunnel. At first, I didn't know how I got there, but hovering over me was a glowing blue giant who assured me that he meant me no harm." Sherman then began an endless coughing fit. Each time he stopped, the coughing began again. After several minutes, he began to talk again.

"After we climbed to safety, we detonated our handiwork and that was the end of the reptile men's hidden underground tunnel. But to this day, I suffer. That's why my eyesight is so poor. In fact, it turned out to be my last tunnel. Because of my eyesight, the Marines sent me to a hospital in Hawaii to recuperate, and several months later, I was put on disability. That's where I met Chester. I kept in touch with Sheldon for several years, and he became blind shortly after leaving the military. I was a little luckier. Despite my disability, I was able to work at labor jobs. Nothing that required driving or reading and writing, but I earned a good pension despite my eyesight."

"What do you think the substance was?" Dr. Clarke questioned.

"I think it was like snake venom. I think it was meant to kill us, in fact, but our protective gear and helmets saved us. When they hissed at us, a long-forked tongue came out of the slit in their tongue and showered us with their venom. As I saw the protruding tongue, I pushed my face into the floor and covered my face. My hands still show the effects of the poison."

Sherman sat up in his recliner chair and reached his hands

across the end table between them. She saw the deep scars on his hand. "That's what the alien venom did to me," he said. "I suppose they thought we would never recover and die in that tunnel."

"Did you tell your commanding officers about the event?"

"Are you kidding? We knew they wouldn't believe us. The medics thought we'd encountered a bio-hazardous material in the tunnel and ordered us into a hospital. I was in several hospitals. Sheldon and I spent six months, first in Germany and then Hawaii, before the military decided to send us home. I told Chester about the event. He's the only person who knew the truth, but now, you. I never thought much about flying saucers and all that stuff. I considered it nonsense. I lived in the real world. But the reptile men were as real as you and me. The Blue Men were as real as you and me. I can confirm there are beings in the universe who do not look like human beings, who are smarter than us and can travel the universe. Some are good; some are evil. That should humble us humans, don't you think?"

Dr. Clarke said that she took Sherman to dinner that night and heard more about his life history over a bottle of expensive red wine. She had not heard from Sherman since her visit with him. She sent him a box of candy for his birthday and the complete works of Tony Hillerman on tape. She received a note from one of the nurses saying Sherman enjoyed the box of candy and card. He was listening to his second round of the Hillerman books. He was doing well and would have written, but his eyesight had grown worse. Dr. Clarke sent him assorted chocolates and wine each month over the next year.

Nanoses's Story
Nanose contacted me (Dr. Clarke) after a former student announced that I was known as the UFO Lady at a local basketball Appreciation Night. He stopped me in the parking lot as I struggled to open the hatch to my Subaru. After assisting me, Nanose told me that he had

an encounter and needed to tell someone. He invited me to have breakfast with him the next morning. When I agreed, a wide grin crossed his face and he shook my hand vigorously. Little did I know that his story was not the usual Star People's encounter.

I watched the tall, broad-shouldered man in military fatigues walk slowly toward my table. He sat down, examined the salt and pepper shakers, tightened them, looked at me, and grinned. He was a handsome man in his mid-thirties. An eagle ring graced his right hand, and an eagle feather earring hung from his left ear, occasionally catching in his long, black hair, which fell loosely below his shoulders.

After we ordered a pot of coffee and donuts, Nanose leaned forward and spoke to me in a quiet voice, "I saw the Blue Men from outer space in Iraq," he said. "In my wildest dreams, I would never have believed that men who had blue skin and glowed like the moon even existed. But I'm here to tell you, there are Blue Men. They come from outer space. They are giants, but gentle, peaceful men."

Dr. Clarke then asked when and where he encountered them.

"I enlisted in the military in 2001 when I was twenty, mostly out of boredom. There were no jobs on the reservation and everyone just hung out, smoked grass, and drank. I got tired of that lifestyle after a couple of years. I wasn't smart enough to get a scholarship to go to college, so I decided to let Uncle Sam send me to school. This is before the 9/11 event, and I didn't expect to end up on the battlefield, but in 2004, I was sent to Iraq." He paused as the waitress appeared with a plate of donuts. "I don't tell strangers I'm a veteran. I don't like to talk about it. Telling you about the Blue Men is my first exception."

Nanose continued his story. "I was in the Middle East for two years and twenty-three days. I've been home now for ten years and one day. The Army offered money to reenlist but there was no way I was taking a chance on going to war again.

War is like hell must be." He paused briefly, looking at the plate of donuts, and chose a jelly-filled roll. "I count myself lucky to have survived. I managed to get out of it what I wanted — a college degree. But it's of little use. No jobs for a fitness trainer on the rez. I suppose I could teach P.E., but I don't think I would make a good teacher. Besides, it doesn't take much for me to be right back there in Iraq in my mind. I recon it will always be with me."

Dr. Clarke asked what happened to him in Iraq.

"Many things, but what I'm going to tell you is not something you will hear on TV. Lost or missing soldiers were not reported. The government closely guarded the deaths of Americans in Iraq. But the reason I wanted to talk to you was to tell you what happened to me and my buddies in Iraq. You can believe it or not, because even now when I think about it, it seems unbelievable." Nanose became quiet and shook his head as if in disbelief. "I'm not a man to waste my time or your time. I swear to you this story is true."

"I make no judgments about the stories I hear. I am here to listen and to record your story."

"Okay. That's what I want to hear. One evening, our advanced patrol unit came under mortar attack. Several of our team were wounded or dead. After falling back and darkness fell around us, our lieutenant called for volunteers to retrieve the bodies of our comrades. My buddy Rense and I set out. It took us maybe twenty minutes to locate the first body. There were four down. Rense and I saw a light come out of the hills. I motioned for Rense to look in the direction of the light, but when I looked at him, he seemed stunned or under some kind of spell. I shook Rense, but he didn't respond. While I was trying to figure out what was going on, my eyes kept moving toward a mesmerizing light — a beautiful blue light. I couldn't determine where it came from, but it held me transfixed. As it came toward me, I made out the form of two men, giant men that were blue. As they approached me, I pointed my rifle at them, but they told me they meant no harm. My rifle slipped to the ground automatically, like some force was telling me it was okay."

"Did they tell you what they wanted?"

"They told me that they could take my friends with them—my dead comrades and they could live again in another world. I didn't know what to make of it. I called out to Rense, but he didn't respond. Then they told me that Rense would have no memory of the events that were taking place and that soon they would return for him."

"Where were they going to take them?"

"They said they would have a good life, but not one on this Earth. I was in a dilemma. I didn't know what to do. I knew their familiar back home would want to bury their dead, but at the same time, the offer of a renewed life was appealing and I told them to take them."

"Can you describe the Blue Men?"

"They had a human form, but they were blue. Their bodies, or maybe it was their suits, were a luminescent blue. A beautiful blue."

"Did you trust them?"

"It's funny. I trusted them completely, and yet I knew they were not of this Earth. I felt total peach and contentment in their presence."

Dr. Clarke asked what happened next.

"The next thing I knew, Rense and I were searching for the bodies. He had no memory of any of the events. We searched for another half hour or so and then returned to our unit. We reported that we couldn't find any bodies." He paused and then finished his donut and coffee, and continued. "I made a decision. I felt a chance for another life was best for my buddies. Maybe I'm wrong, but when I meet St. Peter at those pearly gates, I'll tell him I did my best."

"What about Rense? Did he ever remember that night?"

"Rense was blown up on a patrol the next night. I was with him, but there was nothing I could do. His body came up missing. I believe the Blue Men found him and took him away, too It's strange, you know. It was like the Blue Men knew his fate. They told me they would return for him soon, but at the time I thought nothing of it. I didn't realize they were foretelling his future. They knew he was going to die."

"These events have had a profound impact on your life. How are you dealing with it?"

"I've often thought about contacting Rense's family and explaining that I believe their son is alive and living on another planet, and the I stop and think about how crazy that sounds. Then I think maybe knowing that their son was alive and, on another planet, would be worse than thinking he was dead. I'm satisfied that he had a good life; the Blue Men promised me that. My only regret is that I didn't go with them, too."

"Did they offer to take you?" Dr. Clarke asked. He nodded. Dr. Clarke saw the tears well up in his eyes and decided to change the subject. "You said you graduated from college. Where are you working now?"

"I'm a firefighter. My degree didn't do me much good. No jobs on the reservation when there are no fires. Anything to pay the bills. I have a small cabin out in the country where my grandpa lives. When I'm not working, I watch TV and play computer games. I read a lot. I have a tomato garden that I tend. We don't have running water, so it's small. I'd like to have a big garden, but the lack of water makes it difficult. I like the quietness of the country—no cars, planes, or people; only Grandpa, and he's a quiet man, too. Sometimes we sit at night and watch the stars. I keep hoping that when the good Lord takes Grandpa, the Blue Men will come for me, too. Every night, I whisper a silent prayer for their return, but so far they have not appeared."

Follow-up: *During her next visit to the reservation, she saw Nanose at his home in the country and met his grandfather Abraham. He still keeps to himself and prefers not to talk about the war, but he spoke to Dr. Clarke again about the Blue Men. He still* *hasn't come to grips with his decision to stay on Earth. He said his name, Nanose, meant cougar in English. He believes that his name foretold his ability to go to war stealthily, like the cat of his nomenclature, and make his way through the war-torn country and survive. As for Dr. Clarke, she believes Nanose is a survivor, and his name gives him amazing spiritual powers; he just hasn't realized it yet.*

Matoska's Blue Men Story

Matoska was a twenty-four-year-old army vet who emailed Dr. Clarke while in Afghanistan and told her that when he returned stateside, he would like to meet. He said a most unusual event happened to him while on patrol one night, and it was a story that should be told. They agreed to meet at a pre-arranged site in Colorado, halfway between Dr. Clarke's home and his.

Dr. Clarke met Matoska at a rest stop off the interstate. Dressed in camouflaged pants and an olive-green tee-shirt, she recognized him immediately from his description. Standing well over six-feet tall, he would have stood out in almost any crowd. They sat down at a picnic table at the interstate rest stop. He placed a cooler on the table and said that he always brings food and drinks when meeting a guest. Dr. Clarke took a water and unwrapped her sandwich. He said he was Indian, but she thought he could belong to other ethnic groups.

"I guess you're wondering who I am. For the record, my mama was Lakota and Southern Cheyenne, and my dad was a white man from Finland. That's the reason for my name, Matoska. It means white bear. I was an only child. My mom raised me after my dad decided he missed Finland. She refused to go with him, and we never heard from him again."

"It's his loss," said Dr. Clarke, noting the sadness in his voice.

Matoska sighed and took a bite of his sandwich. He watched an 18-wheeler pull into the rest stop. He suddenly blurted out, "Have you ever heard of the Blue Men?"

Dr. Clarke nodded yes, and Matoska jumped up praising God. "I knew it all along. Others have seen the Blue Men, too!" He reached out and clasped her hands and whispered, "Thank you."

He caught his breath and began, "I saw the Blue Men in Afghanistan. The brightest blue, translucent color you can imagine. I've never told anyone this story but, thank God, I heard one of your interviews on YouTube about Star People.

(Matoska might have referred to my interview with Dr. Ardy Sixkiller Clarke on July 11, 2013, about her book, *Encounters with Star People*) Interview:

https://www.youtube.com/watch?v=aLfFmjBaFFs

"I knew I had to contact you. Thank you for meeting me. I know that meeting a stranger at a rest stop is unusual, but I needed privacy and you know what it's like in an Indian home — too many relatives," he laughed and continued.

"I deployed to Kandahar in January 2010. I was a Communications Operator. I operated and maintained communications equipment from combat radios to satellite phones. We were short-handed in that area of expertise. I shared that responsibility with one other operator, so we had twelve hours on and twelve hours off. In my downtime, I often went on patrol into the city. Part of it was out of boredom, and part of it was because I grew fond of the children in the city. Growing up I always thought Indians were poor, but there's nothing like the poverty and suffering of the Afghani children. One night as I was monitoring the combat radios, I got an urgent message for emergency medical evacuations. Our troops were wounded by a roadside bomb and others were under heavy fire. Under those conditions, Med Air Evac Teams couldn't deploy immediately to pick up the wounded."

"Were American soldiers killed that night?" Dr. Clarke asked.

He nodded. "But you won't hear about it on CNN. So

many things are covered up about what is going on over there. The next day, we were sent out to recover the bodies. I volunteered to go; these men were my brothers."

"What did they discover?"

"We rescued only one soldier, Dustin, who had made it through the night. The other seven were missing. We found some signs of their existence — a rifle, a St. Christopher medal, but no bodies."

"What happened to them?"

"Dustin said he didn't know, but late the next night, he told me an amazing story. He claimed that the Star Men came for them. According to him, he took refuge in a build and decided to wait out the night. The others were outside, and even though he called for them throughout the night, no one came. About an hour after radio silence, he told me he saw a bright light. All gunshots were silenced, and a beam came down, and he watched them recover the bodies one by one and lift them into a tubular craft that rested about the scene."

"Did he remember any other details?"

"He said that as the event was happening, he couldn't take his eyes off it. He yelled at his buddies, but none of them responded."

"Did he tell you what they looked like?"

"He said they were tall, blue men, maybe as tall as eight feet. Very muscular and strong. They told him they were going to take his friends. They also told Dustin his friends would be fine and that he would survive his tour of duty and return home to his wife and children."

"Was he interrogated by his commanding officer? Dr. Clarke asked.

"He never told the brass what happened. He said he couldn't remember."

"Did his superiors believe him?"

"They found no reason not to. Everything was kept hush-hush. There was no way to explain the disappearances of seven soldiers and the press would have a field day. It was covered up."

"What about their families?"

"The most interesting thing about the whole event was that none of the missing soldiers had listed a next of kin. So it was easy to keep it out of the press. Americans never knew what happened that night, only Dustin who was determined to maintain silence."

"Why do you think he kept silent?"

"Do you think anyone would have believed him?" Matoska replied. "Dustin wanted to make a career out of the military. He was probably afraid to tell them what he saw for fear he would be discharged for psychological reasons."

"Did you believe his story?"

"At the time, I wasn't sure what to believe. I knew the bodies were never recovered. It may not have made CNN, but that doesn't mean it didn't happen. I knew those guys. They were my friends, as close as any brother, and they were gone."

So, you never revealed your friend's story until now?"

"Well, that isn't the end of the story. Two days later, I went with Dustin on patrol. As we toured the streets that day, the heat was unbearable. We went into a deserted building to escape the heat. It was so hot in Afghanistan that you could fry an egg on a rock in the sun. It was miserable, and we were wearing heavy equipment and tools. We just wanted a reprieve from the sun and to drink some water." He paused to finish off his sandwich and can of Pepsi.

"Did something happen inside the building?"

"Something amazing happened. After searching the building, we positioned ourselves against a wall and watched the doorway. I remember relaxing a little and enjoying the coolness of the building, and that's when it happened. Out of nowhere, the Blue Men materialized before us. They told us that our friends were fine, and that they were able to save our fallen comrades. All seven were alive and well."

"Alive and well, but I thought they were dead. Isn't that what you told me?"

"They said they took them away to live in another world free of war. Their past memories were gone and new memories in their place so they would no longer remember the war or their life on Earth."

"How did you react to that?"

"At first, I felt angry. I thought they had no right to play God. Just as I was about to tell them this, I realized I was in the presence of powerful beings who were good and humane. They were the best part of what humans could be. Then they disappeared just as they appeared, but before going, they told Dustin that they would put his mind at ease."

"What did your friend say about their appearance?"

"That's the strange thing about it. When I mentioned the Blue Men, he looked at me like I was crazy and said he didn't know anything about Blue Men and wanted to know if I had been sipping the home brew. It soon became obvious to me that he had no memory of the events. I never spoke to him about it again. I don't know why I remembered. But I swear to you on the Bible, which I believe is Holy, this happened just as I told you."

After finishing his sandwich, he walked to the garbage can. "I don't think they were gods, but they were godly men, who monitor our wars and sometimes they choose humans to save."

"What about the young men who were taken? Did you do any investigation about what they may have had in common?"

"It's funny you should mention that. I did do that. One night when everyone was resting, I looked at the files. They were all between the ages of twenty and twenty-four. There were two Mexicans who joined the Army to get citizenship. There were two white guys from Alabama. There was one black soldier from Mississippi. There were two Indians. Both listed their residence as Oklahoma. And as I mentioned before, they listed no relatives. They were alone in the world. Perhaps the Blue Men chose them for that reason. When I thought about it, I felt better. Perhaps the Blue Men chose them for that reason. When I thought about it, I felt better. At least no one was at home mourning them. I think Dustin escaped because he was married with a wife and children."

"Why didn't they take you?" Dr. Clarke asked.

"When they appeared before Dustin and me, I think they came to help him forget. And me, I was a non-combatant. I was a radioman who just happened to go on patrol with Dustin. If they had given me the option to go, I might have considered it, although I do love my mom. I love her a lot. Besides she was listed as my next of kin."

"Do you think they knew that?

"They chose carefully who they took. Men with no ties to Earth."

"So, you see the Blue Men as peaceful and loving—is that correct?"

"I see the Blue Men as men from the stars who love peace and gave my friends another chance. They were in a war not of their making. They were dead according to all reports."

"Would you ever go with them if they returned?"

"Someday when my mom passes. I hope they will return for me. I would like to live in their world."

Follow-up: *Dr. Clarke never saw Matoska again, but he did email occasionally, and never mentioned the Blue Men. He always signed his emails with a quote: "Still watching the sky…White Bear." He was the first to tell her about an encounter with the Blue Men. She cannot help but wonder how many other veterans have had the same experience but remain silent.*

Author's comment: The total number of U.S. military personnel missing in action from the Vietnam War from 1964 to 2022 totaled 1,600. Their bodies were never found. Were some of the soldiers taken by the Blue Men to their peaceful planet? I'd like to think so! How many soldiers have encountered the Blue Men in the many U.S. battles? Were the

Blue Men there for soldiers in the Civil War, World War I, and World War II? Are women taken by the Blue Men now that they are allowed in combat since 2016? Defense Secretary Leon Panetta lifted the Pentagon's 1994 ban on women in direct ground combat roles. But under the Pentagon's cautious, phased approach to opening the careers to women, it wasn't until 2016 that women were eligible for every position. According to the internet, 58,220 United States soldiers died in the Vietnam War.

Winter's Glowing Blue Men

Winter was celebrating his graduation from high school at a friend's party when his dreams of the future were shattered by a car accident fueled by alcohol. He was left paralyzed from the waist down, a paralyzed right arm, and blind in one eye. His dream of studying medicine vanished that night. After two years of surgery and rehabilitation, he suffered from extreme depression and attempted suicide twice. Dr. Clarke had seen Winter and his sister grow up and his parents, both educators, often invited her to dinner when she visited the reservation. It was during a tribal council meeting when he and his parents were there. She sat beside Winter who told her about his life-saving ordeal and the Star People.

Winter greeted Dr. Clarke at home in his wheelchair. His parents were getting ready for a meeting on a resolution to expand tribal membership. He had popcorn and a bottle of Diet Coke waiting for Dr. Clarke. Winter's parents left and then he said, "I asked to talk with you privately. I'm glad you're here. I trust you. I wanted to tell my story to someone I trusted. I've not only known you forever, but I found your books on Amazon and read them on Kindle. There are a couple of stories of encounters in your book that are similar to mine, but not exactly."

Dr. Clarke asked if she could tape his interview and take notes and Winter agreed. "Have you spoken about your encounter with your parents?"

"God no. They have enough to deal with. Look at me. I not only destroyed my life that night, but I destroyed theirs. There are some things I keep to myself. But after reading your books, it got me thinking. If my story can help someone else, I'm willing to share it."

"I'm glad to hear that. Where would you like to begin?" Dr. Clarke asked.

Winter started at the graduation party. "I got wasted that night. In fact, I don't even remember getting in the car with Amelia. She was kinda my girlfriend but nothing serious. I had a singular goal and that was to be a doctor and return here, work at the hospital, get married, and raise a bunch of kids."

Dr. Clarke then said, "I remember that was your goal when you were ten. What happened that night, or do you remember?"

"Actually, I don't remember much. Butch, my best friend told me that two of the guys carried me to the car and Amilia got behind the wheel. She had been drinking too, but they thought she was okay to drive. As you know, the drive to our place is over a mountain road with a couple of hairpin curves, and she missed one and drove right over the embankment. The car tumbled end over end until it came to rest against a tree, now more than ten feet from the river."

"I've seen the site of the accident. The Great Spirit was looking out for you that night."

"I don't know about that, but one thing's for sure, someone was watching out for me," he said.

"Were you conscious when it happened?"

"Not at first. I remember the pain and waking up with blood dripping down my face. I couldn't move. I called for someone to help but got no answer. I was trapped by the back seat, which had collapsed against the front passenger's seat. I called out to Amelia, but she was unresponsive. I learned later that she had died on impact. I feel bad about that. Amelia was my best friend and the smartest girl I'd ever met. It took a long for me to accept her death. She wanted to go to nursing school. When we were little, we often said I'd be a doctor; she would be my nurse."

"So, you regained consciousness after the accident. Is that correct?"

Winter had tears in his eyes as he said, "Yes, but immovable. I had no feeling in my legs and feet. I panicked and pounded on the door. I yelled until my voice rasped. No one came, so I gave up. I tasted the blood in my mouth and knew I was not likely to survive unless help came immediately. That's when it happened."

"Are you referring to the Star People?" Dr. Clarke asked.

He nodded. "Suddenly a bright, iridescent, blue light descended upon the car, and I thought the police discovered the accident. That's when I saw a being engulfed in a strange, glowing blue light. I couldn't make out any features. I thought I must be ad and the ancestors had come for me to take me to the spirit world."

He paused for a moment, poured the Coke into the glasses with his left hand, and offered me the bowl of popcorn. "It's not easy to describe them. The image is fuzzy in my mind. I knew they had the form of humans, but there was a shimmering glow that distorted their image. It was hard to get a clear image."

"Did they speak to you?"

"Not a first. One of them pulled the back door off the sedan and threw it aside like it was a toy. The other one came in from behind me tore the other door off and removed the back seat that was trapping me. The one behind me placed his hands on my head and the bleeding stopped. I felt a healing in my head. My head felt so hot that I thought it would explode. As he covered my head with his hands, he said I should not be afraid."

"Did you feel afraid?"

"Once he touched me, peace filled my body. I was no longer afraid. I knew I was going to survive. They healed the opening in my head. When I got to the hospital, there was only a scar that the doctors could not explain." He leaned forward and parted his long black hair. Dr. Clarke could see the white scar about a quarter of an inch wide and three inches long. "They asked me about it, but I had no idea. But I knew it was the Star Men. They did something to my head. In fact, I think if they had not come to me, I would have died from loss of blood or been mentally incapacitated for the ret of my life. I think they saved my life and made it so I could continue to function mentally."

"If they have so much power, why didn't they heal your paralysis?"

"They removed me from the car and placed me against a tree. They told me that interference with another's destiny was not standard practice for them, but they made an exception in my case."

"Did they tell you why?"

"They said that my destiny had already been decided. I didn't understand it. Days after the accident, I felt angry. These beings were powerful, and I believe they could have healed my physical condition, and they chose not to do that."

"Have you accepted your paralysis?"

"It hasn't been easy. The first year I was angry; so angry that I lashed out against people who tried to help me. I said terrible things to them that I regret."

Dr. Clarke then tried to reassure him. "I think that's normal. The important thing is not to beat yourself up about that," she said, trying to reassure him.

"I still have bouts of depression. I want to die sometimes. But there is one thing that keeps me from doing it. Something happened to me when they healed my head. I hope you won't think I'm crazy. You know I've always been a good student. I graduated valedictorian. But something happened that night that is difficult to explain."

"Please try."

"I have increased mental ability. I can't explain it. In the hospital, I discovered I could read a book in a day. I asked my mom to bring a dictionary, a big one. She brought a huge one from the school library — you know the kind that weighs a ton and generally sits on a table because it's too heavy to move." Dr. Clarke nodded as he continued. "I read the entire thing. I began noticing other things. I had to tone down my vocabulary when I talked to my friends who visited me. My vocabulary was far beyond what I was capable of before the accident. I discovered I learned things more easily and was interested in almost every subject."

"Do you believe the aliens did something that increased your intelligence? Dr. Clarke asked.

"I believe the aliens, when they repaired my head, did something to my brain. Yes, I believe they increased my intelligence."

"Have you ever considered going to the university?"

"I would have to have a caretaker. I can't go to the bathroom by myself," he said with tears forming in his eyes.

"Winter, there are all kinds of help for disabled students including caretakers. Maybe you're not supposed to be a doctor. Maybe the Star Men knew that. You're definitely an intelligent young man. I know you wanted to be a surgeon, but perhaps you should go into medical research. Maybe you'll find a way to reverse paralysis for accident victims. The possibilities are limitless. Perhaps the Star People knew your destiny did not need physical mobility."

A smile crossed his face, and he wiped a tear from his cheek. "I think it was more than that. I wanted to be a doctor so I would be rich. Helping people took the backseat. I used to envision myself with a beautiful wife and beautiful children living in a big house and taking fabulous vacations."

"And now?"

"Beautiful girls don't want anything to do with me. What woman wants to be with a cripple?"

Dr. Clarke then responded. "You're not a cripple in your mind. Some women love men for their intellect. While it's true, that you would need both hands and use of your legs to be a surgeon, there are other ways to make contributions in the medical field. Perhaps the Star People knew that and only improved your mental abilities."

"Do you think that's the reason they left me like this?" he asked.

"Who knows? I'm only speculating. But I think it's time you started counting your blessings and doing something with your life."

"Is this what they call 'tough love'?" he asked, smiling at Dr. Clarke.

"Could be," she responded reaching for Winter's hand. "I've heard of some amazing miracles involving the "Star People's intervention. Maybe they knew that in your case, being handicapped was a blessing. It would give you the right path to achieve your intended goals, even if you didn't know what they were. I hope you will take this opportunity that was given to you and imagine a different future for yourself."

"Maybe you're right. Did anyone ever tell you that you are one smart lady?" he asked and then said, "I'm so glad you've been a part of my life and that you are friends with Mom and Dad. I've always thought of you as my second Mom. Someday I might be able to show you how much you mean to me."

"Find a cure for old age, and I will be thankful forever," Dr. Clarke said with a smile.

"Done!" he replied, twirling in his wheelchair.

Dr. Clarke and Winter spent the rest of the evening finishing off the bowl of popcorn and drinking the quart of Diet Coke, reliving the past and discussing possible options for his future.

Follow-up: *Dr. Clarke and Winter stayed in contact on a regular basis. Each time she saw him, she was reminded that the Blue Men can and do perform miracles. Shortly after her visit, Winter enrolled at the tribal college and completed the core classes in six months* *instead of the two years expected of students. He transferred to the state university and enrolled in a pre-med program. Despite his disabilities, he is no longer the handicapped boy who once told her how his dreams were lost that fateful night. Instead, he is a vibrant, intelligent you man who astounds his peers and his professors with his analytical skills and vast store of knowledge about pharmaceuticals and diseases. He has branched out into the study of robotics and their use in medical science. Dr. Clarke expects great things from him in the future and expects he will make a difference in the world. She believes the Star People knew it, too.*

Madison and the Blue Ball of Light

Madison was an FBI agent on a southwestern reservation and a member of a California tribe. She had requested the post on this reservation because of the drug trafficking problem. Her brother had died of a drug overdose, leaving Madison with no relatives except a distant cousin who lived in Seattle. She vowed to bring down the members of various Mexican cartels operating on reservations. It was the night of one of the stakeouts that she had an encounter; an event that made her re-evaluate her career decision.

Dr. Clarke met Madison during a school lockdown. A student brought a weapon to school and was caught showing it to his friends when the principal ordered the campus closed. At the time, Dr. Clarke was a visiting consultant and was due to be in another school when the event occurred. The tribal police were the first to show up, followed by the Bureau of Indian Affairs (BIA) police. A local representative of Homeland Security arrived and barked orders to everyone who only wanted to flee the makeshift prison.

When Madison, the FBI agent arrived, Dr. Clarke approached her and asked her permission to leave the school premises. Even though she sympathized with Dr. Clarke's situation, there was little she could do. Realizing that she might be stuck there for countless hours, Dr. Clarke found a place at the top bleacher in the gymnasium, pulled out my tape recorder and earphones, and began listening to an interview she had conducted the previous night. A police dog arrived and began searching row by row. Madison was wandering up and down the bleachers. When she saw Dr. Clarke, she came over and sat down.

"Let's see, you look like an Aerosmith fan," she said.

Dr. Clarke stopped the tape recorder and removed her earphones. "You're right. I'm a fan, but I wasn't listening to music, just reviewing an interview from last night."

She held out her hand and after a brief introduction, she smiled, and commented, "Now I remember where I heard your name. You're the UFO lady. I heard you were on the reservation and hoped I would meet you. I've been interested in your work, and I've read your books, but I never expected to meet you."

Dr. Clarke thanked her, and then she asked, "How many people have you interviewed on this reservation?"

"Twenty-three total," Dr. Clarke replied.

Madison asked to hear stories of their encounters. "The people around here call them Star People, and yes, I have interviewed individuals who have had direct encounters." Dr. Clarke went on to tell her how she locates individuals about their stories. "I find them through acquaintances and relatives who refer them to me; other times the individuals seek me out, and on several occasions, I think it's fate. Frequently, I find myself in the right place at the right time and it's as if the story just comes to me. It's destiny. I can't explain it. I meet strangers who suddenly tell me they have a story of an encounter. It's like someone is intervening so I can tell their story."

Madison asked if she believed in destiny.

Dr. Clarke nodded.

"I do too. Perhaps it was fated for the school to be locked down because that would bring me here as part of the response team. And perhaps it was just fate that you happened to be caught in the lockdown. Fate or destiny?

"I'm not sure I'm following you."

"I have a story, too. I had an encounter that has made me question everything I've been taught. But I can't tell you now. I have to join the others. I don't think there is anything beyond the young man showing off to his classmates, but we have to be sure." She pulled out a business card. "If you're free tonight, let's get together over drinks. Call me later. My cell number is listed there."

Two hours later, the principal came over the intercom and announced that the lockdown was lifted and that guests were free to leave.

Dr. Clarke and Madison met at 8 p.m. that night at her home in the government housing section of the reservation. "Part of the perks of the job is housing," she said as we walked into her living room. "The house is far too big for me, so if you ever need a place to crash, feel free to give me a call."

Dr. Clarke sat down as Madison handed her a virgin strawberry daiquiri while she had one with alcohol. "You know, I'm breaking the law right now. This is a dry reservation and alcohol is forbidden. Of course, nine out of ten houses have alcohol of some kind, but that doesn't mean there isn't a law forbidding it. But there are times I enjoy being naughty," she said with a chuckle.

Dr. Clarke pushed the record button on her tape recorder as Madison began. "One of the worst things about my job is the waiting. I spend countless hours on stakeouts, and the waiting is boring and more often than not fruitless. One night a few months ago, I was on a stakeout of an alleged drug dealer. I suspected he was an illegal who was shacking up with a reservation girl and had ties to a Mexican cartel. I'm not sure how he came to be on the reservation, but it was not long before he found a woman, and with his green card, he was free to move back and forth across the border. That's a common practice among the drug runners. They can be found all over the west. Their method of operation often involves finding a local woman which gives them freedom of movement around the reservation and with a green card they freely move across the border."

"Do you carry out the stakeouts alone?"

"I'm the only FBI agent on the reservation. I keep the BIA police, who are also federal, advised on my operations when I go on a stakeout, but they don't assign anyone to work with me."

"How did you encounter the alien?" Dr. Clarke asked.

"On this particular night, I had been on stakeout for seven hours. By 4 a.m., I was getting sleepy and decided to return home. There were two small hills along the highway with a one-lane bridge over the river. I crossed the first hill with no incident, but just as I approached a curve in the road, I noticed a brilliant blue ball hovering along the side of the road. I slowed. Frankly, I was mesmerized by the light. I wasn't sure what I saw, and just as I slowed, I saw a brilliant blue ball dart into the underbrush along the side of the road. I immediately stopped and shined a spotlight in that direction. I got out of the car, drew my weapon, and walked toward the edge of the road."

"Did you call in your position to the police?"

"No. It happened too fast. I kept walking up and down the edge of the highway until I came to the bridge. After the bridge, there is a warning that alerts drivers about the next hill. There are barriers on each side of the bridge and steel posts to prevent cars from going into the river. As I shined my flashlight into the darkness beyond the bridge, I saw two men standing on the other side of the posts. When I ordered them to raise their hands and come toward me, a shot rang out missing me by inches."

"I thought you saw a blue, glowing ball. Were there men, too?"

"As I found out later, I had come across some drug peddlers, and at the moment they were shooting at me."

Dr. Clarke asked if she was frightened.

"I'm trained to take care of myself. I wasn't afraid at the

time, but my bravery was short-lived. Suddenly, I was aware of the glowing blue ball circling me. Just as I started to turn around, the ball of light engulfed me, and even though I could hear gunshots, they seemed to ricochet off the blue ball. At that point, I struggled to escape the light and ran for my vehicle, but suddenly an entity grabbed me and the next thing I knew, my feet were off the ground, and I was being escorted through the woods. I felt a sense of peace come over me and I did not resist."

"Did you ever see the entities that kidnapped you?"

"Only glimpses. They appeared human, but they were engulfed in this blue, shimmering light. They communicated in my head and told me not to fear. The next thing I remembered was returning to the edge of the road. Suddenly the two drug traffickers walked up to the bank with their hands raised. They asked me to arrest them. They had been so frightened by the blue light that they feared for their life. I called for back up from the tribal police. After an hour of searching, we recovered their stash of drugs."

"Did you have any idea who kidnapped you? I asked.

"No. I saw no one. I only saw the blue glow. They carried me about a mile through the forest. As a person trained to observe, I tried to remember every single detail about my surroundings. I heard the river and saw a relay tower in the distance. At that point, I think I passed out." She paused and lit a cigarette. "That's my story. Have you heard anything similar?"

"I've hard of both the balls of light and the Blue Men."

Madison relaxed and said, "The experience has changed my life forever. I know that life exits away from Earth. It might be different, but it exists."

Follow-up: *Madison left the FBI after meeting with Dr. Clarke. She returned to the University and received a PhD in archaeology a few years later. The last Dr. Clarke heard of Madison, she was somewhere in the jungles of Guatemala. She was part of a team* *excavating an ancient city in the rainforest.*

Rayen's Story: Saved by the Blue Men

Rayen was a thirty-year-old mother of five-year-old twin girls and a seven-year-old son. She was a full-time homemaker and her husband, Russell, was head of the sanitation department on the reservation. The two married shortly after high school, graduated from college, and delayed having children until they could make a down payment on their home and Rayen could quit her job. Rayen called Dr. Clarke one night as she was settling into her bed at a shabby reservation motel room. She heard rumors that Dr. Clarke collected stories about UFO encounters, and she wondered if she could tell her story.

Before Dr. Clarke knew it, Rayen knocked on her motel room. Rayen had a short, stylish haircut and wore baggy sweat pants. Rayen said how much she appreciated Dr. Clarke seeing her late that night.

"I hope you don't mind if I tape your story," Dr. Clarke said.

Rayen shook her head. "I don't mind, but no names please. I don't want anyone to know who I am." She proceeded to remove her shoes, pull up her legs and feet on the couch and rest her chin on her knees. "I never much thought about UFOs. You'd have to live under a rock if you didn't know that people are abducted and UFO sightings are quite common, but I always paid little attention. I guess I really didn't believe the stories were true, except maybe the photos of the UFOs I'd seen on the History Channel or the internet. They looked real. But about a year ago, I became a believer."

"Can you tell me how that came about?"

"My encounter happened in the fall of last year. I went to the city to shop for school clothes and supplies for my kids. My mother-in-law told me she would babysit, so I left the kids at home. Russell, my husband, was working that day so I went alone. I had a great day shopping by six and headed home. I had a two-hour drive ahead of me. I expected to arrive home by 8 p.m. Russell promised to feed the kids and put them to bed."

"Did you have your encounter on your drive home?"

"It was on an isolated section of the road near the railroad crossing in Burgess. Have you ever traveled that road?"

Dr. Clarke replied, "Many times."

"Well, then you know how quiet and remote that place is. The whole town is no more than a city block. It was particularly dark when I came through the town. Generally, I see lights in windows and a lighted beer sign at the bar, something to show there was life. On this night, it was very dark. No lights, no people, not even a light in a house. It gave me an eerie feeling. I remember the hair standing up on my arms like static electricity. I slowed at the railroad crossing, looked both ways to make sure there was no train, and pulled onto the tracks. Suddenly, I heard a thunderous sound, and my Suburban began rocking. I looked up and a train was speeding down the rails with no lights. It was headed directly for me. No barriers across the road. I stomped on the accelerator. There was no way I was going to make it. Then out of nowhere, I felt my car levitating."

Dr. Clarke was flabbergasted and repeated the word levitating.

"You know — lifting off the ground. I opened the car door but there was nothing below me but darkness, but I swear, my car was moving upward and there was no place for me to go."

"Were there any unusual smells or sounds that you remember?"

"Nothing. After that, I must have passed out. I woke in an unfamiliar place. There was nothing like it I had ever seen in my life. It wasn't long until I discovered I was on a spaceship. I found myself in a hot, humid, barely lit room. It was moist and smelled like rotting trees. My car was missing, and I kept thinking that I still had two years to pay for it. I worried about how I would get home. It wasn't long until these strange entities — five of them entered the room."

Next, Rayen was asked to describe the entities.

"They were blue. I know that sounds incredible, but they were huge beings, human-like in appearance, but glowing, luminescent blue. They spoke to me in English in my head. I heard a voice in my brain."

"Did they tell you why you were on the spaceship?"

"Only that they had been observing the Earth, and they watched as I approached the crossing. They realized the train was going to collide with my vehicle and they decided to save me."

"Did they give you a reason?"

"No, and I was too hysterical to ask. I just wanted to be home. I knew they had saved me, but I just wanted to get away from them."

"Did anything else happen to you while you were on the craft?"

"I'm not sure. I tried to stay awake, but I couldn't. The next thing I remember, I was sitting in my car on the other side of the crossing and my car was running. It was almost midnight when I pulled into the garage. Russell opened the kitchen door and yelled at me, demanding to know where I had been. I told him the car quit working, and I was stranded on the side of the road until someone came along and restarted my battery. I was almost four hours late."

"So you lied. Why?"

"Because at the time, I thought it was more believable than what really happened. I know I should have told the truth, but I can't bring myself to do it. Can you tell me, have you heard of blue space men? I can get them out of my mind."

Dr. Clarke replied, "I've heard of the blue men many times. I assure you it is more common than you might imagine."

Rayen grabbed Dr. Clarke's hands and held on tight for a

long time. "Thank you. That's all I wanted to know, and thanks for talking to me. I needed to know I was not alone and that there were others who had similar experiences. It means a lot to me."

Follow-up: *Dr. Clarke saw Rayen a few times since the interview. She never told her husband the truth, and they never spoke of that night again. Knowing that others have seen the Blue Men has helped with her nightmares. So far, the Blue Men have not returned.*

Sylvia's Story: A Blue Man saved me
When Dr. Clarke first met Sylvia, she was leaving an Alcoholics Anonymous meeting at the Tribal Community Center. When she noticed Dr. Clarke, she approached her and said she recognized her from the cover of her book, "Encounters with Star People." Sylvia had read and reread the book at least a dozen times and wanted to know that she knew the stories were true because she had also experienced an encounter. When Dr. Clarke asked if Sylvia would like to tell her story, she asked her to call when she had time to talk. They met the next evening at an off-reservation McDonald's.

Sylvia, who was named for her great-grandmother, Sylvia Red Feather, was a twenty-year-old tribal college freshman. She admitted to being a former drug addict and an alcoholic. She had been sober for twenty-two months at the time of their meeting. A petite young woman with troubled eyes, she spoke openly and without hesitation, as they sat at a rear table in the back of the McDonald's dining area.

Sylvia said she had brought shame on her family. There was nothing to do on the reservation. She was bored as a teenager hated school and chose the wrong crowd. "Every time I got high, I knew it was wrong and I hated myself, but I was not able to give up the drugs and alcohol. Twice I went to rehab but nothing worked. The draw of drugs eventually led to prostitution. I would do anything to get my fix. If it hadn't been for the Star Man, I would probably be dead today.

Now I'm trying to make amends to all the people I wronged, but it's hard to face my family. I've hurt them deeply and I don't know if they'll ever fully recover from my behavior."

Dr. Clarke asked her to clarify what she meant about the Star Man saving her.

"It happened almost two years ago. I had a dreadful day. I had gone to town in search of some Johns. I needed money in the worst way. Drugs are not cheap, and I needed a fix. I earned about two hundred dollars and was going to head back to the reservation and get high when another client stopped me and offered me a fifty. Not one to turn down money, I got in his car, and he drove out to the country. I knew the area. I had gone there before on camping trips with my family. It was near a state park. Before I knew what was happening, he attacked me and beat me unconscious. Later, I discovered that he raped me, stole my money, and left me for dead."

"Did you report it?"

"That's not something you do around here. The white cops would've blamed me and thrown me in jail. When I became conscious, I started walking down the road. That's when I encountered the Star Man."

"Did you see a spacecraft?"

"No. He was just standing there in the middle of the road. There was a strange, blue brilliance about him. Almost a glow. I never really knew if it was the reflection of the moon or if he was a natural brilliance."

Dr. Clarke asked Sylvia what she meant by brilliance.

"It's very difficult to explain. It was more like neon than a glow. That's the reason I think it might have been a reflection, but I'm still not sure. You have to remember, at the time, I was almost beaten to death."

"What did the Star Man do?"

"He told me not to be afraid. He said he was there to help me, but in return, I must change my life."

"How did he help you?"

"I remember a rushing stream that ran beside the road. He led me there and washed the blood from my face and hands. There was warmth to his touch despite the cold mountain water that he used. I know my face was bruised and battered, and I could barely see out of one of my eyes. He ran his hand over my face, and honest to God, I swear the swelling and pain went away While he worked on my face, his hands glowed a bright orange. I hurt too much to resist and I just let him do his thing. Then he asked me to like down in the grass by the stream. I obeyed."

Dr. Clarke asked Sylvia how she communicated with him.

"I think we just knew each other's thoughts without talking. He continued to run his hands over my body. When he reached a place where I had a lot of pain, he stopped for a moment and the pain went away." Sylvia's attention was drawn to two men wearing dark glasses and white shirts and ties in McDonald's. "I've seen them before," she whispered. "Do you think they're following me?"

Dr. Clarke suggested they were probably Mormon missionaries who worked the reservations, trying to convert the Natives.

Sylvia, feeling paranoid, said she had seen them four times in the last two days. They were standing in front of the AA meeting last night and she had seen them that morning walking down the block where she lives.

Dr. Clarke then asked, "You were telling me that the Star Man healed you with his hands. Can you tell me more about that?"

Sylvia reiterated how the Star Man hovered his hands over the injured areas. A hot, orange glow came from his hands. Soon the pain disappeared. The next day, I went to the IHS (Indian Health Service). The doctor told me that it appeared that I had four broken ribs, a broken bone in my right leg, and a broken pelvic bone. He couldn't believe that I had been injured in less than twelve hours. He said I was healing perfectly."

"You're telling me the Star Man saved your life?"

Sylvia said yes, and then told Dr. Clarke there was no machine involved, just his hands. "He told me that he found strange substances in my blood and those substances were going to kill me, so he removed those, too."

"Are you telling me that once he healed you, you were no longer addicted to drugs and alcohol?"

"That's what I'm telling you. It was like I'd never used drugs. I felt strong and without any desire to find a dealer. The next day, I went to the tribal college and enrolled. I plan to study nursing, but I'm putting in my first two years at the tribal college so I can do some things to help my mom before I leave the reservation."

"After he healed you, can you tell me what happened?"

"He told me that he would check on me from time to time to make sure that I was healthy. He took me to the middle of the road, and I saw a blue ball move upward toward the heavens. I looked around me and I was standing at the reservation line. I walked home. When I appeared at the doorway, my mother looked at me and almost didn't recognize me. I never told her how I became sober. I go to AA because that's what she wants me to do, but I really don't need it. I'll never do drugs again."

Follow-up: *Dr. Clarke visited her again and they always had dinner at McDonald's and laughed about the two strangers who were "following her." It turned out they were visiting Mormons on their mission. She had seen others like them before in their shirts and ties on the reservation, attempting to convert American Indians to their faith. Sylvia, who had a 4.0 grade point average at the tribal college, looked forward to attending the university next fall. Dr. Clarke wrote that she'd miss their trips to McDonalds. Sylvia is not the first-person Dr. Clarke has met who has been saved by the Blue Men, but she is certainly the first to tell me about being healed of drug addiction. Perhaps there is hope for the world after all.*

Kenneth's Story: The Star Men taught me to use my power
Kenneth was nineteen the first time he was visited by the Star People. At the time, I spoke with him, he was sixty-eight and the visits had not ceased. The owner of a convenience store and gas station combo on the reservation, he remained a bachelor all of his life. A leader in the traditional religious community, Kenneth often talked about the importance of remembering the old ways, telling the legends, and practicing the religion. He frequently held ceremonies, both on and off the reservation. I met him at a pow-wow in Bozeman, Montana. He had traveled far to conduct a sweat lodge ceremony. I had been invited to participate. During the ceremony, small balls of light entered the lodge. Kenneth told us not to fear, the Star People were visiting us. Later, I asked him about the Star People. He invited me to visit him on the reservation where we would talk.

During Dr. Clarke's next trip to the reservation, she stopped at a bakery and ordered a box of fruitcake cupcakes. There she met with Kenneth on Sunday at a prearranged time. When I arrived at his home, he was standing at the doorway waiting for me. He welcomed me into his home and immediately opened his gift. He smiled and said how much he loved fruitcake. Then he put on a fresh pot of coffee. Kenneth had long, black hair parted in the middle that fell to his shoulders. His piercing brown eyes and his striking smile set off his face, which was mostly wrinkle-free, red suspenders held up his beltless, tan work pants. A red and black buffalo-checked flannel shirt, too big for his small frame, was stuffed neatly inside his pants. He poured two cups of coffee and then unwrapped a cupcake.

"You are the first person to ask me about the Star People," he began. "When I perform a ceremony, the Star People are always with me. They frequently come into the sweat lodge and participate. They enter the sweat lodge and touch the participants. In some cases, they assist with healing. They are always with me."

Dr. Clarke then asked, "When I was in your sweat lodge, I saw the small balls of light. Were those the Star People?"

"Yes. They come in many forms, but sparks of light, balls of light, are common. They can also take human form. But in the sweats, they mostly appear as light."

"Tell me about the first time you saw them."

"I was in the military. This was back in the days when the draft was in place, and after I graduated high school, I joined the Marines. I was proud to serve my country. I arrived in Vietnam in 1965 and I was nineteen at the time. We were sent there to secure U.S. airbases, but we ended up in combat operations instead of a defensive force. After that, the war escalated, and the rest is history."

"You said your first encounter was while you were in the military. Did it happen in Vietnam?"

"I was a gunner on a helicopter. We would fly into the Delta to pick up fellow Marines. My job was to protect my comrades as they boarded the helicopter, among other things. On one occasion, there were several wounded. Those who were not wounded were having difficulty getting the wounded to the helicopter. I jumped out to help when the helicopter came under heavy fire. The pilot had no choice but to leave. I tried to move the wounded to a more secure location with the help of two other marines."

Kenneth grabbed a second cupcake and refilled his coffee cup and offered to refill Dr. Clarke's cup. After he sat down, he continued his story. "This next part is unbelievable, but I swear it did happen. All of a sudden, it was like we were in a bubble. I could still hear the gunfire, but it was like it was in the distance. We were suddenly bathed in a bright light, and we were taken upward. At the time, I had no idea what was happening. There was no helicopter, but we appeared to be in a transport of some kind. Then, we were on the ground again, and the helicopter was approaching. There was no gunfire. We loaded the wounded onto the copter, and we were flown to safety. It was like for one moment the war stopped."

"You said there were two others who were not wounded. Did they remember anything?"

"Nothing. They had no idea that the event occurred," Kenneth said.

"What do you think happened?"

"I don't know. After I returned to the states and made my way home, I put the event behind me. I got married to a wonderful young woman, who was more patient with me than she should have been. I kept having flashbacks to that moment. I never slept through the night. Finally, we both agreed the marriage was not good and she left. I moved here and built this cabin. It's where I belong."

"When did you realize it was an intervention by the Star People?"

"After my wife left, I did a lot of soul searching. One night, I built a fire in the backyard pit, which I do most nights, and I saw my first UFO. As I watched, captivated by the sight, the craft descended slowly and landed in the field to the south. Two figures approached me. They told me not to be afraid. I tried to stand, but I was too weak to move. They said that we had met before. Then they revealed that they had saved me in Vietnam."

"Were they talking about the event that occurred on the ground?"

"Yes. They proceeded to tell me that they saved me for a purpose. They said I was destined to be a healer among the people. They would help me. I had to forget the war and make something positive out of my life. Then they were gone."

"Can you describe your visitors?"

"I never saw them in full light the first time they came, but the next time, they took me on board their craft and that's when I saw them. They were tall, maybe as tall as seven feet. They were very muscular. They shimmered, and their skin was light blue."

"Light blue?" Dr. Clarke questioned.

"The shimmering light around them was blue, but their

skin appeared a lighter shade of blue. They were peaceful souls who traveled the world and healed pain. They taught me to channel their energy and to use my own energy to heal. We all have that ability but do not use our power. The star men taught me how to use my power and to tune into theirs. They changed my life. I'm no longer the man that came back from Vietnam. I'm not the boy that joined the Marines. I'm a healer."

"Do the Blue Men frequently visit you?"

"They are always with me. If I'm in the sweat lodge, if I'm called to pray for someone, if I'm alone in my cabin, their presence is always with me. They healed my PTSD. I am not the man who came back from 'Nam. I am thankful for them."

"Do the Blue Men appear in different forms to you?"

"They can appear in solid form, but they are mostly balls of energy. You saw them in the sweat lodge in Bozeman. Because they are energy, they prefer that form."

Follow-up: *Dr. Ardy Clarke visited Kenneth again and brought him his favorite fruitcake cupcakes. She heard about his miracle healing during their last meeting. Kenneth transformed from a Marine who suffered PTSD to a gentle, caring man and he believes the Blue Men are the ones responsible for his transformation.*

CHAPTER TWELVE

NANCY RED STAR'S STORY

Another Native American writer of Cherokee ancestry, Nancy Red Star, has written about extraterrestrial contact in her book *Star Ancestors* © 2000. Her account of her people began in Atlantis when the continent began to break up which started the migration of the red-skinned people through Mesoamerica, Egypt, and America. The Star Beings showed them where we came from. They taught the people how to read the stars, how to build pyramidal ceremonial centers, and how to keep cosmic calendars. They taught the people how to honor our place of origin from the stars, how to reconnect with it, and with those who seeded them here.

Red Star writes that the migration stories contradict conventional anthropology, which claims Indians came from

Asia, across the Bering Strait into Alaska, and down into America. Some Indians contend that it was the other way around — the migration came through Mesoamerica after the sinking of Atlantis, which makes far more sense than coming from the Bering Strait and down to America. It certainly answers why there were Maya, Aztec, Inca, and Olmec pyramids and huge mounds built by unknown people in America.

Red Star spent several months interviewing elders in the United States about UFOs, ETs, and sky deities. One of the five interviews was with Troy Lang aka Rolling Thunder, born of the Red Paint Clan in Asheville, North Carolina. His mother was a full-blood Cherokee, and his father was a black man from North Africa. He is a charter member of the International Treaty Council, which holds a seat in the United Nations. It's been eighteen years since Red Star wrote this book and I searched the internet for Troy Lang and it's as if he never existed — perhaps he has since passed. However, a photo of him was included in the book. I feel it is important to relate to Troy Lang's story.

"The way my grandparents and parents talked and lived was the Indian way. They took us out at night to look up in the sky and would say, "The sky is our camping ground in the stars. That is where we went, and that's where we came from." It was always taught that we came from the stars. Yes, our ancestry is of the stars. All Indians will say the same.

"I believe the Star Ancestors are already here. My relatives didn't use the words *extraterrestrial* or *space travel*. They spoke of the Little People. In our language, we say *tsunsti*, 'ancient astronauts.' We know what is happening in the skies. At one time we lived in Dayton, Ohio. People of all colors in that part of the world know that UFOs are a reality. We used to set out lawn chairs at my house on summer nights and stare off toward the airbase. We saw colored lights like you've never seen on Earth, moving faster and shining with an intensity that defies description."

Troy Lang continued, "My only fear is that I will die before I fulfill my work helping to heal the races. Dying is not the end, however. It is the beginning of the new."

Nancy Red Star had her first craft sighting in 1970 in Roxbury, Connecticut, when she was twenty-year-old and attending the New School of Social Research in New York City. She witnessed lights through the skylight in her apartment and was told to travel out of the city to an isolated location in the country. She thought it best to bring a witness to confirm what might happen there.

When she and a friend arrived, a triangular formation maneuvered on the horizon. Then one craft came forward and the light disappeared. The craft proceeded to directly where she was standing; it hovered some two hundred feet above her head. A field of energy transmitted information to her at the same time.

Nancy was told that she had work to do pertaining to them. Although she felt there were no living beings in the craft, she sensed the ship had been sent from a large craft. At no time did she ever feel threatened or afraid. Instead, there was a tremendous sense of well-being and confirmation of a more highly advanced technology and presence.

Years later she found her cousin, Shona Bear Clark, 74, who is a powerful Indian medicine woman. She was born of the Wind Clan and raised on the Creek Indian reservation near Oklahoma City. She descends from a proud line of medicine women.

As a young woman of twenty, she died from uncontrolled bleeding during childbirth, and because she has 0-Rh-negative blood (Lisa from Canada and many other abductees claim they have been abducted and their 0-Rh-negative blood is evidence of their alien DNA). Because 0-negative blood is so different, a donor was difficult to find. As the blood drained out of her, she shot out of her body and found her astral body on the ceiling, surrounded by a warm light of pure love. She said, "I saw all that I'd always seen and what I had only vaguely glimpsed. There was nothing I didn't completely understand. I knew the secrets of the universe. Then I felt an odd sensation. I became aware that someone was tying a tag and someone was saying the Lord's Prayer. Then suddenly I was back in my body. I had been dead for seven minutes. I was in pure light. I didn't see or hear anyone in the light, but ever since then, I have been able to hear people thinking [telepathic]. I can see a person's spirit floating above their heads, which tells me a great deal about the person."

She didn't see a spacecraft until she was twenty-five when her daughter had been badly bitten by a dog. She and several family members and friends left quickly in a couple of cars, driving to the hospital as fast as they could. On the way, a saucer-shaped object came down from the sky and hovered a short distance above them. It was silver and looked like two saucers, one over the other, with a line around the middle made of windows. They pulled over and got out of the car, all ten people. Above them, they could see figures in the windows. Everyone got scared except my daughter and me. They all returned to the cars and were yelling for Shona and her daughter to come back, but we had left our bodies and entered the craft.

Shona described her encounter with alien beings: "The Blonde aliens I knew from earlier in my life were there, enveloped in a pale blue light. They examined my injured daughter, and either cured her or determined that she was not in danger. Then the saucer rose up and disappeared, as if through a hole in the sky. When I looked down from the hole, my daughter and I were on the ground again, staring at each other in amazement. Everyone else had driven off. The next night the craft came back and hovered over my mother's house for nearly two hours. We weren't afraid."

Shona felt that the UFO beings had done something to her daughter, and they didn't leave their physical bodies but were transferred into the shift in their astral forms. The Blonde

Beings returned when she was forty-three and her father was ailing from pneumonia.

One day she went to check on her father and a white man was standing in the front yard of her father's house. She assumed he was a preacher because he was in a light-blue suit and what seemed to be a clergy's collar, and black patent leather shoes. She walked within three feet of him, paused, and then asked him who he was. He just smiled and said, "Everything is going to be fine." Then she blinked and he was instantly gone.

As soon as she entered the house, she could see her father had greatly improved. She asked her mother who the white man was, and she looked out the window but didn't see any man. Later she told her father about the incident, and he just laughed and said, "Maybe it was my guardian angel." Shona went back outside and looked for the man but there weren't any tracks in the snow.

Another incident happened in the middle of the night at 3:32 a.m. and Shona's room was lit up by some unknown illumination. She looked down at her foot — there was a piece of it missing, about one-inch deep and three inches long. The inside of her foot looked silver, but there was no blood. All at once she became aware of two men standing next to her, on each side of the bed. They had blonde shoulder-length hair and blue eyes and looked to be around fifty years old. Their skin was a bronze color as if they were tanned, and they wore robes, one red and white with gold roping, and the other man wore a blue robe. The one wearing the blue robe passed his hand over my foot and said, "Shona, you are completely healed." The man in the red robe put his hands on each side of her head without touching her and said, "We will be back when you need us."

As soon as they had disappeared Shona's foot looked normal, but the strange light remained until around six in the morning. The whole time she felt as if she was bathed in love. She felt that they had great power and that she was given this power to heal. They also told her to paint hides. They wanted her to paint hummingbirds, deer, and pyramids—full of diamonds and half diamonds. Now, the pyramid shape is predominant in her artwork.

Shona said, "So few Earth people understand what is happening. Earth is being destroyed, and the people will go with it. I try to wake them up."

Again, one night she was visited in her bedroom at 11:30 p.m. to find a similar being with long blonde hair, blue eyes, and wearing a white robe and gold roping around his neck standing beside her. He said, "We are giving you back your memories." That's all he said. He stood there all night as I slept on and off. That's when she began leaving her body on a regular basis.

"I have lived a long life, continually aware of the existence of other realities and of strange, magical beings that can traverse the dimensional barriers and enter my world. These are things Indians rarely speak about to White men. But we are changing all that now.

"When I got my memories back I saw their world. I saw their home. They let me visit. I saw a world that had three suns, and the land looked orange. It was sandy. I saw Earth; there were seven rings around it. The Blondes live in one of those rings, one of those realms. They interact with humans, but they aren't angels. They are a race of beings that would not go against the Creator and the original instructions. They would prefer death than to go against the Creator, who allowed them to stay there. They interact with humans, trying to help humans, to save them. Human beings are so fragile and so self-destructive at the same time. I've painted these blonde people; my children have seen them. They dress completely in white, and sometimes they have children with them."

One time Shona locked both sets of her keys inside her truck. Her son suggested breaking the window, but she decided against it. Then she said aloud, "Well, if you're here, help me find the keys." All of a sudden something took her hand and dragged her to the back of the house, to her bedroom. Her son watched as she went to a little basket on the dresser and was drawn to a white stone in it, about palm size. Her hand thrust into the basket, and when she brought it out the stone was in her hand. Under the stone was one key, which opened the door to my trunk. She opened the truck door and found the keys, but the one that opened the truck vanished.

Shona's Vision of the Future

Shona believes something is going to happen. She sees dark skies like it is before dawn. The wind is blowing; it must be blowing two hundred miles an hour. Trees and houses are pitching over like match sticks. "I'm watching this, and I realize when I reach up and touch my hair that it's raining horribly. I see all this chaos and debris, but my hair is not even blowing, not even wet. I'm not being affected by this. I'm just watching.

"I realize that this is something that is going to take place. I meet many people who have no checkpoints in reality. They see this world as going on forever. I know differently. From what I have been told telepathically it won't take long — within twelve or twenty-four hours the [Earth] shift will be made. A lot of people will leave the planet at the time of tribulations. The cycles are changing. The civilization of higher knowledge came over, driven by greed, and lost their way. With greed, you lose your power as a light being and become totally human. Power misuse will be the fall of human beings.

"The beings whom I have communicated with telepathically have told me that women will rise to take back the power and lead the way. The good news is that the world is being cleansed. Where there is land now there will be water. Earth is literally going to flip during this cleansing. Everything is going to be different. That is the cleansing of the world. People will have to start all over again. I think the people who will be saved from this will be the teachers. We have a Creator who will instruct the chosen few."

She added, "Now is the time for our teachings to be shared. For our planet. For the future of all beings."

Dana Pictou's Story of The Little People

Dana Pictou is a member of the Acadia Band of the Mi'kmaq in Nova Scotia. Born of the Turtle Clan, Dana is a traditional ash-basket maker and teacher of that art. Nancy Red indicated that Dana lived in Vermont with his family at the time of the publication of her book.

The Little People are believed to be alive in spirit on islands in Nova Scotia and Maine. It's said you can find these beings in rocks that have all these little holes in them. Only very special people find these rocks. The holes are not natural,' they're carved. The Little People carve them and leave them for those who come into their circle during a vision time. The Little People have always been guides for the Mi'kmaq.

"At my vision time, I cleared a piece of earth — cleared it of all that was standing and rooted and half-buried in the ground. I made sure it was smooth and there wasn't anything impure in that little circle with the hole in it. I put it in my bad and showed the elder who was helping me to the vision. He said, 'Well, you got visited by the Little People.'

As a child he was standing in the vision circle for the second night, gazing into the south. This is his rite of passage, guided by his teacher and grandfather, Wayindaga.

"I was looking into the south; it was two or three o'clock in the morning. I was having a lot of visions. I saw these lights like comets coming down from the sky. Then they would stop, and I could see Little People dropping from the sky in the distance, just far enough so I couldn't make them out once they reached the ground. (Dana's description sounds eerily like Dawn and Steve Hesses description of hundreds of beings dropping from the sky in the Mojave Desert.) Then they would come running out of the woods. I tried to look without blinking to make sure I wasn't "seeing" things. When I would look up I would see them dropping from the sky again. This lasted for forty-five minutes or an hour, Little People just dropping from the sky. I was looking to see where they landed, but I couldn't find the place."

CHAPTER THIRTEEN

THE TUJUNGA CANYONABDUCTIONS

Ann Druffel's book, *The Tujunga Canyon Contacts,* was published in 1980. The book detailed the encounters of five young women who lived in the Tujunga Canyons of Southern California starting in 1953. The women were linked more or less in intimate personal relationships that took place for two decades. Druffel investigated their cases for five years, and later parapsychologist D. Scott Rogo worked together on the book's publication. This was the second book written about so-called "alien abductions."

Druffel concluded the UFO entities were attracted to this particular group of women for two reasons: (1) All the Tujunga close encounter witnesses were interested in metaphysical studies and other mind-expanding activities. In general, UFOs seem attracted to individuals displaying psychic talents or whose minds were otherwise open to higher knowledge; (2) some of the Tujunga Canyon close encounter witnesses were members of the gay community. The UFO entities appeared concerned with the reproduction (and evolution) of the human race and were possibly investigating them to obtain details about this non-creative lifestyle.

In summary, therefore, Druffel felt that UFOs and their occupants are an essential part of God's creation. They are intellectually superior to humans, at least in our present state of evolution, and they are also superior in they are not bound by the confines of our material world and exist in other realms.

D. Scott Rogo's Summary on the UFO Abductions

Ann Druffel's friend and co-author of *The Tujunga Canyon Contacts*, Douglas Scott Rogo, was a writer, journalist, and researcher on subjects related to parapsychology. Rogo was murdered in 1990 at age 40. His case remains unsolved to this day. I felt Rogo's research and hypothesis on UFOs have real merit and should be considered.

Rogo's summary of aliens and UFO cases:

"When we first began to work on the *Tujunga Canyon* case, Ann and I didn't know where our research would eventually lead us. Since popular interest in the UFO mystery only dates back to the 1940s, researchers such as ourselves usually spent more time trying to prove such appearances than explaining them. It should be noted that not every abductee believes in the extraterrestrial hypothesis, and some have come to believe that other forms of other-worldly intelligences interrupted their lives.

"Many contemporary ufologists—including J. Allen Hynek, Jacques Vallee, Ann Druffel, Jerome Clark, and Ivan Sanderson, have given up on the idea that UFOs are some sort of nuts-and-bolts craft visiting our world from some distant galaxy. Quite frankly, these investigators have come to realize that UFOs and their occupants just don't behave like alien visitors to our realm. For one thing, they often seem at least partially immaterial. They sometimes change shape at will as they maneuver, shrinking or imploding into nothingness or literally growing or blowing up like a balloon; and they sometimes seem sensitive to the very thoughts of their viewers! UFOs are also natural mimics.

They have been seen to change shape in midair and imitate the appearance of airplanes and even helicopters. But they also seem to be bad mimics. They will sometimes change shape and 'turn into' an airplane or helicopter but will forget to include a cockpit or propeller and will continue to fly about without making any noise whatsoever! UFOs are often accompanied on their flights by mystery [unmarked] helicopters and distorted-looking airplanes that, from the standpoint of design, couldn't possibly fly.

"All these facts indicate that UFOs are not purely physical objects. They seem to be only partially physical, and partly ethereal at the same time. This fact is a major clue to the nature of the UFO mystery.

"A second major clue about the true nature of these flying objects was first made known to us by John Keel in his *book UFOs: Operation Trojan Horse.* When we think about UFOs, we invariably envision saucer or cigar-shaped objects flying about the skies. Keel, however, found by checking recent historical records that UFOs have not always appeared in these shapes. He points out in his book that as our own aeronautical technology has improved, UFOs have changed shape accordingly!

"For example, the first major UFO flap recorded in the United States came in 1896-97. The UFOs seen at this time were not discoid in shape, but zeppelin-like. Although these phantom 'blimps' were seen from California to Kansas, man-made zeppelins did not take to the air until a few years later.

So, these UFOs seemed to be presaging the upcoming invention and development of the zeppelin. Yet they behaved very much like the later, typical UFOs — they appeared with huge beacon lights underneath, often flew at incredible speed, and often in a zigzag motion. (Why do aliens need lights on their ships?). Another major UFO wave struck the United States in 1910 and lasted into the 1930s. These objects were shaped like airplanes, but they flew at incredible altitudes during weather conditions that would ordinarily ground any conventional aircraft. Nor could they be tracked. They would even show off by flying in curious 'hopping' motions, much like present-day UFOs have been observed to do. In 1946, a UFO flap invaded Scandinavia. But these UFOs were shaped more like missiles of the sort that had been developed during World War II than anything else. They would appear mysteriously in the northern skies and disappear just as suddenly. They would appear on the radar and then just vanish off the screens. Nor could they be captured, no matter how many jets were sent in pursuit of them.

"In retrospect, there seems to be a definite plan behind the way UFOs have changed shape over the years. They literally appear to be imitating our own technology. In other words, UFOs seem to be somehow symbiotically linked to our planet and our own culture. The UFO mystery seems to be a cosmic reflection objectifying man's own technological concerns and potential into physical existence.

"The idea that UFOs are somehow linked to our minds gains added credence when we consider the people have had close contact with them. A close encounter with a UFO and/or its occupants is not always a once-in-a-lifetime occurrence. It often preludes what may become a lifelong ordeal of continued alien contact or psychic attack. For years, UFO researchers have been aware of what is popularly called "paranormal fallout' — often a person who has interacted with a UFO will experience psychic events for years to come, apparently as an indirect outcome of his experience. Some UFO victims also become poltergeist victims.

"Parapsychologists have learned that poltergeists have violent telekinetic (or psychokinetic) displays that occur when a family, or member of the family living in the besieged house, cannot deal with psychological stress."

Rogo also wrote that some UFO witnesses have psychic experiences after UFO or abduction encounters, while others have a lifetime history of psychic abilities. But he asks if UFOs are only quasi-physical, how the occupants (aliens) be explained? Rogo felt that they didn't seem to be flesh and blood beings because they could disappear into thin air, walk through solid walls or closed windows, and have been known to run over muddy fields without leaving footprints.

But they must be flesh and blood if they die in crashes like the Roswell incident in 1947. How could the military have their corpses if they were not flesh and blood beings? It makes more sense that either they can manipulate our minds like magicians, or they can manipulate time and space – or perhaps both.

Astrophysicist and author Jacques Vallee believes that the UFO phenomenon is the product of a mechanism that controls human consciousness, much the same way as a thermostat regulates the temperature in your house. He does not believe that UFOs are a phenomenon in their own right but represent only one manifestation of the control mechanism. He feels that religious "miracles" such as the appearances of the Virgin Mary at Lourdes and Fatima, as well as fairy visitations witnessed during the Middle Ages, are also manifestations produced by this control system. Vallee compared this idea to the way psychologists modify animal behavior by constantly reinforcing certain modes of response. UFOs "are the means through which man's concepts are being rearranged."

Rogo felt that Vallee's ideas were brilliant, but he objected to them because of how UFOs often drastically affect the people who have been abducted or interacted with them. However, there is little evidence, he wrote, that they have created any great social impact.

The aliens had an impact in 1947 at Roswell with the general public becoming aware of the UFO mystery nationwide. But Steven Spielberg's movie *Close Encounters of a Third Kind* probably made a more significant impact than all the UFO sightings put together.

CHAPTER FOURTEEN

LISA'S AMAZING HYBRID STORY

Lisa is a strikingly attractive blonde with hypnotic green eyes, who stands 6 foot 3 inches tall, and claims her mother gave birth to twins after a bizarre encounter with two gray aliens. Lisa, whose surname is not revealed in the video, says her mother was supposedly pregnant with a boy in 1975 when she was born. She is now convinced she was implanted into her mother by aliens after they "visited her while she was pregnant".

Her bizarre story was revealed for the first time by UFO researcher Luigi Vendittelli from Montreal, Canada, on the Earth Mystery News YouTube channel. Vendittelli said, "Lisa's mother, who was living in St. Jerome, Quebec, was eight months pregnant and decided to go upstairs into the bedroom to take a break." The moment she hit the bed she was immediately paralyzed, and she started seeing this metallic gray object and two tiny aliens walking through the wall. They spoke to her telepathically. One said, 'she's not ready yet,' and the other said, 'she's ready.' Lisa's mom was frightened and told them to leave her alone and her other children. They vanished soon after.

One month later Lisa's mom was at the hospital giving birth. She had always gone to her obstetrician for checkups and everything looked normal, until that day. She gave birth to a healthy boy, but a few minutes later the nurse went screaming to the doctor to return to the room that the woman was giving birth to another baby—a twin. That's when Lisa was born. The doctor was stunned and stated there was no way another baby was there—nothing indicated a twin throughout her mom's pregnancy.

Many years later when Lisa was a teenager, her mom was visited by a tall human-looking alien. The alien had red hair and wore a type of white jumpsuit with a doctor's type of white coat on top. What caught my attention about this story was the insignia on the coat—a coiled snake. Could the coil snakes represent reptilians, or the medical symbol used today?

She was taken to a round room where she asked the alien's name. He replied, "John," in English—not the expected French version of John which is 'Jacques.' The room felt like a pharmacy with many vials. The alien appeared to anticipate her next question and said, "That's all the medicine that can cure humanity, but we're never going to give it to you because you are not supposed to be sick."

Through the years Lisa has experienced strange visions. In one vision she became a lizard and felt the ground beneath her feet. But other than her strange visions, she leads a normal life as a wife and mother.

Luigi has conducted alien abductee/experiencer meetings and support groups in Northern Quebec. At one of Luigi's support groups, Lisa met Sarah for the first time, an experiencer from Great Britain. Although they had never met before, somehow they sensed an instant recognition as if they were long-lost friends. After the meeting, Lisa was given a crystal by a friend. Sarah took the crystal and said to Luigi, "Please ask Lisa if her blood type is O negative."

Lisa answered in French, "I am O negative."

Sarah said she knew that and said, "So am I."

The strange part about this story is Lisa's mom is O negative, Lisa's O negative, and her daughter's O negative. A great number of hybrids claim to have an O-negative blood type. Luigi asked a physician friend if there was anything unusual about Rh-negative blood. The physician replied that a woman who has this blood type and is impregnated by a man, not O-negative needs a vaccine. He said it's more complex than that, but if a vaccine isn't given the baby will probably die. There's a high risk of losing the baby.

The YouTube video did not mention if Lisa's father was Rh-negative.

Today Lisa and Sarah have a spiritual connection and have the ability to carry on conversations without an interpreter and understand each other. So what does Lisa think about all this?

"I have a reason for being here and it is a little different than other people but I feel there are a lot of people like this. There is something to be done. We need to change things and it's a very heavy burden to have," Lisa said as she tried to grasp the mystery of what she feels within.

If thousands and maybe millions of people are hybrids then what is their mission? Will Lisa and others suddenly awaken to the alien's agenda one day? Was John's insignia of a coiled snake similar to our Bowl of Hygieia used as a symbol by pharmacy professionals since 1796 or was it the insignia for a highly intelligent reptilian/dinosaur species as I theorize in my book *Ancient Serpent Gods?*

About the RH Factor

Just as there are different major blood groups, such as type A and type B, there also is an *Rh factor*. The Rh factor is a protein that can be present on the surface of red blood cells. Most people have the Rh factor — they are Rh-positive. Others do not have the Rh factor — they are Rh-negative.

If a woman with Rh-negative blood becomes pregnant with an Rh-positive baby, her body will produce antigens signaling to her immune system that her fetus is essentially toxic. Oddly, the woman's body will kill its own fetus, unless given a rare antibody known as Rh-D immunoglobulin. This complication is known as hemolytic disease.

Theories on Rh-Negative Blood

Some believe Rh-negative blood is simply a mutation that came about at some unknown time in our evolution. But, as strange as it sounds, others have speculated the possibility that it may have come from an alien species that interbred with humans or engineered us in some way, producing a hybrid bloodline.

When we look at hybrid animals in other species, there are similar incompatibilities and sometimes even complete infertility. When a horse and donkey mate, the genetic differences result in a sterile mule. The same goes for a liger – the progeny of a lion and a tiger — the two species' chromosomes don't match, so they produce infertile offspring. Could there be a similar incompatibility between Rh-negative mothers and Rh-positive babies?

About 15 percent of the world's population has the Rh-negative distinction, with the D-antigen absent in their veins. But this percentage of the population is not spread evenly across all areas of the planet. While humans are thought to all share a common ancestor, originating in sub-Saharan Africa, the number of Rh-negative Africans is disproportionately low compared to others – about three percent. In Asia, that proportion is even lower with only about one percent of the population possessing this rare blood type. The gene that produces Rh-negative is largely present in Caucasians, with the highest concentration found in a small region on the Iberian Peninsula between France and Spain, known as the Basque region. Here, straddling the Pyrenees Mountains, up to 40 percent of the population is Rh-negative, and that's not the only distinguishing feature of the region.

Those from the Basque are also the only people of Western Europe who continue to speak an indigenous Indo-European language—an isolated tongue not spoken anywhere else in Europe. But this language is not just isolated; it's completely unrelated to other European languages.

A more mundane explanation for the homogenous traits of people from the Basque region is the idea that early farmers, during the start of the agricultural revolution, mixed with local hunters, before becoming isolated for thousands of years preserving their language and genetics. Others have posited the idea that the Basques could have been the pure descendants of the first modern humans to arrive in Europe.

But another theory that falls in the more ethereal category is that the Nephilim of biblical lore are responsible for Rh-negative blood types. In the Book of Enoch, the Nephilim, also known as the Watchers, descend from the heavens and mate with humans, creating a human-angel hybrid. This group of angels and their offspring were wiped out in the great biblical deluge, though some were said to have survived, leaving the Rh-negative blood distinction.

Another otherworldly theory is that the Anunnaki, the extraterrestrial race that helped establish ancient Mesopotamian civilizations, engineered or crossbred with humans and that some part of this process created the Rh-negative blood type.

It's alleged that people with Rh-negative blood have distinct physical features paired with a predilection for psychic phenomena and alien abductions. Some of those features are:

- Higher than average IQ
- Lower body temperature
- Higher blood pressure
- Red or reddish hair
- Extra vertebrae
- Sensitive vision and particular sensitivity to sunlight
- Elevated intuition

Everyone on the planet has either O, A, B, or AB but a sub-category to this is whether an individual is Rh positive or negative.
The Rh level refers to the Rhesus factor, which brings a specific antigen into the blood — if your blood does not carry the antigen, you are Rh-negative.

Some 85 percent of people are Rh-positive, and according to a startling claim, the remaining 15 percent of us could be descendants of aliens.

Consider this: Researcher Lara Starr states that if everyone had truly evolved from apes, we would all have the same blood type. In an article for *The Spirit Science*, she writes: "In the study of genetics, we find that we can only inherit what our ancestors had; except in the case of mutation. "We can have any of numerous combinations of traits inherited from all our ancestors. Therefore, if man and ape had evolved from a common ancestor, their blood would have evolved the same way. Blood factors are transmitted with much more exactitude than any other characteristic. All other earthly primates also have this Rh factor."

"If we had all evolved from the same ancestor, we would all have the same blood."

The author of the article goes on to say that several personality traits are associated with an Rh-negative carriers including higher than average IQ, lower body temperature, sensitive vision, and higher blood pressure.

Starr goes on to say that women with Rh-negative blood will be unable to carry the child of a man with a Rh-positive type. She states: "If you do, you get something called Hemolytic disease. This is the same allergic reaction that occurs when the Rh-negative mother is carrying a Rh-positive child.

"Her blood builds up antibodies to destroy an alien substance (the same way it would a virus), thereby destroying the infant."

However, scientists have dismissed the bizarre claims, stating that the Rh types are simply a by-product of evolution.

The scientific website archaeology review writes that a study "seemed to indicate that there is an evolutionary advantage for a population to have the RhD deletion within it. "This isn't dissimilar from other genetic expressions that are seemingly harmful to individuals but can have some overall positive benefits to a population. The sickle-cell trait is one such expression.

Dawn and Steve Hess (from the book *Mojave Incident*) thought their daughter was a hybrid after Dawn became pregnant during or after the alien abduction in the Mojave Desert. Dawn also said that her daughter has Rh 0 negative blood, which is interesting, but not conclusive that she's an alien-human hybrid.

Betsey Lewis

CHAPTER FIFTEEN

ABDUCTED BY REPTILIANS

UFO eyewitnesses have encountered reptilians over the last several decades. They are described as beings who stand six to nine feet tall with long torsos, a lizard-like face, and long tails. Some claim they have only three fingers with a thumb and others say they have four-to-six digits and claw-like hands. Their thick skin is either dark brown or green scales; others report smoother skin with a sheen that changes colors from dark green to brown when they move. Other witnesses claim they have a forked tongue, and in an earlier chapter, Dr. Ardy Clarke said a U.S. soldier in Vietnam witnessed reptilians in the jungles deep underground who emitted a venom that blinded his fellow soldier. They aren't your friendly ETs and from many stories, their agenda on Earth isn't benevolent for humans.

John Carpenter, an alien abduction researcher, describes the reptilians as having faces like snakes and golden vertical slit eyes, and their hands are webbed. He stated they are a highly intelligent race with well-developed telepathy; and use mind control on their abductees. He also maintains they are among the most feared species of the universe.

Thomas Castello, a former Dulce, New Mexico base security technician, claimed that Dulce was a secret base operated in New Mexico by military humans as well as reptilian aliens and their worker class, the Grays.

In my book *Ancient Serpent Gods* ©2016, I wrote about Castello's encounter with the reptilians and grays. In the early 1960s, a subterranean nuclear blast occurred about thirty miles southwest of Dulce, right off U.S. 64. This nuclear blast was conducted under the umbrella of project Plowshare and was named 'Gassbuggy.' It was alleged that this particular subsurface nuclear blast was used to create a hollowed-out chute or chimney for the development of a substation for a super-secret tunnel system attached to an underground Black Book Project base.

According to Thomas, this particular under-world city operated with humans, reptilians, and gray aliens. Experimentation projects took place there, primarily genetic experiments on kidnapped men, women, and children. Could this account for thousands of humans simply vanishing without a trace?

There is or was a myriad of other specialty science projects taking place at the Dulce base including, but not limited to atomic manipulation, cloning, studies of the human aura, advanced mind control applications, animal/human crossbreeding, visual and audio wiretapping, and the list goes on.

Dulce, New Mexico is a strange place. It's a sleepy little town perched upon the Archuletta Mesa, just south of the Colorado border in northern New Mexico. Tourists passing through sometimes see little more life in the town other than a small town. Those who have tried to investigate the town claim that upon entering the town, black vehicles with heavily tinted windows tailgate them until they are outside the city limits. It is also said that Native Americans living in the surrounding area refuse to talk to strangers about what they have seen or the stories they've heard.

In addition, several other sources, who want to remain anonymous, have reported oddities in their work with operation 'Plowshare' during the 1960s. The project was created under the guise of the use of atomic bombs during peacetime, and forged ahead under the umbrella of "Natural Gas Exploration." Several of these multi-kiloton blasts were used as a rapid way of developing huge sub-surface chambers for facility development. It is reported that the technology to clean radiation is available and already in use for such projects.

The Dulce base floor plan was illustrated by Thomas Castello and John Rhodes in Las Vegas, Nevada. Its layout, when inspected carefully, appears to be futuristic. According to Rhodes, from a vertical viewpoint, it resembles a wheel with a central hub and corridors radiating outwards like spokes. This 'hub' is the focal point of the entire base. It is surrounded by central security and extends through all levels of the base.

Rhodes said, "I believe this core to be the center of the entire facility. It probably contains fiber optic communications and power lines. This would justify its highly guarded and central location as well as explain its vertical continuation through all levels. With all communication lines and power lines focused towards the hub, it is possible that any one level could be completely "locked down" by its security or the security hubs from either above or below its own level. This would provide maximum control over the entire facility.

"The 'spokes' or corridors radiating away from the central hub, lead to numerous other labs in five different directions.

Connect the spokes and a pentagon is revealed in its design. From above, this base resembles the layout of the Pentagon in Washington D.C. complete with halls, walls, and military insignias! Since we do not have the exact heading on its corridors, magnetic alignments are impossible to determine.

"When viewed laterally, its appearance takes on the look of a tree with a trunk at its center and its floors extending outwards like the branches. If this is a facility of science, then one could easily say that its lateral appearance is like that of the tree of knowledge. Was this purposely designed this way or does it just happen to be a coincidence?

The overall design of this facility reminds one of a multi-stacked subterranean Hopi Indian kiva. Although I believe that it's somewhat of a disservice to the Hopi to mention this in association with a facility full of horrors like the Dulce base.

"As cultures around the world tend to bring their own styles of architecture with them during periods of migration, so perhaps did the advanced civilization that 'originally' built the Dulce Base. If the reptilian influence over man is as great as archaic documentation and myth would have us believe, then there have to be other subterranean dwellings similar to this in other locations."

(Note: The following are some additional facts and comments concerning the late Thomas Edwin Castello. These have been 'paraphrased' from the research files of John Rhodes):

In 1961, Castello was a young sergeant stationed at Nellis Air Force Base near Las Vegas, Nevada. His job was as a military photographer with a top-secret clearance. He later transferred to West Virginia where he trained in advanced intelligence photography. He worked inside an undisclosed underground installation, and due to the nature of his new assignment, his clearance was upgraded to TS-IV. He remained with the Air Force as a photographer until 1971 at which time he was offered a job with RAND corporation as a Security Technician, so he moved to California where RAND had a major facility and his security clearance was upgraded to ULTRA-3. The following year he met a woman named Cathy, they married and had a son, Eric.

In 1977 Thomas Castello was transferred to Santa Fe, New Mexico where his pay was raised significantly, and his security clearance was again upgraded — this time to ULTRA-7. His new job was as a photo security specialist in the Dulce installation, where his job specification was to maintain, align, and calibrate video monitoring cameras throughout the underground complex and to escort visitors to their destinations. Once arriving in Dulce, Thomas and several other new 'recruits' attended a mandatory meeting where they were introduced to the BIG LIE, that:
"...the subjects being used for genetic experiments were hopelessly insane and the research is for medical and humane purposes."

Beyond that, all questions were to be asked on a need-to-know basis. The briefing ended with severe threats of punishment for being caught talking to any of the "insane" or engaging in conversations with others not directly involved with one's current task. Venturing outside the boundaries of one's own work area without reason was also forbidden and, most of all, discussing the existence of the joint Alien/U.S. government base to any outsider would generate severe and, if necessary, deadly repercussions.

Thomas did his job as his superiors demanded. At first, his encounters with actual gray and reptilian beings in the base were exciting, but soon he became acutely aware that all was not what it appeared to be. Thomas slowly began to sense that there was an underlying current of tension existing between him and some of the personnel. Once in a while, he would walk around the corner, interrupting serious discussions between coworkers, and, as Thomas was a security officer, these talks would die off into a short murmur and individuals would part company.

One particular part of his job was to go into various areas of the base and align the security monitoring cameras when it was necessary. This allowed him to venture out and witness things that would stagger the imagination. Later he was to report seeing laboratories that investigated the following: Auraic energy fields of humans; astral or spirit-body voyaging and manipulation; psi studies; advanced mind control analysis and application; human brain memory recognition, acquisition, and transfer; matter manipulation; human/alien embryonic cloning; rapid human body replicating by use of energy/matter transfer (complete with an individual's memory from the neural network computer memory banks) and other scientific advances.

Once in a while, Thomas would see some of the horrifying genetic creations that were housed in separate sections of the base. These, he knew, couldn't have had anything to do with mental illness or health research. Thomas didn't want to look any further. Each time he discovered more pieces to this underground maze, it became more and more overwhelming to accept. His curious mind, however, implored him to search for the truth regardless of his desire to turn away in horror.

One day, Thomas was approached by another employee who ushered him into a side hallway. Here he was approached by two other men that whispered the most horrifying words: that men, women, and children that were labeled as mentally retarded were, in fact, heavily sedated victims of abduction. He warned the men that their words and actions could get them in big trouble if he were to turn them in. At this, one man told Thomas that they were all observing him and noticed that he too was 'uncomfortable' with what he was witnessing. They knew that Thomas had a conscience, and they knew they had a friend.

They were right; Thomas didn't turn them into his commanders. Instead, he made the dangerous decision to quietly speak with one of the caged humans in an area nicknamed "Nightmare Hall." Through their drug-induced state, he asked their name and their hometown. Thomas discreetly investigated the claim of this 'insane' human during his weekends out of the facility. He discovered through his search that the person had been declared missing in their hometown after vanishing suddenly, leaving behind his traumatized family. Soon he discovered that hundreds, perhaps thousands of men, women, and children were listed as missing or as unexplained disappearances. Thomas knew he was messing with something extremely dangerous and so were several of his co-workers. All he could do, until somehow the situation changed, was to be alert and extremely guarded with his thoughts. The gray aliens' telepathic capabilities allowed them to 'read' the minds of those around them and if he revealed his intense anger, it would be all over for him and his new friends.

In 1978, tensions within the Dulce base were extremely heightened. Some security and lab technicians began to sabotage the genetic experiments. Increasingly frail nerves and paranoia finally erupted into what is commonly referred to as the Dulce Wars. It was a literal battle between the reptilians and the humans for control of the Dulce base. It was the reptilians more than the human scientists that were pushing the "Big Lie," and insisted on using humans in their experiments, and those who did not survive the experiments were used as sources for the liquid protein tanks which fed both embryonic gray fetuses as well as full-grown grays, as a source of nourishment. The initial "Dulce War" conflict began on Level Three.

No one is exactly sure how it started, but we do know through Thomas' account that it involved base Security Forces armed with beam weapons known as "Flash Guns," machine-gun-toting U.S. Military personnel, and the gray alien species (that were playing both sides against each other). When the smoke cleared, sixty-eight humans had been killed, twenty-two were completely vaporized and nineteen escaped via the tunnels. Seven were recaptured and twelve remain in hiding to this day.

Thomas returned to his post awaiting his escape. But in 1979, the intense pressure brought upon Thomas by his job finally made him break the code of silence. He told his best friend, by a hand-passed note, that he was working in a sub-surface, huge installation outside of Dulce, New Mexico. He also told his friend that he was working side by side with Gray aliens that consider themselves "Native Terrans" (possibly short for terrestrials) and that the upside-down black triangle with the inverted gold-colored "T" inside it was the insignia of the project.

Thomas knew that he had to leave the job for his peace of mind, however now that he knew the truth about the abductees being held below, it would be almost impossible to live a normal life. He would always be under observation and threat until the day he died. He also was aware of the fact that old age may not be his downfall. His demise could easily be expedited by certain individuals like so many other people who have tried to get the truth out to the citizens of the world.

After one of his weekends away from the facility, he decided to return to work, but this time through one of the less guarded air shafts, unannounced and into the base by way of secret passages. Once inside, he proceeded to appear as if he was working his normal duties while taking charge of every thought as he passed by Grays. During this time inside the base, he removed still photographs of the facility and treaties signed, with authentic signatures, between California Governor Ronald Reagan, several other individuals, and the Grays.

Thomas also managed to retrieve a 7-minute black-and-white surveillance video of genetic experiments, caged humans, and Grays, as well as schematics of alien devices and complex genetic formulas. These items, he felt, were not only his chance to a seat at the bargaining table when the need arose, but also, there were things that the public needed to know about.

He made copies of the films, photographs, and paperwork, packed several 'packages', and instructed several different people who he trusted explicitly to bury or hide them until the right time. He was then made aware through certain sources that his wife, Cathy, and son, Eric, had been forcibly taken from their home to an undisclosed underground facility for 'safe holding' until he decided to return with the items. At this point, he knew that even if he did return everything to the Dulce commanders, that his wife and son were probably never going to be the same again, if they even returned at all, after being manipulated by aggressive mind control. He also knew that he and his family would become permanently missing due to some tragic accident. Thomas was at zero option. He quickly dissolved into a lonely life on the run—from state to state, border to border, motels to sofas. Always looking behind him and trying his best to look ahead.

This website information as of 2009 or 2010 claimed Thomas Edwin Castello was currently living in exile in a European country, that for obvious reasons cannot be named. He is living under an identity that protects his well-being and allows him to live a 'normal' life. Thomas, at the time, was diagnosed with terminal cancer and was compiling what he called "a final document" detailing his experiences as a Senior Security Technician at the Dulce underground facility in New Mexico. If this story is true, I assume that Thomas Edwin Castello is deceased, and we may never know the truth of his fantastic, and very frightening story of human abduction for genetic experiments conducted by grays and reptilians (Terrans) aided by U.S. scientists/military.

If this base is ever revealed to the public or another subsurface habitation similar in appearance to the Dulce base is found, it might connect them to the Hopi reptilian or snake legend. Could the Skinwalker Ranch in northeastern Utah be another Dulce? Investigators believe it is.

Phil Schneider's Terrifying Encounter at Dulce

Thomas Castello's story of Dulce, New Mexico took place in the early 1960s. But another incredulous story, with similar overtones, was told by Phil Schneider who detailed the firefight with gray aliens at an underground facility in Dulce, New Mexico in August 1979.

Phil Schneider at the time was a U.S. government geologist and Skunk Works aerospace engineer assigned to tunnel a mile into the Earth when they hit the alien complex. He was a self-taught geologist and explosives expert. Of the 1,477 underground bases around the world, 129 deep underground facilities of which were in the United States, he claimed to have worked on thirteen. Two of those bases were huge, including the much-rumored bioengineering facility at Dulce, New Mexico.

Schneider always maintained that gray humanoid extraterrestrials worked side by side with American technicians. But in August of 1979, a misunderstanding arose, and a firefight ensued. He was contracted to take part in a deep drilling operation at Dulce, New Mexico. During the sinking of the initial four shafts, it became apparent that many of the lasers and mechanical components of the tunnel boring machine (TBM) were coming up broken. Phil and several other geologists were elected to travel down the shaft via a basket to determine what the problem was. Upon arriving at the bottom of the shaft (2.5 miles deep), a horrifying discovery was made. They had broken through into a large cavern infested with alien creatures. Phil also claimed the government had known and worked with one of the eleven alien beings that are here — who are mostly malevolent. Some of the small gray aliens are controlled by the reptoids, he said.

The government knew about these creatures but failed to

inform any of the geologists working at Dulce in 1979.

The creatures were described as seven-foot-tall grays. Immediately Phil fired on them and killed two of the creatures, but he was hit by a light green cobalt radiation beam that was fired by one of them. Badly injured, burned, and missing two fingers, but still alive, Phil was placed in the elevator basket and began the long trip to the surface, while an intense firefight raged in the cavern below. When it was over, a total of sixty-six secret service agents, FBI members, and black berets were struck and killed by the alien creatures. Phil and three others survived the bizarre event. This alleged event has come to be known as the "Dulce Wars."

Phil believed that the beam-weapon blast to his chest caused his later cancer. Many people confirmed that a large scar indeed existed on Phil. During his lifetime made many outlandish claims. He stated vast underground cities and tunnels run through the world, built by laser technology, that can vitrify rock in an instant, turning it into a solid-agate-like substance.

Phil Schneider died on January 11, 1996, under mysterious circumstances after revealing his bizarre story the year before during speaking engagements. He was discovered in his Portland, Oregon apartment with a catheter wrapped around his neck three times and half-knotted in the front. Although his death was ruled a suicide, his ex-wife, Cynthia Drayer, believed he was assassinated especially after he received numerous death threats before his untimely death.

My research uncovered how ancient civilizations worldwide worshipped reptilian or serpent gods. *The Ancient Book of Dzyan*, probably the oldest of Sanskrit sources, speaks of a serpent race that descended from the skies and taught mankind.

Madame H.P. Blavatsky (1831-1891), an occultist, spirit medium, author, and co-founder of The Theosophical Society in 1875, spent three years in Tibet, Bhutan, and Skkim, accumulating thousands of Sanskrit sources which were compiled into *The Book of Dzyan.* These sources concern the ancient people called Nagas or Sarpa which were semi-divine beings with a human face and the tail of a dragon. Blavatsky believe that these Sarpa are the Seraphim of the Old Testament; the Seraphim would thus have the same etymological roots as the Sarpa of ancient India.

One of the greatest stories of East Indian legend was the Ramayana, the story of *Sita,* the bride of a northern Prince called Rama, who is abducted by Ravana, the serpent king of Ceylon, which is now modern Sri Lanka.

Throughout the story, Ravana is described in barbaric terms as "feeding on humans and drinking the blood of his foe." He is formidable in battle and almost defeats Rama when he uses his special Naga weapon, described as a "Naga-dart serpent noose," which seems to paralyze his enemies and drain their energy and life-force. Like all divine and semi-divine beings in mythology, Ravana had access to sophisticated weapons.

Ceylon, the island kingdom of Ravana, was the stronghold of the Nagas. It was described as the home of the Nagas in ancient Chinese sources. In one of the first literary references to Ceylon, when it traded with China before the Aryan occupation of India, it was described as a land of strange reptilian-like creatures. Because of its gems and spices, and its convenient location as an entrepot (a port city), it became popular with Chinese merchants.

The Hopi Indians described a race of reptilians called the *Sheti,* or "Snake Brothers," who lived underground. The Maya spoke of a reptilian race, often called the "Iguana-Men," who descended from the sky.

According to Cherokee legend, the great warrior *Aganunitsi* killed *Uktena,* described as a lizard-snake-like monster, and brought back the shining seventh scale from his chest, which resembled a large, transparent crystal with a blood-red streak and possessed mysterious power. In Columbia, *Bachue* (the primordial woman) transformed into a big snake and was called the "Celestial Snake."

But these aren't all the extraterrestrials visiting Earth from ancient times to the present time. Some abductees have seen Insectoid beings, Praying Mantis beings, Ant beings, and other bug beings. Some are said to be good-natured and humble, and others are described as aggressive.

Insect beings play a wide variety of different roles in the legends of Native American tribes. One of the most intriguing legends involves the Hopi and the Ant People, who were crucial to the survival of the Hope in both the "First World" and the "Second World." During the destruction of each world, virtuous members of the Hopi tribe were guided by the Sky god, *Sotuknang*, who took them to the subterranean caves where they found refuge and sustenance. The Ant people were portrayed as generous and industrious, giving the Hopi food when supplies ran short and taught them the merits of food storage. Their legend says the reason why ants have such thin waists today was because they once deprived themselves of provisions to feed the Hopi people.

For thousands of years, serpents played a major role in religions, folklore, and superstitious beliefs. In the Bible, Isaiah 14:29, reads, *Rejoice not thous, whoke "palestina, because the rod of him that smote thee is broken; for out of the serpent's root shall come forth a cockatrice, and his fruit shall be in a fiery flying serpent.*

A cockatrice is a mythical beast, essentially a two-legged dragon, wyvern, or serpent-like creature with a rooster's head.

Other Native American legends tell of the struggle between man and snake people that resulted in the snake people destroying mankind with a flood and a large number of humans with what was described as nuclear weapons.

Clinton's Story and Star Lizards
Dr. Ardy Sixkiller Clarke met Clinton through his cousin who served on the BIA Police Force. Clinton had trained to be a police

officer, but after his raining, he decided to open his own security company on the reservation. He had a cadre of young men located throughout the reservation who worked for him. While his firm had clients from the business community, most of his business came from individuals who wanted their houses patrolled when they were out of town on business or on vacation. According to his cousin, Clinton told him of an encounter with three monstrous aliens on one of his routine patrols. Clinton agreed to meet with Dr. Clarke for a late lunch at the local reservation café to tell her about his encounter.

Dr. Clarke greeted Clinton at the café where he was sitting in a back booth. He was a tall man with black hair cut in a short, military style. "I don't know what my cousin told you," Clinton began in a low voice."

"Not much, only that you had a terrifying encounter, and he thought if you talked to me, I might be able to help you put everything into perspective."

Clinton continued after taking a bite of his taco and a sip of tea. "It was a subzero night in January when I got a call from Joe, one of the guys who worked on the east side of the reservation. He said he was sick and unable to patrol several unoccupied houses on his rounds. I didn't have anyone to cover for Joe," he continued, "so I decided, despite the distance of fifty miles, I would cover for him and get one of my in-town guys to cover for me. The heater on my pickup was on the blitz, and my windshield kept fogging up with ice crystals. I had a bottle of anti-freeze behind my seat, and I stopped periodically and poured the fluid across the glass. I remember it was below zero, and twenty miles into the drive I wished I'd stayed in town."

"How long did it take you to arrive at your destination?"

"It took nearly two hours. Not having a heater was the biggest problem, and the snow-covered roads had turned to ice. When I arrived at the driveway of the first house on my round, my pickup suddenly lost power. The driveway was about a quarter mile long. So, I checked my flashlight and started the long trek to the house."

"What happened to your truck?" Dr. Clarke asked.

"I don't know. It just quit. The lights went out, the radio stopped, and the engine died."

Dr. Clarke asked if his flashlight still worked.

"Yes, but I didn't need it. There was a full moon, and once my eyes adjusted to the night without the headlights, I was able to see quite well. As I walked up the driveway, the house and barn set at the top of a small hill. I saw a light toward the back of the house. It was a powerful light, shining a wide beam. I thought it was a burglar with a flashlight. Then I saw another light and then another. There were three of them. Fortunately, I had my revolver. I pulled it out of my holster and decided to creep around the opposite side of the house to get a drop on them."

"Do you always carry a firearm?"

'Usually. I have a legal carry permit from the tribe, which allows me to defend myself, although I've never used it. This night was different." Clinton continued to explain what he found after Dr. Clarke asked if he found any burglars. "When I reached the house, I crept along the side, hoping to surprise them. Just as I planned to get the jump on them, their flashlights turned toward me, blinding me. I knew they were advancing on me as the spotlights moved in my direction. I raised my gun and ordered them to stop. I no sooner got it out of my mouth than I felt a hand on my neck."

He paused and finished off his glass of iced tea. "This wasn't a burglar. Look at me. I'm a big guy. I am six feet four and weigh two-hundred-and-forty pounds. I work out and bench press three hundred pounds. But whatever had a hold on my neck lifted me off the ground like I was a toy. I couldn't see who or what it was, and the more I struggled, the more my assailant squeezed my neck. I finally gave up, and once I relented, I saw the faces of the others. They were not human. I don't know what they were, but they were not human."

"What happened when you saw them?"

"They were communicating among themselves. I think that's what their grunts and whistles, almost like hisses, were. Then suddenly my assailant in the back picked me up, threw me over his shoulder, and walked toward the darkness. That's when I saw the ground shimmering with light. I couldn't tell where it came from, but I was surprised at the light. Then I became aware that this monster was carrying me up some sort of ramp. He carried me inside a structure and locked me in a room. I was alone in a dimly lit place no bigger than a bathroom. I searched for an exit, but the walls were strange like a sponge, porous and wet with no evidence of a door. There was no escape. I no longer had my gun. I don't know what happened to it. I had nothing to defend myself."

"Was there anything else about the room that you remember?"

"Just a dim light filtering down. I ran my hands along the walls. They were warm and smelled like swamp water. When I banged on the walls, it left imprints, but they quickly disappeared."

"How long were you in this room?"

"I have no idea. Maybe a half hour. I know it was not long until I had the sensation that we were airborne. There were no windows, and I could not confirm my suspicions, but a few minutes later one of them came in and took me into another room. There was a viewing center in one corner, and I watched as Earth faded away. It was then that I realized that I was in far more trouble than I could have imagined."

"Can you describe the creatures that abducted you?"

"They were huge, scaly, figures with flat faces, big wide mouths. They looked like lizards. They must have stood eight feet tall. I felt like a dwarf next to them. They wore no clothes, although they had some kind of belt around their waist. They had flashlights and what I assumed were weapons strapped to their arms. And their arms were huge. Twice the size of my leg and they possessed tremendous strength. Their eyes were the scariest part of all. Huge oval-shaped eyes that wrapped partially around the sides of their heads. Their pupils were yellow and oval-shaped."

"Were there any other creatures in the room at this time?"

"No. I was just deposited in this room with the viewing center, and again, I was unable to find my way out. To tell you the truth, I never expected to see Earth again."

"What happened?"

"I don't know. The next thing I remember, I was lying outside my client's house. My pants and shirt were gone. I was in subzero weather without any clothes but my underwear. I was freezing. I ran to my vehicle. I had left the key inside when I walked up the driveway. That saved my life. I managed to turn around and make it back to town."

"How were you able to do that with no heater in your car?"

"I had an old hunting coat in the pickup. I put it on, but the strangest thing happened when I started up the engine — the heater suddenly came on. Before long, I was warm. When I got to town, I headed for the HIS [Indian Health Hospital]. I was lucky that there was no one else in the waiting room. The doctor on call examined me and asked about the claw marks on the back of my neck."

"What did you tell him?" Dr. Clarke asked.

"I told them I got tangled up in some briars while hunting. He looked strangely at me, put some antiseptic on it, took a few stitches, and released me. He gave ma a pair of doctor's pants."

Dr. Clarke then asked if the doctor asked how he lost his clothes.

"I told him I lost them in a poker game," Clinton said with a smile.

"Do you really think he believed that?"

Clinton shrugged. "The ER sees lots of strange characters at night. If he didn't believe me, he said nothing."

"Did you have any other injuries?"

"Bruises, but no significant injuries other than my neck.

When I got home, I fell into bed. I kept having all kinds of nightmares about the creatures. I don't remember much. I kept waking up every time the dream got too unbearable. All I know is that they did things to me. Things I don't want to think about. And why? Why would they do this to me? Or to any human. We don't think that lizards could have these kinds of brains or fly in a spaceship. But these ones did. It makes a man think about what other kinds of creatures are out there landing on this planet. We are the babies to them as far as advances in space travel. And what were they doing at an old ranch house on an Indian reservation? It makes no sense. Nothing makes sense. In Sunday School, the teachers taught us that God made man in his image." He paused and looked at Dr. Clarke as if waiting for a response. "I mean, this is the space age. Isn't the idea that we evolved?"

"Maybe God made other intelligent beings too, just not in his Image."

Clinton agreed.

"Did you have any other marks?"

"None that I noticed. My neck is another story. It's painful every day. I can't work like I used to, and my fitness program has taken a back seat. What do you think they wanted with me?"

"All I can tell you is that you are not the first person to tell me about encounters with lizard-like people. And as in your case, most of them can be quite aggressive. Let me ask you this — did you ever go out to the site where it happened?"

"The very next day. I measured the footprints around the house. They were twenty-four inches long and six-inches wide. I found one that looked more like a claw print. But the sun had come out and was melting the snow. I found the spot where the spacecraft landed. All the snow was gone. There was an elongated spot with a semi-circle at the front. I measured it. It was nearly one-hundred feet from end to end. I assumed that was the length of the craft."

"Did you take any photos?"

"Never thought to take a camera, and my phone is a simple TracFone. No photo capabilities. I'm not into smartphones. I don't need somebody tracking me all the time. I keep things simple."

"And your gun?"

"I found my gun and flashlight up against the house, probably where I dropped it. Funny thing though, the gun was useless. It was like something very hot had melted the firing mechanism. I took it to a gun dealer in the city, and he said it was beyond repair. Although he said he'd never seen anything like it, he offered me seventy-five dollars toward a new one if I'd give it to him. I took the deal, but a few hours later, I got to thinking that someday it might be important, so I went back to the gun dealer, but he refused to return it to me."

"Anything else?"

"Nothing I can remember. It sure made me rethink my occupation. After that, I decided to go back to college and become a teacher. I don't want to be responsible for the same thing happening to my guys [his employees], and I sure don't want to go through that again. The tribe is considering buying my business. That would be good for me. I could go to school without borrowing money."

"Anything else?"

"Yeah, when I go out at night, I stay away from isolated places. I never leave home without a handgun and generally with a friend. I think there is safety in numbers." He laughed and scooted sideways in the booth and stretched his legs into the aisle. "I have a lot of trouble with my neck. It hurts like hell every day. By evening, I'm on heating pads. Chiropractors and doctors haven't helped. Guess that's my souvenir from my encounter."

"Do you have scars from the ordeal?" Clinton turned around so that his back was facing Dr. Clarke. He pulled down the collar of his shirt, and I saw the large white scars around his neck. They reminded me of a bear mauling victim that she met in northern Montana. Even if he wanted to forget about that night, his scars and pain were a constant reminder.

Follow-up: *Dr. Clarke visited Clinton a few times since telling the story. He was now a junior at the state university and was studying to be a math teacher. There had been no more encounters with the lizard people, but the memory is ever-present in his mind. He still has trouble with his neck and admits that he has to limit his time on the computer, despite the fact that many of his courses require him to go online. There is no question that Clinton's encounter with the star lizards changed the direction of his life and his health as well. For Clinton, his encounter did not have a positive outcome.*

Maone's Story
One of Dr. Clarke's former students, who was head basketball coach at the reservation high school, requested that she stay over on a Friday night and attend one of his games. Little did she know that she had been invited to the game because it was "Appreciation Night." In other words, at half-time, the student-athletes and coaches recognized the most influential person in their lives outside their families. When it came time for the coach to announce his choice, he called her name. She was also surprised that he added that she was known as the UFO lady in familiar circles, and if anyone had a story, they should contact her. After the honoring, Dr. Clarke made her way to the top of the bleacher carrying several gifts bestowed upon her by his family. Afterward, Maone approached her introduced himself, and offered to help. When she sat down, he deposited the blankets, moccasins, and jewelry on the bleacher in front of her, and told her that he had a story to tell. She visited him at his family ranch the next day.

Maone came from a very traditional family who practiced the old ways, including adhering to the Native culture, speaking the Native language in their home, and practicing the Native religion. He belonged to the wolf clan of his tribe, thus the name Maone, meaning Red Wolf in English. He sported a gold belt buckle indicating he was a champion bull rider. Although he stood no more than five feet eight, he was a giant of a man who reveled in his ability to teach the younger generation about their ancestral history.

Dr. Clarke comments on how she had heard about his work with at-rick youth. "It is a good thing you are doing."

"Before I begin, I want to make sure one thing is very clear. There is a difference between the Star People of my grandfather's day and the star visitors I have met. That being said, please bear with me. I believe kids need to know where they come from. Without that, you don't know where you are going or where you've been."

Maone spread out a horse blanket on the ground and invited Dr. Clarke to sit. He was a gentle man who spoke softly, often hesitating as though choosing his words thoughtfully. "

"You told me you had a story to tell. Would you mind if I taped it?"

"Not at all," he said. Everyone should know the truth about the star visitors."

"When did you have your first encounter?"

"I've had them over the years since I was a teenager. I've been exposed to many things, far too advanced for a man like me. I'm nobody, but the star visitors have shared many things. I think it's because of my traditional upbringing. I believe they would like to change my resolve, to break me, in other words, or make me submit."

Clinton continued. "I have witnessed the most advanced technology that is possible to imagine. I have seen them use technology to interface with the mind and body and the results of their experimentation. It's beyond the scope of what humans can imagine. I've seen them take the human body and make it half machine and half human, and then control it to the point that the person will do anything they want them to do."

"I don't understand," replied Dr. Clarke.

"The star visitors use mind control and energy harvesting to control those humans they abduct. From my perspective, it has extreme spiritual implications. They are not spiritual beings, and they show their power by destroying spirituality. Whether you're spiritual or not, you have to believe in something. I believe in the Great Mystery, God, and the Great Spirit. I will not be intimidated to give up my religion, nor erase my belief in a future life. I hold fast to my beliefs. The star visitors have no beliefs; therefore, no consciousness."

"Why do you say they have no beliefs?"

"In their world, they have erased emotions and individuality. They are all alike and respond as one. They no longer speak orally. They read each other's mind and have no free will."

"You said they practice mind control. Could you elaborate?"

"As I said, they control their population through mind control. Everyone thinks the same."

"What is energy harvesting?"

"They abduct people to harvest their energy. All of us have this power within ourselves to control everything around us, and yet humans have not used that energy for centuries, and when they do, it is often misguided. The star visitors have machines that capture this energy and basically turn humans into mindless persons who will fall for anything. They can make a person forget all the teachings of their parents and grandparents and follow a leader with some bizarre notion of what is right and wrong. It is the basis of radicalism. Throwing away the old and instituting a new way even though it is not what we have been raised to believe."

"Are you saying through the energy harvesting they change people to be someone they were not raised to be?"

"Yes. Once they have completed the energy harvesting, those individuals are subject to manipulation that causes them to act in ways that would shock humanity. Riots, serial killings, torture, human trafficking. These events have become common around the world. We are losing our humanity. And it is the aliens who have brought that upon us with the assistance of power-hungry individuals who work in consort with them."

"Do you mean politicians, government employees? Dr. Clarke asked.

"Some are politicians. Many are extremely wealthy in society. They've given their souls to gain their wealth. They cooperate with the enemy."

"But what about someone like you?"

"They've not touched me. I have a strong resolve of who I am. I know where I come from, who I am, and where I belong. That is why I teach the young. It is the only way to protect them. Even if they capture you and try to perform their ungodly experiments, they can't change a person who has a strong sense of person and individuality."

"Can you describe the star visitors?"

"They are like lizards. Their faces are long with a snout like a lizard or snake. They have a long tongue that can lash out like a lizard. I have seen them eject some kind of venom from their snouts to paralyze and kill an enemy. They are frightening creatures. They terrorize those they kidnap. I'm one of the lucky ones. They found my resolve to be something they rarely encountered."

"What do you think they want?"

"I think they plan to one day control the Earth. They already are doing it just a little at a time. We are not alone in the universe, and there are forces at work that we do not understand or can even begin to comprehend. I believe the government knows about them, but they have lied to people so long, they can't find a way to tell the truth."

"Do you think the government will ever tell the truth?"

"If and when the truth is revealed, it will change the way we view ourselves both religiously and physically. Humans will undergo such a transformation that we will no longer be human again. Not the human that you and I know."

"Have you shared your stories about UFOs with anyone?"

"No, only you. I think the truth of what is going on would be too difficult for most people to understand. I think they would regard me as some crazy Indian, but I'm not."

"Why tell me?"

"As Indians, we need to guard who we are. We teach our children the Red Way. It is our only hope. Your books reach more people than I can hope to reach and maybe some will take my words to heart."

Follow-up: *Dr. Clarke only met with Maone once since their first meeting. He is a true believer that the old ways will keep his people alive for many generations to come.*

Tennesy's Story: The Soul Takers
Tennesy contacted Dr. Clarke through email and asked to meet with her if she ever took a trip back East. She took him up on his invitation when she went to a family reunion. They agreed to meet at a truck stop off the interstate. When she arrived, he recognized her from her photograph and welcomed me to a back booth in the large restaurant. Tennesy, whose name in Tsalagi (Cherokee) language means mighty warrior, appeared to be exactly that. After we ordered lunch Tennesy wasted no time telling his story.

"The aliens I met were more like reptiles than humans, although there were some human qualities," he began. "I get excited and forget that you do not know the circumstances of my encounter."

"Please, just start at the beginning. By the way, I hope you don't mind if I tape your story."

"I don't mind. I live in the mountains, not too far from here. I love the mountains. As a boy, I walked every inch of the hills behind my home with my dad, who was Cherokee. He knew the mountains like the back of his hand. He knew the herbs for healing, the plants that come in the spring that you can eat, and those that provide food and healing in the fall. He was my teacher. Now I roam the mountains alone and collect those items. My dad passed last year, but I know he still walks with me."

"I'm sorry to hear about your dad, but it appears you have many fond memories of him."

Tennesy nodded.

"Was it in the mountains behind your house where you encountered the Star People?"

"If you want to call the Reptile Men, Star People, then yes. I don't regard them as the Star People of our elders. They are a different race; not human-like. There is a canyon that runs behind our house. The gorge is very deep and difficult to maintain a footing. I have only been down to the bottom of the valley once on my own power. It's difficult to climb back out of the canyon. Even though I'm pretty good shape, it's a challenge."

Dr. Clarke described Tennesy as muscular with rough hands suggesting he was a construction worker. His black hair was parted down the middle fell to his shoulders and outlined his chiseled, bronzed face.

"If you have only been to the canyon once on your own power, have you been to the canyon by other means?"

"Many times. The area is a heavily forested region. The valley is closed to the public, and special permits are required to enter because of the danger. For years, my people have heard unusual sounds from underground. There are legends about it in the area. But there is one area where glowing lights have been seen. The only way to reach it is by foot, but few have ever attempted it."

"Did you?"

"Yes. That's where I met the Reptile Men. I decided to investigate the glowing lights I'd seen the night before. I wanted to find out for myself what was going on. I was thirteen at the time. When I got to the bottom of the gorge, I discovered a long, silver, pencil-shaped craft sitting at the opening of a waterfall. Behind the waterfall was a concealed cave. Once I spotted the craft, I cautiously approached it."

Dr. Clarke asked if there were any signs of life. "Not at first," Tennesy replied. Once I got near enough to the craft to touch it, I reached out my hand and the craft disappeared before my eyes. One minute I touched it, and the next minute it vanished. That's when I saw the large reptiles. I can't tell you how scared I was, even at thirteen. I didn't scare easily. I tried to speak, but nothing came out of my mouth. I tried to move backward, but my legs wouldn't move and then the most scary thing of all happened: I was paralyzed like a stone statue. I couldn't move, and then they got inside my head."

Dr. Clarke asked him to explain.

"I could hear them communicating in my head, but I didn't understand. Finally, one of them, I think was the leader, came forth and spoke to me in Cherokee. He said I should not fear them. They were here from another world and had stopped to refuel and maintain their craft. He told me I would not remember seeing them, but that if I was interested, they would show me many wondrous things. Over a period of three years, they showed me many things."

Dr. Clarke then asked for a description of the beings.

"They stood about eight feet tall. Their faces were a cross between a snake and a lizard. They had a snout for a nose. They wore vests with an insignia of a snake in yellow. No other clothing. They all seemed to be the same sex, although there were no visible sex organs. They had huge muscular arms with six-digit claws for hands. Their legs were equally muscular. They had a funny way of moving forward and backward using a rather short, powerful, thrusting motion that seemed to propel them backward and forward."

"How did they speak to you?"

"Like I said, they got inside my head. They took me inside the cave. It was like a big cathedral with huge stalagmites and inside this huge cathedral sat the craft I touched outside. They told me the cave was a tunnel to the universe and allowed them to travel to many worlds."

"Did they explain what they meant by traveling to other worlds?"

"They didn't have to tell me. My grandfather used to talk about a tunnel that allowed the elders to travel to other worlds and contact various races in the universe. These privileges were only for the seers or the elders, but they regularly made contact in the old days before time began."

"Did they take you into the tunnel?"

"Several times over the next three years. They took me to other worlds and showed me advanced races and cultures. I saw the Reptile Men interact with humanoid and non-humanoid creatures. Everywhere we went it seemed the Reptile Men were the masters, and the other creatures were subservient to them. Other beings appeared afraid and anxious in their presence, but I observed their interactions from a human perspective, and that might not be what was going on at all. But yet, I feared them. I don't believe they are on Earth for any humanitarian mission."

"Why do you say that?"

"I've seen them torture humans and non-humans. I've seen them steal their souls. They have machines that take your soul. At least I think that's what they do. Once a person or creature is put into the machine, they follow orders blindly. They have no will of their own. It worries me."

"Were you ever put into the machine?"

He nodded and said, "But it didn't work on me. All I know is they kept trying, but it only increased my resolve to not allow them to take my soul."

"How did you manage that?"

"You are probably going to think this strange. I recited an ancient prayer my grandfather taught me when they put me in the machine. My Pops taught me this prayer as a means to overcome fear. Over and over again, I recited the prayer. The machine didn't work. I think the words of my grandfather were too powerful for them. I think that is the key. They have no spirituality. But humans by nature are spiritual. At least those of us who know the old ways."

"Do you think other prayers would have the same effect?"

"I don't know. I never tried it. I stayed with what I knew the best. My grandfather's prayer is powerful. It comes from the ancients in the time before time. He learned it from his grandfather, who learned it from his grandfather. It has been passed down through the ages of time. I will stick with it. It's what I know."

"Can you tell me why you contacted me?" Dr. Clarke asked.

"I wanted you to tell my story because I believe the Reptile Men have plans for Earth. I think they want to make humans subservient to them. If you write my story, tell the people that if they are taken, to pray their own prayer to prevent the Reptile Men from capturing their souls. Perhaps if everyone did this, we will discourage them. This is why I tell you my story. It's maybe the most important thing I will ever do."

"Do the Reptile Men still visit you?"

"They gave up after I joined the Army to try to get away from them. But I know they are out there kidnapping others and performing their soul-taking project. They must be stopped. Just tell everyone to remember to recite their most powerful prayer if they are even taken."

Follow-up: *Dr. Clarke kept in touch with Tennesy by email. At the time, he still worked in construction although he received a master's degree in business administration. When he wants to talk about the "soul takers," he calls Dr. Clarke on a TracFone for fear the government might locate him. He became engaged and plans to marry in the spring. So far, the Reptile Men have not returned.*

Buck's Story: They're the Devil's Children
Buck, whose legal name was Horatio, a moniker given to him by a Catholic nun at a boarding school in South Dakota, worked as a legal aide for an advocacy group representing American Indians in federal prison. As a liaison with the prison and trusted by both the

incarcerated and incarcerators, Buck spent most days investigating the stories of convicts and preparing briefs for lawyers for appeals. Dr. Clarke caught up with him during a visit to his grandmother's house. He explained that he kept his encounters private due to the nature of his work. He felt his encounters, if made public, would be fuel to discredit him, and his work was too important to jeopardize it.

Dr. Clarke had been friends with Myrtle, Buck's grandmother, for many years. She was one of the first Indian teachers on the reservation. Over the year they became friends. It was Myrtle who convinced Buck to study pre-law at the university. While lack of money and family obligations put an end to his goal of becoming a lawyer, Buck appeared content in his role of advocacy. As they sat around Myrtle's cramped kitchen table enjoying herbal tea, Buck talked passionately about his work and the injustice in the state.

"In South Dakota," he explained, "Indians make up sixty percent of the federal caseload, and yet we are only eight-and-a-half percent of the total population. Now, do you call that justice or racism? It's the same in all the states with an Indian minority: North Dakota, Montana, Minnesota, and Oklahoma. There is no justice."

He set down his teacup and smiled, and then reached for Dr. Clarke's hand. "Sorry, sister, I know you didn't come to hear about the prison system. You're here for another purpose — UFOs and aliens. I've had more than a half dozen encounters. Where do I begin."

Dr. Clarke suggested at the beginning when it all started.

"When I was about nine years old, I was staying with MawMaw [grandmother]. I did that a lot. She was my rock. At night, I began see these monster men who often roamed MawMaw's house at night. I was a night owl boy — had a hard time sleeping, and the summers were so hot, and in the evenings, it was hard to sleep. We had no fan in the house and it was reserved for the living room. At night, I would go there, relax on the couch, and quietly turn on the fan. MawMaw didn't allow me to use the fan much. She said it ran up her electric bill, and in those days even being a teacher didn't pay much. The Tribe set the salaries, and teachers were at the low end of the totem pole." Dr. Clarke then asked about the monster men and Buck continued. "I saw them the first time when I was a boy, but every encounter has been with the ones I call the monster men. They are the same.

"Always before I saw them," he said, "I would see a bright light that lit up the night sky and the Earth below. It gave the appearance of a bank of bright lights, all pointed at the windows of the house. After that, the monster men came. I would watch them as they walked around at night. I would see their shadows as they passed the window. I was afraid. It took at least several weeks before I got the courage to go outside and check them out. At first, I hid in the shadows, and what I observed were really monsters. They were taller than any man I had ever seen. They walked funny, like when they set their foot down, it came down with a thud. They seemed strange to me, like someone learning to walk for the first time. They walked a lot like toddlers who were unsure of their balance, but they were huge beings walking like that. To a nine-year-old this was confusing, but at the same time, I was fascinated. I wanted to know where these monsters came from. I wondered if they were demons from hell that the Father talked about in church."

"Did you ever reveal yourself to them?"

"I did, but not on purpose. One night, I heard a frightful sound coming from the barn. I knew something was scaring my mare, Betty. I heard her kicking her stall and neighing loudly. I rushed out the door only to come within a foot of one of the monsters. He reached down and caught me in one hand and held me aloft like a rag doll. He sniffed me. He actually sniffed me like an animal might do when they are unsure of something. Then he dropped me from his grasp and walked toward another monster who was about twenty feet away. I jumped to my feet and headed for the barn."

"Was anyone in the house while all of this was going on?"

"MawMaw, but she was asleep and didn't walk up." He reached out and held his grandmother's hand. "When I entered the barn, I picked up my BB gun that I always kept at the door. I didn't expect it would stop the monsters, but I could at least put one's eye out. I was a good shot. That's how I got the name Buck. I could always be counted on to bag the biggest buck when deer hunting."

"Were there any monsters in the barn?"

"I didn't see any, but I smelled them. They had a terrible stench about them like rotten eggs. They were there and gone I guess. I tried to calm Betty, but nothing could comfort her. I finally gave up."

"Can you describe the monster who grabbed you?"

"At the time, I couldn't see much. It was dark, but two weeks later they returned. This time, I was ready. I had my 12-gauge, a box of shells, and my flashlight. After the first encounter, I was ready. I was so naïve. It was about midnight. At the sign of the first lights, I went outside and climbed into the loft of the barn. It wasn't long until I saw this long tank-like craft descent from the sky and land. I saw four beings emerge from the craft and walk toward the small creek that flowed on the west side of the property. A few minutes passed, and they began walking the property, making what appeared to be a circle around the place. It was like they were searching for something."

"Was there anything special about your property? Any minerals, rocks, or something they would want?" Dr. Clarke questioned.

"Geodes. Tons of geodes, on the ground, under the ground. Our property was on the site of an ancient riverbed. Lots of geodes. I loved cracking them open and bringing them how to MawMaw." He pointed to a shelf along the ceiling of the small kitchen. "That's a part of my collection. I don't know why they would be interested in geodes. They did not appear to be beings that were interested in their aesthetic.

"What can you tell me about them?"

"They reminded me in some ways of a huge snake, at least their heads did. Their body was more human with arms and legs. They seemed to be able to communicate with one another, but I could not understand them. They made hissing and grunting sounds. It was nothing I understood, but it looked like they understood each other. Their heads were huge, like the size of a buffalo head, but there was no neck. Just a head that grew out of their body. When one of them came close to the barn, I shined my flashlight in his face, and he had the weirdest eyes, big, slanted eyes that reflected red in the light like a wild animal. His mouth was like a big snout, nothing like a human. When he opened his mouth in response to the light, I realized he could eat me with one bite. The light in his face caused him to back away, and I fired a shot. Not directly at him, but close enough that he knew I meant business. To this day, I remember the sound of the shot, the kick of the 12-gauge, and what I interpreted as fear in the reaction of the monster man. At once, he headed toward the others who had assembled together in a circle. For a moment they stood there. Then they walked back to their spacecraft and disappeared. Then they walked back to their spacecraft and disappeared. I watched them leave. I stayed in the loft until they were no more than a star in the sky."

"Have you had any other encounters with the monster men?

"Several. It is always here on the property. I worry about MawMaw who refused to leave this house. But they are explorers, nothing more. I have since learned they come for the quartz. I don't know what they do with it, but as I understand it, it is a valued commodity in the universe."

"So, you have communicated with them?"

"Only on a nominal basis. They can plant ideas in my head. I don't think they mean any harm, but they do not want to reveal themselves to humans. They fear humans will try to destroy them."

Buck went on to describe more about them after seeing them on several occasions. "On this planet, I think they would be considered relatives of the lizard. Their appearance from mid-torso to their heads is very lizard-like. They do not have scales, but they have translucent skin that looks brown and green at the same time. From their torso down, they have huge legs making it difficult to walk. Their arms are monstrous where they join their bodies, but then taper off to small claw-like hands. It reminds me of pictures I've seen of dinosaurs. Maybe they are a mix of dinosaurs and lizards. It is hard to describe something that doesn't exist, at least not on this planet."

"Do you believe they are of superior intelligence?'

"That's obvious, isn't it? If not, how do they come here? They are definitely intelligent, and it would be hard for humans to accept that these monstrous lizard men are smarter than they look. They are also carnivorous. I've seen them capture and eat deer while the deer was still alive. They are powerful, too. Humans would not stand a chance with them in combat."

"Why do you remain silent?"

"Who would believe me? Maybe you and MawMaw, who has seen them too."

"Do you have anything you can add to Buck's story?" Dr. Clarke asked addressing Buck's grandmother Myrtle.

She nodded and then quietly said, "They're the Devil's children. God didn't make those creatures."

Follow-up: *Dr. Clarke visited Buck and his grandmother frequently. They'd talk late into the night about his work and the monster men. She believed Buck's story as a reliable and honest observer of the reptilian creatures that have been reported by others. While his encounters did not seem to terrify the adult Buck, it was obvious that as a nine-year-old boy, he was terrified of the monster men.*

Barbara Lamb and Reptilian Encounters
Barbara Lamb has hypnotized ET experiencers since 1991 and has uncovered stunning information from more than 560 people and at least 1,800 regressions to reptilian alien encounters. In the book, *Alien Experiences,* by Barbara Lamb and Nadine Lalich, they uncovered twenty-five cases of close encounters. The following cases are condensed from the book.

Marie's Regression
Barbara Lamb conducted this regression on July 16, 2006, with the subject Marie, asking her to describe her encounter and abduction.

Marie began, "I'm on a ship and standing in a room with only females—female humans. Everyone seems pretty out of it with their arms hanging down at their side. This experience has something to do with babies and war. They're showing us smoke and bombs. Will they rescue Earth's babies at a time of war? The DNA has been altered in some of the Earth babies, and they have added some of their own DNA into them, to change the human race and get rid of the aggression. Only some of the babies are going to be saved from the planet when the disaster comes. The extraterrestrials alter their DNA when they're inside the pregnant mother by injecting DNA into the womb of the mother with the baby inside. We are the protectors of these babies.

"Oh, there's something wrong. Three races of extraterrestrials are here right now and one of them is a reptilian race. I think there's something wrong with them and maybe they're dying. I can see different types of beings in different types of vehicles now and it's the reptilians that have the cigar-shaped crafts. The little grays and the big white ones with big heads are here, too. Who is it that's dying?"

Marie continued to describe why they were dying. "They're telling me that their cells are dying because they have exposed themselves to conditions here that are different from their own conditions. They might have to mix their cells with human cells to survive here for very long because they can't stay here for very long at any one time. They take the blood from the babies who have been genetically altered, and they inject it into themselves so they can stay here physically for longer. They need some ingredients of our immune system to be okay here."

Louise's Regression May 4, 2004

Louise had experienced multiple contacts with extraterrestrials that she stated were reptilians, with bumpy, mottled green skin that was soft to the touch. She also described them as having tails. Barbara Lamb hypnotized Louise to an event that took place in 1992 where she had been taken. It was a large, round room with strange, indirect yellow lighting that didn't have a source. She recalled seeing gold, reptilian eyes very close to her face, and feeling that there were several other beings in the room with her.

Louise felt she was being controlled. At one point she was shown an unusual baby that looked like a reptile being that appeared to have been taken from her own body and slipped into a jelly-like substance. As she described the experience as wonderful, she became very emotional and wept.

After the regression, Louise said she felt exploited and disrespected by the reptilian beings who behaved as though they were superior to humans. There were times when she experienced paralysis and, there were times when she was sexually aroused. The shocking revelation from Louise was the reptilian beings conveyed to her that she was connected to them and was very valuable to them. They explained to her that although they do have the capacity for emotion, including love, it is quite dissimilar to human love in that they experience feeling at a lower, more dense frequency than humans do.

Rita's Experience

Rita first contacted Barbara on January 11, 2001, after her husband urged her to because he thought she was experiencing alien contact. He, too, was an experiencer and recalled seeing Rita on craft during several of his encounters.

Rita had also experienced ongoing dreams of extraterrestrials and, when waking from these dreams, felt the memory carried a strong sense of reality. In one experience, she described seeing a nuclear missile hit Los Angeles and people dying from radiation. It's common for abductees and experiencers to be shown apocalyptic visions by the grays and reptilians. During the event, her sister was also present, and they both observed a giant spaceship and helicopters flying overhead. She also recalled being shown a written plan for ETs coming to live on Earth's surface.

But what if they are already on Earth and living beneath us? I have no doubt numerous species of ETs have visited our planet for diversified reasons, and perhaps these ETs are at odds with the grays and reptilians. This hostility and wars between alien species might have begun millions of years ago on planet Earth and continues to this day.

In another dream-like experience, Rita was in an institution-type building with a large group of people huddled together. A big, lizard-type being with a long, thick tail walked up to her and the people. He wore no clothing and carried a clipboard. The group, now in a trance, was led in a line into a larger room with rock formations along the side. There they were shown enactments of violent scenes, including sexual relations between a human female and a reptilian being. Although the scenes appeared real, Rita felt they were holographic.

During this enactment, the reptilian noted their emotional reactions from a distance, writing on the clipboard.

Separately, Rita was taken into another room where she encountered a second reptilian being with dark, rough skin and yellow eyes with vertical pupils. He forced her to look through an interior window into a room where a third reptilian male forced a vulgar-looking woman onto a medical table and sliced open her abdomen with its talon on his finger. Immediately, she became unconscious.

Rita felt that the scene was created to get her emotional reaction to them of shock and disgust. At one point, Rita was in contact with a familiar being with huge, solid black eyes, who wanted to communicate about creation to her. Then several other beings brought to her that she felt was a hybrid infant that was hers. It appeared more human but had thin, pale skin and dark almond-shaped eyes. The baby's nose and mouth were small, and she had tiny tips. Her head was larger than a normal head and was hairless.

Rita didn't feel it was her infant but felt a strange love connection for it. She was surprised that the hybrid infant responded to her as the other beings observed her reactions. The beings then told Rita that they needed to remove tissue from one of the veins in her arm to inject into the baby to improve its health. Oddly, her husband revealed to her that he, too, had an identical scar on his forearm, but was never regressed by hypnosis to find out why.

Ken's Ant People Encounter
Ken's experience did not involve the reptilians, but the ant people (legends exist of the Ant beings by the Hopi Indians) and the small grays. During an encounter with them, he recalled standing on a shoreline and looking across a body of water at a city in ruins and building collapsed. He stood along a ridge of land where a twelve-foot-high gash had been cut away by some catastrophic event. The being told Ken that various kinds of catastrophes would be happening on Earth and that he, and others of his kind, would be removed from the planet — humans with whom they had been working with. He would be one of those special people.

The destruction of our planet and the extinction of humanity is a common message given by aliens or reptilians to their captives. Many experiencers/abductees, depending on how the experience is viewed, are often greeted by Nordic, human-looking beings, or angelic beings like Dawn Hess was shown, perhaps to ease their fears. Could these be extraterrestrials or holographic images shown to humans throughout the ages to control us through religious imagery, like the story of the three children who witnessed an angel and the Blessed Virgin Mary in Fatima, Portugal in 1917 for six consecutive months and always on the 13th day and at solar noon?

Nancy's Abductions

Nancy had a strong interest in space and ETs, but she also feared that she had been abducted her entire life. Under hypnosis, Nancy revealed that she was abducted by the large-eyed grays and was given an exam to treat her womb with something that would prepare the cells of the lining, in preparation for the future when they would implant her with another child. The procedure would provide some type of protection for her and the baby.

Nancy also stated that the beings tried to convince her that they were her guardian angels, and although they seemed to behave in a caring manner, she distrusted what they were saying.

The extraterrestrials explained that there are six dimensions of reality and that they had come into the third dimension from another plane, intending to impart information through the humans with whom they worked (military?). Like thousands of other abductees, Nancy was told she was one of their chosen people and they would be guiding her on a special mission on Earth. She felt they were always watching her.

CHAPTER SIXTEEN

REPTILIANS WORKING WITH MILITARY

UFO investigator Preston Dennett included this story in his book *Onboard UFO Encounters* about the bewildering alien encounters of Ramon (pseudonym). Although most of the stories in his book give alias names, this story involved my friend MUFON investigator Ann Druffel and was listed in the MUFON archives.

Ramon began to have UFO encounters at the age of six while living in a government housing project called Basilone Homes, located at the base of Hansen Dam in San Fernando in Southern California. It wasn't far from the infamous Tujunga Canyon alien cases that Ann Druffel and D. Scott Rogo investigated beginning in the 1950s. Although MUFON investigator Idabel Epperson was involved at first with Ramon's case as an adult, Ann Druffel later took over probably due to her extensive investigation into the Tujunga Canyon abductions and her own UFO sightings off the coast of Southern California.

Growing up Ramon was abducted countless times. Then in 1964 he joined the Marines and was sent to Camp Pendleton near San Diego. Although he never completed high school, he was put through IBM training and told that he was assigned to "Headquarters and Service."

Not long after he arrived, Ramon was at his desk when he overheard two officers talking outside his door. They were discussing a UFO in the military's possession, being held in a hangar and guarded by officers with M60 machine guns. They also mentioned strange blue lights.

The men were not disturbed that Ramon overheard the conversation and he found that odd because it seemed to be a private and possibly top-secret conversation.

A few days later, Ramon and a small group of other young privates were called into a meeting with a Marine Corps sergeant. The sergeant began telling them that they were going to participate in something that would be for the betterment of the country. The next thing Ramon knew he and eleven other marines were boarding a Navy bus. He had no idea where they were going because the windows were painted black with black curtains over them.

The Navy bus went through checkpoint after checkpoint to get to their destination. It appeared they were in a top-secret military area that was well guarded. What puzzled Ramon most was the green fatigues everyone was wearing. One minute he was awake and the next minute he and the other men were wearing yellow jumpsuits. Again, he fell asleep. He later learned that yellow jumpsuits are used when entering a radiation area.

Ramon was concerned about how his clothes kept changing without his recall. They finally reached their destination — an isolated hangar in the desert at an undisclosed location (Area 51?). Along one wall was a row of six or seven condensing units, each about the size of a refrigerator and fully active, making a high-pitched humming noise.

Ramon and the other privates stood at attention when the sergeant entered the room and gave them the same talk about their mission and how important it was for the country. Two doctors in white coats also accompanied the sergeant. Each man was put in a chair where their blood was drawn, and they were hypnotized with a spinning black and white striped wheel. Then Ramon was injected with something that sedated him and he assumes the other men were too. It appeared Ramon and the eleven privates were going to be guinea pigs for some military experiment.

One of the doctors assured them that they would remain in the room at all times. Finally, the hangar door opened and revealed a UFO of dull gray, not the one he recalled as a child that was glossy gray. Suddenly, several reptilian-looking humanoids marched into the hangar and walked up to the sergeant as if they had been working together for a long time.

One of the reptilians walked up to Ramon and the other men and just stared. Ramon described the being as seven feet tall, muscular, and wearing a blackish-green uniform. He remembered the face was scaly somewhat, like that of a snake and he wore a featureless uniform except for a large badge depicting a dragon-like creature. The group of marines (more than Ramon recalled at first) were frightened and broke rank. The next thing Ramon recalled was waking up in his barracks at 3:00 a.m.

Upon awakening, Ramon felt confused and disoriented, and he couldn't move. Another marine assisted him back to his bunk and he fell into a deep sleep. Ramon began to realize that since the age of six, he had been in some weird experiment involving UFOs, extraterrestrials (perhaps terrestrial beings) military, and mind control.

Through the years the abductions continued, and his family, friends, and co-workers began to see UFOs, and sometimes aliens.

By the 1990s, Ramon began to be harassed by unmarked black helicopters circling above his home. Abductees Betty Andreasson Luca and her husband Bob Luca described the unmarked black helicopters that have visited through the years and continue to this day, the menacing phone calls bugged phone calls, and men breaking into their home which detailed their experiences in a self-published book, *A Lifting of the Veil*. These unmarked helicopters have been seen after a cattle mutilation.

Ramon began to have flashbacks of his time when he served in the Vietnam war. A strange-looking man with elongated eyes was always at the mess hall at 3:00 am. Ramon thought he looked human but wasn't. The man appeared many times and then one night he brought another man with him who also had a peculiar appearance and elongated eyes. He looked at the back of his neck and was shocked. The human man or alien had translucent skin and under the skin was a Jello-type substance, pinkish-white and pulsating. He could see inside its body!

Many segments of his military time were blurred, but he believes he was taken to meet the reptilian beings. He recalled being taken to big trailers with military personnel where they wore badges with the insignia of eagles. During one of Ramon's interactions with the aliens, he recalled how they tried to force him to have sexual relations with an attractive-looking human woman. He refused. Whether this woman was a real human or alien hybrid was unclear to him.

He recalled during one abduction where he saw human babies alive in tubes.

Ramon also discovered he could affect light bulbs by exploding them. Some imploded. He discovered that he could make the volume on a television and radio increase, and he went through a time when he'd receive a garbled metallic-type voice in his head.

The years of UFO abductions and experiments have taken a toll on Ramon. He had his first wife divorce him because of the UFO and alien activity, his dog was killed by what he believes was a UFO that came to visit his home while he and his wife were gone. At night, his young son at the time would wake up screaming in terror.

As of 2020, Ramon continues to be haunted by these creatures. He believes that the grays are fallen angels, and there will be a battle between Good and Evil soon that will determine the fate of Earth and all humanity. He still wonders what role the U.S. military plays in all of this — are they the good guys or complicit with the reptilians in human DNA and God knows what other experiments? He did discover that the grays disliked him using the word God around them. The mention of God seemed to agitate one of the grays. It kept saying, "Your God? Your God? Where is your God?"

All the while they experimented on him or took him in the middle of the night, they'd always say, "We won't hurt you." Ramon is convinced that millions of us are part of one big giant experiment.

Ramon (alias name) contacted the National UFO Reporting Center in Davenport, Washington on December 23, 2011, and gave this report in 2011. Occurred: 12/23/2011 21:00 Reported: 12/25/2011 9:25:34 PM 21:25 Location: Palmdale, CA Shape: Other Duration: 2 minutes
While on the North/14 Antelope Freeway, my passenger noticed an octagon-shaped, while my wife was driving the winding mountain range. This craft seemed to pace the flow

of traffic as we traveled northbound just before Acton, CA a small township community that rests in a small bowl-like valley. At arm's length, this craft seemed to be approx. the size of a standard house large ceiling air vent, at 500 feet high over the freeway. The craft gave off a brilliant array of white/ red/ (blue/green) colors. I noticed a large spotlight-type light in front and to the rear of the craft, which may or may not be the direction of travel of this craft, as when I first noticed the UFO it traveled in the north by north/west direction, within a split second it shot northbound out of sight approx. 1/4 mile only to return over our car in less than a second. I opened my sunroof in our ML-350 Mercedes Benz and lost sight of the craft for a second or two but noticed the craft seemed to ! be pacing our car, I should make mention this SUV/ML-350 has radar function which may have helped the craft pace our car at the beginning of the sighting and just before speeding forward the 1/4 mile, again hard to tell because of the octagon shape.

Moreover, the spotlight in the front and end of the craft always remained on, the circumference of the craft displayed red lights over box-like windows which were white, and blue lights circled the craft. This craft then traveled in a north/west direction and gave the appearance of rest on top of a medium-size hill 1 & 1/2 miles away. In conclusion, I have a history of childhood UFO abduction, inside the craft which was investigated by the late Dr. J. Allen Hynek, in 1973, in turn, my case was transferred to (MUFON) Beverly Hills, CA MUFON Chapter, investigators the Late Idabel Epperson and her investigator daughter Marylin Epperson. Finally, it should be noted in 1964/67 while serving my country as a United States Marine, Camp Pendleton, San Diego, CA I was subjected to a (MILABS) experience, along with other Marines, as we were taken via military bus with blackened windows & black curtains over the black painted

windows. We went to a desert location where a UFO craft
was housed.

It's unsettling that our military is in bed with malevolent
aliens, and they seem to allow genetic testing and horrible
experimentation on humans. What purpose could the
military have besides gaining highly sophisticated
technology, perhaps thousands of years ahead of our human
technology, in exchange for allowing experimentation on
millions of humans?

A time is coming when the dark reptilians will be forced
from our planet.

Betsey Lewis

CHAPTER SEVENTEEN

STARGATE PORTALS

Most of you probably can't comprehend dimensional portals on Earth and throughout our universe, yet they exist, and people have seen them. They've been here for eons, and legends of them have been passed down by indigenous peoples.

Chaco Canyon is located 72 miles south of Farmington, New Mexico, and is the location of monumental structures built by a mysterious people called the Anasazi (or Puebloan people). They built their structures in a hostile environment 1,100 to 1,200 years ago. They left behind rock drawings and petroglyphs of monsters, spirals, dragons, and giants with six toes. The Anasazi were well-versed in mathematics and astronomy.

Chaco Canyon, New Mexico

The Navajo people have legends of the Anasazi people who fought off red-headed giants as tall as 40 feet high who were cannibals. Their stories include a reptilian race called "The Deceivers," and a great flood. The Native Americans in New Mexico believe the spiral petroglyphs tell the story of portals or stargates in the area where bizarre beings travel to and fro from their place of origin in the cosmos.

Dr. David Morehouse, Ed Dames, and Mel Reily decided to investigate Chaco Canyon in the early 1980s and find out if there was any truth to a portal above the Mesa. What they discovered there was beyond their wildest imagination.

Dr. David Morehouse served in staff and command positions ranging from Airborne rifle company commander to commander of an elite Airborne Ranger Company. He was Aide de Camp to two generals, the Battalion Executive Officer of the 680-man 2nd Battalion, 505th Parachute Infantry Regiment, as well as the Chief of Training for the 13,500-soldier 82nd Airborne Division. From 1987 to 1991, David Morehouse was assigned to several highly classified special access programs in the US Army's Intelligence Security Command and the Defense Intelligence Agency's Directorate of Science and Technology as a top-secret Psychic Spy or

Remote Viewer. He holds a Master of Military Art and Science Degree, a master's degree in administration, and a Doctorate in Education. He resigned his commission in 1995 after his decision to write *Psychic Warrior* resulted in the filing of unfounded charges against him, which ultimately were dismissed as baseless by an Army discharge review board.

From 1987 to 1991, Morehouse was assigned to several highly classified special access programs in the US Army's Intelligence Security Command and the Defense Intelligence Agency's Directorate of Science and Technology as a top-secret Psychic Spy or Remote Viewer.

Retired Major Ed Dames was a decorated military intelligence officer, an original member of the U.S. Army prototype remote viewing training program, and a former training and operations officer for the Defense Intelligence Agency's psychic intelligence collection unit.

In the 1980s, Dr. David Morehouse, Ed Dames, and Mel Reily decided to investigate and substantiate the existence of a portal in the southwestern United States near the Abiquiú area, located 53 miles north of Santa Fe. New Mexico. Ed targeted an area in New Mexico where subterranean extraterrestrials supposedly exist.

Eventually, the three men were guided to another area by two Native Americans who told them there was another place to go. They said it was a special place and to expect things to happen at night. At twilight, the men noticed a bright light moving vertically above the horizon and vanished as if it went into the ground. They saw bursts of light and brief objects going from one dimension to another dimension.

Later they went to another area where they were permitted by a Park Ranger to stay in a certain area. Laying on their backs, the three men witnessed the sky become what could only be described as circular translucent water or cellophane as it distorted the night's starlight. They theorized it was a dimensional stargate where space folds in on itself. It was not an atmospheric phenomenon, Dr. Morehouse said. It remained for several minutes, and then collapsed and vanished. It opened three more times in two and half hours, remaining stationary in the sky for fifteen minutes and then closing. Morehouse theorized it remains open for a certain time and then closes if nothing is coming or going through it.

They were unable to capture the phenomena at the time, forgetting cameras. Also, cell phones were invented in 1983, but could not take pictures or videos like the ones used today.

Who were the giants that feasted on Native Americans? Legends of the giants exist throughout the world. Dr. Morehouse in an interview said that archaeologists had discovered bones in Chaco Canyon clearly showing humans were cut up as if feasted.

According to reports of Northern Paiute oral history, the Si-Te-Cah, Saiduka, or Sai'i were a legendary tribe of Northern Paiutes who fought a war with red-headed giants and eventually wiped them out or drove away from the area, with the final battle having taken place at what is now known as Lovelock Cave near Lovelock, Nevada, where they burned them alive.

When you understand how portals exist on Earth and that a plethora of aliens and dimensional beings dominate these portals, you will understand what is currently happening worldwide as humans move closer to World War III. Evil beings have orchestrated the current events. The Mideast has been a major portal where entities control humans and ignite wars, and they feed on human fear, hate, and anger.

Proof Portals Exist at Skinwalker Ranch
During Season 4 of *The Secret of Skinwalker Ranch*, Dr. Travis Taylor and his team believed they found evidence of a portal in what they call the Triangle area on the Ranch located in northeastern Utah. In Season 4, Episode 13, the Skinwalker Team witnessed a large rocket vanish into the Triangle Area of the Ranch at 1:52 am at 10,000 feet, traveling at 800 mph. It

broke the sound barrier. Something invisible exists about the triangle, and the team wants to know what it is.

Dr. Travis Taylor, a scientist and engineer, theorizes a transversable wormhole exists above the Triangle where the rocket vanished, and where orbs vanish into the Mesa. The explanation for a transversable wormhole is that if a particle can enter through one side of the wormhole and it can exit through the other, then the wormhole is traversable. Thermal images after the rocket vanished an orb materialized and then the orb split into and then turned into five spheres. UAPs have been seen sliding in and out of the rock Mesa as if it were Jello. Indigenous tribes in the Utah region, Navajo and Utes, have legends of portals and stargates where orbs appear and vanish in an instant.

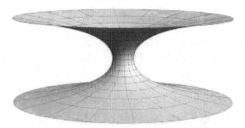

Transversable Wormhole

Thousands of people have witnessed ETs walk through solid objects and into mountains and Mesas. They can manipulate time and space.

Skinwalker Ranch's owner Branden Fugal and the Skinwalker team say that The Secret of Skinwalker Ranch, Season 5 will "break our reality and change world history."

Better stay tuned!

UAP/orb captured over the Skinwalker Ranch Mesa on a 24/7 live stream camcorder.

During another chips and salsa informal chat on October 5, 2023, Brandon and his team met to answer questions for Skinwalker Ranch members. Brandon said Robert Bigelow, the previous owner of Skinwalker Ranch, would never step foot on the Ranch again after seeing the paranormal things there and the hitchhiker effect where poltergeist activity happened in his home.

Dr. Travis Taylor was asked about how UAPs can go through solid objects such as mountains and water without making a wake or breaking the sound barrier traveling at impossible speeds. Taylor called it a pocket reality and mentioned supercavitation.

Supercavitation is the use of a cavitation bubble to reduce skin friction drag on a submerged object and enable high speeds or UFOs have an electromagnetic field around them. What if they can shapeshift from a material object into a non-material object with advanced technology? Not only can UFOs go through solid objects, but so can extraterrestrial beings that can walk through walls.

Most often UFOs have a blue aura around them which indicates high voltage. If UFOs were entirely in this dimension, the laws of centrifugal force would be entirely valid for them. Since it is obvious that the effects of centrifugal force have no bearings on their space, and they are moving in time and space.

As Brandon Fugal said, "humanity is not alone in the Universe." It's ridiculous to think we are the only ones on this little planet in the entire Universe.

Writing-on-the Stone Park Stargate Portal

Nestled near the border of Montana and Canada is the *Writing-on-the-Stone Park,* located in the province of Alberta, Canada. The park contains the greatest concentration of rock art on the North American Great Plains. There are over fifty petroglyph sites and thousands of other works that date to 9,000 BCE.

In Dr. Ardy Sixkiller Clarke's last published book, *More Encounters with Star People,* published by Amazon in 2016, she wrote about how she drove alone to Stone Park in Alberta from Montana. There she met an Indigenous man who was camping there. The man named Tom asked Dr. Clarke to stay and talk for a while over a pot of campfire coffee. Tom explained that the Park has a spiritual significance, and the whole area is sacred. He said he had studied with holy men. Dr. Clarke had heard that a portal exists there and if you walk through it, you travel to another place and time.

Tom said, "There is such a portal and it's not always open. You have to be in the right place at the right time. The Star Travelers stop and visit with me." He said they looked human. He used to come to the place with his grandfather, a healer and spiritual man. "There are other places like this in the world. There is a place in Peru, one in Mexico. one in Bolivia, and one in Alaska. The others, mostly stay hidden. Only those who have traveled the universal highway know of their existence. There is a place in Iraq. My united was deployed there, and I came upon it by accident. A star traveler saved my life there."

Tom and his unit were dispatched to a town in the Iraq desert. When they arrived, there was an ambush. He hunkered down in an abandoned building when he was suddenly peppered with gunfire from above. Suddenly sand began to swirl from the abandoned building's floor and a tunnel appeared. He entered the passageway and was greeted by a human-like being. The aliens offered to take him away from the war, but Tom refused, saying that his absence would be considered desertion.

Tom continued to tell Dr. Clarke more, "There are places all over the world that are sacred. These places were often the portals to the universal highways, but as centuries passed and populations moved or were destroyed, people forgot about them. They are like a network of invisible sky roads that lead across the Milky Way to other worlds. The Maya knew about these portals, and so did the Inca. Many American Indian tribes knew too. That is how the UFOs come here. That is how they leave. Without the highway, they would be unable to travel such distances in such little time. There are portals throughout the world. There is one in Navajo Country and it's near Chinle, Arizona. There is one in Arkansas, and another one in West Virginia. There are three in Nevada near the area known as Area 51, as well as one in Dulce, New Mexico, and there is one near Livingston, Montana." (Mt. Shasta, Skinwalker Ranch in NE Utah, and Southern Colorado should be included).

Tom cautioned Dr. Clarke that when the portal opens, there is no way to know when they will open, and there is no guarantee that you will ever return. There are times when the portals close and you cannot return to the place of your entry." Tom said there are benevolent aliens who blend in with humanity. They are calm in the face of adversity, and always kind and look for the good in all situations. "There are many species in this great universe, Dr. Clarke. They, too, travel the universal highway. There is no control over that. Some of the species (malevolent) who visit Earth have other agendas."

Universal Portals

Stargate, wormholes or portals, whatever you want to call them, exist worldwide and on other planets throughout our Universe. Besides UFOs diving into the ocean, there are stories and legends of deep underground alien bases throughout the world where humans are taken for genetic experiments. Theories suggest some of the areas known for UFO activity and mysterious disappearances of people, ships, and aircraft are known to be portals or stargates to other dimensions. Stories include well-known alien abductees who were taken to undersea cities or bases.

Portals or gateways could be hidden entrances to other dimensions or worlds. Several places around the world are known to be energetic hotspots from ancient megalith stone structures to Ley Lines that are alleged to produce hyper-dimensional gateways. Some of these renowned places exist at Mt. Shasta in Northern California, Alaska, Sedona, Arizona, the Skinwalker Ranch in southeastern Utah, the San Luis Valley in southern Colorado, the Bermuda Triangle off the coast of Florida, and a prime portal in the Middle East, where they have a major base underground.

If you think back over the history of Earth, you will recognize how many dramas of religion and civilization have been introduced in the Mideastern portal. It is a huge portal — with a radius of a thousand miles or so. Other stargates or portals exist in Mexico/Central America, Mount Fuji, Easter Island, Lake Titicaca, Sinai, Tibet, Uluru in Australia, Peru, and the Nazca Lines. Ancient crystal skulls found near these portal areas are believed to hold the resonance of the Earth's grid.

For example, the Tibetan monks accessed the portals near their monasteries and temples in the Himalayas, learning of the evil plan to invade their country by the Chinese, and so they quickly hid many of their most sacred documents, treasures, and artifacts years before the invasion. China continues to seek this knowledge from the monks through torture.

While we don't exactly know how to open a portal to another dimension, there is evidence the phenomenon could exist. And now it seems science may be catching on to the possibility. Typically, portal areas have some type of electromagnetic significance and are located near large deposits of quartz or other minerals with piezoelectric properties. So, it came as less of a surprise when NASA announced in 2012 that the University of Iowa's physicist Jack Scudder found hard evidence of portals created by the interaction between the Earth and the Sun's magnetospheres.

These portals are extremely volatile and unpredictable, opening and closing in a matter of an instant. But Scudder found markers, called x-points or electron diffusion regions, which allowed NASA probes to locate and study them.

These energetic locales are considered sacrosanct because they represent areas where our inner temple — the mind can access higher states of consciousness, connecting with extradimensional entities or invoking out-of-body experiences. Whether these areas always represented dimensional portals for the mind, or a portal for the physical body is up for debate.

Graham Hancock wrote about native shamans traversing planes of consciousness using a psychedelic substance such as ayahuasca. Within this ecstatic state, shamans report meeting teachers and guides, who provide advice and wisdom for living within the everyday realm of our existence. But Hancock also says he believes it is worth considering that there may be something otherworldly to these portal areas; something beyond materialist comprehension.

One location that seems to fit this description is Puerta de Hayu Marca in Peru. Situated on a plateau just off the western banks of Lake Titicaca, Puerta de Hayu Marca translates to the

Gate of the Gods. Reaching 23 feet in both height and width, Hayu Marca appears to be a doorway to nowhere carved into a rock face in a remote area known as the Valley of the Spirits or Stone Forest.

Hayu Marca rests on what is believed to be on a Ley Line, and the famous Gate of the Sun at Tiwanaku also lies in nearby Bolivia, along with several other important Incan archaeological points. This huge mysterious door-like structure in the Hayu Marca Mountain region of Southern Peru near Lake Titicaca lies 35 kilometers from the city of Puno and is found in an area that has long been honored by local indigenous people as the "City of the Gods." Although no actual city has ever been discovered, the area is known as a Spirit Forest, or Stone Forest, made of strange rock formations that resemble buildings, people, and other artificial structures (Simulacrum).

Ley Lines are Mother Earth's energy points that connect worldwide. The Ley Lines are electrical currents that are like veins in the planet, and it is believed ancient humans accessed these energy points that coil around the planet. Ley Lines are known to crisscross around the globe, like latitudinal and longitudinal lines, which are dotted with monuments and natural landforms, and carry rivers of supernatural energy. Along these lines, at the places they intersect, there are pockets of concentrated energy, that can be harnessed by certain individuals.

The Indigenous Indians of the region have a legend that spoke of "a gateway to the lands of the Gods", and it said that long, long ago great heroes had gone to join their gods and passed through the gate for a glorious new life of immortality, and on rare occasions, those men returned for a short time with their gods to "inspect all the lands in the kingdom" through the gate.

Another legend tells of the time when the Spanish Conquistadors arrived in Peru and looted gold and precious stones from the Inca tribes. According to one of the legends, an Incan priest of the Temple of the Seven Rays named *Amaru Meru* (Aramu Muru) fled from his temple with a sacred golden disk known as "the key of the gods of the seven rays", and hid in the mountains of Hayu Marca. He eventually came upon the doorway which was being watched by shaman priests. He showed them the key to the gods and a ritual was performed with the conclusion of a magical occurrence initiated by the golden disk which opened the portal, and according to the legend, blue light did emanate from a tunnel inside.

The priest Amaru Meru handed the golden disk to the shaman and then passed through the portal "never to be seen again." Archeologists have observed a small hand-sized circular depression on the right-hand side of the small entranceway and have theorized that this is where a small disk could be placed and held by the rock.

Visitors to Peru's Hayu Marca have reported unusual energy fields there with some claiming they can feel pulsating energy from the rock when placing their hand in its center. Many who have reviewed the ancient site online also mention this feeling of elevated or intense energy there.

Lake Titicaca nearby was revered by the Incas and considered to be the birthplace of their civilization. It is also among the deepest lakes in the world, rumored to contain a lost city and a plethora of treasures looted by the Spanish. In 2000, the lost temple of Atahualpa was discovered deep below the lake, adding to the mysterious nature of this ancient culture. It has been noted that the structure superficially resembles the Gate of the Sun at Tiwanaku (Tiahuanaco). It is also said to be aligned by five other archaeological sites which together form an imaginary cross with straight lines crossing each other exactly at the point where the plateau and Lake Titicaca are located.

According to Barbara Marciniak, a new age writer, planets also have doors through which you can enter portals composed of corridors of time. The Tibetans, until the 1950s, maintained an energy doorway. Over hundreds of years, they have acted as guardians and emissaries for those who ventured through. According to the same source, Tibetans have been working with extraterrestrials for eons.

The Maya and Aztecs hid their gold caches. They understood that Gold is part of what allows dimensional doorways to be opened. They anchor portals and bring about transmutations. The gold caches around the globe contain great secrets that are utilized to open stargates and anchor energy. There are huge veins and rivers of gold conducting frequencies throughout Earth that are an essential part of life. Gold is often found accompanied by quartz crystals, which are modern-day founding stones in all our communication devices.

Harvard psychiatrist John E. Mack (1929-2004) had a conversation with the Dalai Lama about aliens in 1994. Mack wasn't naïve about extra-terrestrials. Having already spent decades conducting research with hundreds of extraterrestrial experiencers and abductees in North America, he had built a career on trying to make sense of the alien abduction experience.

The Dalai Lama knows a thing or two about aliens as well. He explained to Mack and a small group that aliens were sentient beings in the universe. He also corroborated Mack's theory that these entities were making contact because they were disturbed by humans' destruction of the environment.

A few years later in 1999, Dr. Mack met with the Dalai Lama again in Dharamsala, India, as part of a symposium on world peace. During this visit, Mack recorded an interview about his interview with the Dalai Lama and aliens. According to Mack, for high-level Tibetan lamas like the Dalai Lama who "live at the level of "mystical formlessness," dramatic alien contact and abduction were unlikely.

Realized beings like the Dalai Lama were already used to being contacted by "a vast array of entities and beings that are very real for them in the cosmos" and so they took for granted a contra-materialist, contra-Western worldview where "things can cross from the unseen world into the material world." It simply didn't make sense for them to have the kind of shattering, consciousness-expanding abduction experiences that were typical of Mack's more run-of-the-mill North American research subjects.

The Dalai Lama's level of consciousness was so advanced, so other or 'alien' to mainstream thinking, that it made encountering an avant-garde alien consciousness redundant. Simply put, the Dalai Lama was already on the aliens' wavelength.

The biggest question is who are these beings that watch us, fly their drones or craft at hypersonic speeds, abduct humans and animals, and buzz our military and our missile sites? Perhaps we should look to Earth and not the sky for the answer to their origin. Ancient people throughout the world have shown us petroglyphs dating thousands of years old that depict alien creatures, and there are ancient Vedic texts that describe flying machines. What if a species evolved millions of years ago on Earth and went underground because of a cataclysmic event 65 million years ago? They created undersea and underground bases worldwide and their technology evolved over 200 million years.

This might be one explanation for the millions of people who have vanished without a trace, stories of whole villages that vanish, and planes that never return.

CHAPTER EIGHTEEN

BETH'S ENCOUNTERS

Beth originally contacted me through email about her sister's orb encounter in Sedona, Arizona. She wrote, "As far as the blue orb, she photographed it on February 2, 2024, at 8:28 a.m. She let me know that she stood in the same spot, and she did not move. However, through deductive reasoning, she figured out that the orb was moving. She clicked her camera three times without waiting and these are the images that she photographed. I asked if she lost any time, and Beth said not.

I sensed that both Beth and her sister had strange childhood experiences, which she confirmed in an email.

orb photo #1

orb photo #2

orb photo #3

My sister and I had an experience in our shared bedroom when we were five and six years old, and again when we were eight and nine years old. When we were younger, we both saw a man with a black suit and hat. We were frightened and covered our heads and never mentioned it to our parents. We believe that our dad was trying to scare us.

Later we encountered a silver orb in our room that was spinning at an enormous speed. It was silvery and it hovered in our room for at least one minute. We screamed the entire time and when it disappeared, we ran downstairs to tell our parents. They never heard our screams and thought we were dreaming. That was at ages eight and nine.

"My sister saw Paramahamsa Yogananda walking in the nearby park. She also had several visions of orbs in her lake home in Wisconsin. The paranormal encounters continued when she moved to Arizona during her walks. I have had visions as well of a black-caped figure next to my bed where red and green lights revolved around its head. My life changed dramatically for the better after this event, and I have seen strange phenomena in the sky. My late mother continues to be at my side and proves it by turning our lights on and off in our Sun City, Arizona home. She also did this in the *house in Anthem, Arizona.*

It's possible that we had missing time during the Silver Orb incident, however, I cannot swear that happened. Please feel free to include our stories in your book. I think that more readers will be able to relate to their own similar events. It may add comfort for them to know that these things happen to many others in this strange and wonderful world of ours.

I asked Beth if she had any miscarriages which many female abductees have discovered but no fetus. She wrote to me again, and said this:

Hi again. I had miscarriages between pregnancies with her two sons. Now that I am thinking about the encounters, my son, Tom had an encounter at age 17 when a gray alien appeared at the foot of his bed. When Tom moved out and my fiance's son, Eric, moved into the same bedroom. Eric also claimed he was visited by gray aliens. These encounters impacted Eric emotionally to the point where we had to obtain a therapist for him.

It wasn't long before I received another email from Beth about a UFO sighting on April 8, 2024, at 4:15 in the afternoon, the day of the solar eclipse. She was at Paloma Park, in Peoria, Arizona, and took a photo of the clouds with her cell phone. She was shocked when she looked closely and saw a large blue orb on the right side of the photo with an energy field that surrounded it in a semicircle. Below, just above the ground was a small black object hovering in the sky.

Original photograph of black UFO in the lower portion of the photo.

Enlarged photo of black UFO.

Beth and her sister have been abductees since childhood, and they are still having visitations. In the future, I hope that Beth will consider regressive hypnosis to uncover more about what she and her sister experienced with the aliens and their reason for abducting them.

Arizona has been a hotspot for UFO sightings for decades and even longer according to Native American legends. Phoenix became a major news event on March 13, 1997, as thousands of people stood outside to view Comet Hale-Bopp. Lights of varying descriptions and shapes were seen from the Nevada line, into Phoenix and to the edge of Tucson, Arizona between 7:30 pm and 10:30 pm MST. actor Kurt Russell, an amateur pilot, reported the strange UFO lights to air traffic control.

Lynne Kitei, M.D. also witnessed the lights that night. On the evening of March 13, Lynne looked out her bedroom window over Phoenix and saw something that would change her life. Strange lights appeared in the sky over the nighttime city. Amber orbs in formation. It was a massive triangular array of lights moving silently but in unison as though they were connected. Was it an optical illusion? Unlikely. Military aircraft? That's what the U.S. government wanted her to think. UFOs? That's what her evidence and subsequent years of careful research, interviews, and documentation, including photographic proof, strongly suggest. The result became her book, *The Phoenix Lights*, a well-researched account, both personal and scientific, of the story behind the lights, of the theories and cover-ups, the facts and denials that surrounded this event. Over the years, Lynne became an advocate for public disclosure by the government about the subject of unexplained phenomena.

Two years ago, she joined my talk show again and said that she experienced a healing from the Phoenix Lights event, and others claimed to have had healings.

According to Lynne, Native American tribes in Arizona find it amusing that people were so excited about a UFO sighting over Phoenix when they have known about the Star People for centuries, but they are usually silent about their experiences and encounters. Dr. Ardy Sixkiller Clarke said to me that she was able to get the stories from different tribal members because she has Native American heritage, and tribal people trusted her.

On a darker note, there are stories of people who have vanished in Death Valley and the Phoenix area. People have observed UFOs hovering over a park in Death Valley and people who travel alone to that place vanish without a trace.

The following story was taken from Dr. Clarke's book *More encounters with Star People: Urban American Indians Tell their Stories* © 2016.

In 1933, Death Valley National Monument was declared a U.S. National Monument, placing the area under federal protection. Fifteen years later, two prospectors reported seeing a UFO crash in Death Valley. Reportedly, the disk hit a sand dune, and two small creatures hopped out and ran off into the desert. However, there are other stories from Death Valley, untold stories that never make the headlines. David

Paulides author of the 411 Books has researched areas where there is a high number of people who simply vanish in National Parks. Death Valley is one of those places.

Death Valley is a desert valley located in Eastern California in the Northern Mojave Desert. It is one of the hottest places on Earth during the summer.

Dr. Ardy Sixkiller Clarke ventured to a campground in Death Valley, alone. She met an American Indian at the campground called Jim Gray Dog (not his real name) who has seen some scary stuff. Many people ventured to Death Valley to watch UFO activity or just hike into the wilderness, and vanish, never to be seen again. Jim said, "There are other parks, but this is the best place. Few lights make for a perfect view of the sky. At night I watch for those little grey bastards. They're mean, you know. They take people. I seen'em do it, too. They don't think anyone is watching, but I watch. I keep a tally too. It happens one or two times a month. Only five times they did not return. They're always alone. Some are backpackers who travel with all their belongings on their back. Others are young women traveling alone. No one ever comes looking for them, but there has been someone out there missing a son or a daughter. At least I remember. I keep a record."

Jim warned Dr. Ardy Clarke. "Never wander in the desert at night, not even this close to the campground. When they take you, you'll not have any chance to run away. They have such power they will make you think they're your friends,"

Jim was abducted by the grays as a teen and strapped onto a cold mental slab with three of the bug-eyed monsters examining him. He discovered they can shapeshift too. They can look like humans or anything they want to imitate. "I saw a young woman, real small-like and frail walk to the very spot where you sat last night. She wore a red print dress that dragged the ground. She raised her arms toward the sky, and they took her. It was through she was expecting them to come for her," he said.

Jim told Dr. Clarke that people vanish in and around Phoenix, Arizona too. He knew of fourteen people who were taken. He said mostly men are abducted.

Betsey Lewis

CONCLUSION

Our universe is filled with wonders beyond our imagination. It's expanding and will never end. How many universes are there and how many dimensional worlds exist? That means other intelligent beings look like something out of the Star Wars Cantina scene. The creatures we take for granted here like insects and ants are highly intelligent beings in another world.

There are three types of aliens visiting Earth — benevolent, malevolent and benign and over 300 species. Each of them has a different agenda for Earth and humanity. There are ancient legends of serpent beings. There are stories of the Anunnaki, Billy Meier's Plejaren, Pleiadians, the short and tall grays, two or more species of Reptilians, the Ant people, the insect people, the Blue Men, the human-looking Nordics, the Red-headed humanoids, and Betty Andreason's Elders, and that's not all.

The Grays and the Reptilians appears to be the most powerful and the most evil when it comes to abducting humans for genetic purposes and mutilating Earth's creatures. They have no emotions or compassion.

There are 300 stories gathered by Preston Dennett in his book, *The Healing Power of UFOs*, about aliens healing humans for many types of ailments. Are the aliens doing this for their compassion or experimental reasons? Preston wondered if the people who are healed have something to do with our individual soul's destiny on Earth or perhaps it's simply a matter of luck.

Betty Andreasson Luca believed the aliens were angels even though they looked like gray aliens. Also, Betty encountered the Elders, human-looking giants who appeared alike, wearing long robes, and the little grays worked with them. On several occasions, she watched the Elder conducting rituals that produced rings of energy. Betty and her husband Bob Luca were told about the future and humanity, the need for us to have both evil and good in the world for our spiritual development. Bob Luca under hypnosis was told, "There will be the haves and have-nots. There will be conflict. However, there will come a time when evil will be wiped away. That time is not close at hand."

When asked when that time comes, will our growth cease?"

Bob replied, "When that time comes, our growth will not cease. Rather, we will advance into further planes of existence. Right now, the type of society that you speak of is not possible because the people of this plane as a whole are not very advanced spiritually. Technology is advancing. Spirituality, unfortunately, is not keeping pace. Man is developing many things which are harmful to him, which he does not understand."

Countless abductions tell of pain experimentation of humans and the removal of sperm and fetuses. Women who had fetuses removed later claimed they met their children, human-gray children with large heads, big eyes, and sparse blonde hair. Abductees are told they are creating hybrids after humans destroy themselves. Betty Luca was told "We create hybrids because as time goes by, mankind will become sterile. They will not be able to produce because of other pollutions of the lands and the water, and the air and the bacteria and the terrible things that are on the Earth. Man is destroying much of nature."

The Blue Men stories described by Native Americans are baffling. They seem to be more transitional spiritual beings who help people in need and never harm others no matter how evil they are, including reptilians. They appear benevolent, but why did they journey to Earth from a planet they describe as idyllic? Do they only assist Native Americans or have other veterans encountered the Blue Men and kept their stories secret?

The gray aliens seem to be working with a variety of higher species. The small grays appear to be workers, while the taller grays appear to be hybrids and conduct experiments on humans.

The most disturbing extraterrestrials are the lizard beings or "Lizzies" who can easily overpower humans. They conduct experiments on humans, but to what end. As we know reptiles aren't the nicest creatures on Earth, even during the reign of the monstrous dinosaurs that roamed Earth 252 to 60 million years ago. Perhaps the reptilians are related to our ancient dinosaurs, or they placed them on Earth as an experiment.

One Native American suggested that humans can resist the reptoids by stopping them from controlling us by saying a prayer over and over in our minds or perhaps a song. He felt they wanted to steal souls, but humans have ancient powers that we have forgotten how to use. We can use those ancient powers to defeat the Lizzies and their evil plans to take over Earth.

Legends or myths tell of subterranean worlds from the ancients worldwide. The U.S. Navy knows that the tic tac objects seen on radar off the coast of Southern California and the East Coast are aliens who have deep undersea bases as well as underground bases.

The Cherokee Indians tell the stories of a race of benevolent, blue-skinned people who lived in the southwestern United States and took care of their gardens. They harvested the food and took it underground to their cities. These people were small, had blue skin, and large black eyes. The sun's rays were too harsh for them, so they built their cities underground and only came out at night using the light of the moon. The Cherokee called them "Moon People."

In the coming years, those who come from the skies or

underground or underseas will not all be members of the Family of Light. They will be the mirror of those upon the planet. Our lesson will be about empowerment and authority and to stop giving over our decision-making process to governmental people or parents or teachers or sky gods. It is time for humans to become sovereign. Many of you may find that you will be very frustrated. You will see things that others will not see; you will see a mass mania occurring upon the planet, and you will not be able to live with it.

What we need to know is that the space beings on and around Earth that we believe are "bad guys" and with whom our governments have made deals. They are beings who are reflecting our beliefs and drama. They are accused of performing heinous acts—mutilations and abductions upon humans, and that is true, but think about what atrocities humans commit daily on our own species and the creatures of Earth. These beings act as a mirror to show us how we acquiesce to and what we allow our evil leaders to do all over the world. How is that any different from aliens mutilating a cow?

The present states of humanity worldwide allow leaders to do as they wish in their name because they do not rise up and shout, "It is wrong to control us." There is complacency on Earth, and it must stop.

Aliens are cunning, except for the Elders experienced by Betty Andreason Luca and the Blue Men, but perhaps they deceive us. Once they reveal themselves to humanity, there will be those who will worship them like they did in ancient times.

Those of you who have studied and used your own discernment will be shocked and appalled at the foolishness of ideological worship that the rest of the human race will express toward certain space beings, especially the Lizzies because they appear massive and powerful and have bodies that do not look like ours. They will perhaps cure certain diseases that they helped to create in the first place by teaching germ warfare to your planetary scientists. They may disguise their appearance with holographic images so real no one will be able to tell what is reality and what is holographic.

Many will become disgusted with society as they are now when they learn that world leaders are colluding with the Lizzies. So, hold on to your seats, because you have no idea what is coming. There will be those who play on both sides like they do now.

The creator gods have their own creators, and all are working toward evolution. The creator gods are jugglers of realities, but who is juggling their realities and putting them through their creation in all of these worlds in the first place?

The stories gathered by Dr. Ardy Sixkiller Clarke about the Blue Men is an enigma about their reason for saving the lives of military men in the Vietnam War. They promised veterans that they spirit away fallen dead soldiers with the promise of a new life on another planet. If one dies, doesn't the soul leave the body? Would the fallen soldiers then be soulless?

We can only theorize the Blue Men are benevolent in saving lives, while some are malevolent with a dark agenda for humanity. Many aliens view us as laboratory mice to be studied, shifted, and changed. Some view us with the kindest of intentions, and who watch us flourish and accept us for who we are. Others see us as naive children who need parenting, and they are here to support us, not punish us. They want us to learn our lessons with kindness.

Should we fear them? No.

Over 2,000 years ago, Jesus said, "Truly, I tell you, if you have faith as small as a mustard seed, you can say to this mountain, 'move from here to there,'" and it will move. Nothing will be impossible for you." Matthew 17:20-21. Jesus meant that literally!

Preston Dennett wrote in his book, *Onboard UFO Encounters,* that Ramon while serving in the military watched as reptilians worked side by side with the U.S. military. Our military allows them to conduct whatever experiments they want in exchange for their superior knowledge. That takes away our freedom and free will, and that is wrong.

We know that humans have been implanted with tracking devices. Some have been removed. But what if the implant device is used for more than tracking and has a more insidious ability to control millions of minds? Have you noticed how humans changed after 2020 — they are quarrelsome, angry, full of hate, and appear hell-bent on destroying the United States. Are the Lizzies behind the curtain controlling a great portion of humanity, steering us into self-destruction? Our precious children are being targeted and lacking in higher education. College students are being programmed into DEI (Diversity, Equity, and Inclusion), which is another word for racism. We are divided now more than ever, and no one seems to agree on anything especially when it comes to protecting our borders from cartels, drugs, and terrorists.

I listened to New York best-selling author and abductee Whitley Strieber's interview two years ago on Alex Ferrari's *Next Level Soul Podcast*. I was shocked by his story and the warnings given by the visitor about our world.

It was in 2001, that Strieber was promoting his book, *Communion*, in Toronto, Canada, when someone knocked on his hotel room door at 2 a.m. Hesitant, he answered the door to find a white-haired man, maybe in his late sixties or seventies, wearing gray pants. The intruder pushed his way into Strieber's room, went to the window, and said, "You are chained to the ground." During the conversation, the stranger presented Strieber with a "New Image of God." The conversation went on for two hours discussing the Holocaust during World War II, sudden climate change, the Afterlife, Psychic Ability, UFOs, and using the Human Soul in machines.

The man did not give his name and Whitley never saw him again. The visitation became his self-published book, *The*

Key: A True Encounter.

The visitor said that we were not allowed to leave the planet because of the Holocaust. Whitley questioned his remark. The visitor said, "It reduced the intelligence of the human species by killing too many of its most intellectually competent members."

Strieber agitated, responded, "You could say that about any war. Wars kill good people. World War One stripped us of the whole and best of European civilization. And World War Two did even worse, and yet we all survived. The civilization survived."

Then the visitor or as Strieber later called him, 'The Master of the Key' got more specific. "Because of the Holocaust, it is why you're still using jets after their invention. Now it's 100 years later, and you're still using them."

Strieber, at this point, was ready to throw the visitor out, but he stopped when he said, "The understanding of Gravity is denied you because of the absence of a child; the child of a murdered Jewish couple. This child would have unlocked the secret of gravity, but he was not born because his parents went, and the whole species must stay now."

Souls are given a mission, and if they don't have a chance to reincarnate at a certain time, they may wait for centuries before coming back to Earth again. That mission may never come to fruition again.

The visitor also talked about a huge upheaval underway on Earth. How many will survive the upheaval is unknown but there will be fewer humans left on this planet.

When you think about how each life is sacred and how each soul has a specific mission in life, but if that life is cut short and doesn't have a chance to survive, it can't fulfill its mission. We have probably been robbed of an unknown number of brilliant souls that could have made great advances for humanity, but couldn't incarnate for various reasons, one of them being abortion. We are already living in a world where abortions are paramount for women who want abortions up until birth. What if Nikola Tesa had not been born and given us the many inventions that have changed our world? What if German-born scientist Albert Einstein, (1979-1955), a Jew, was killed by the Nazis, we would not have the theory of relativity, equation $E=Mc^2$, which states that energy and mass (matter) are the same thing, but in different forms. He is also known for his discovery of photoelectric energy, which won a Nobel Prize in Physics in 1921.

Einstein is held as one of the greatest and most influential scientists of all time, and Robert Oppenheimer, a Jew, (1904-1967), gave us the atomic bomb that ended World War II. Many Jews and non-Jews died in World War II which could have changed our world. Why is there such anti-semitism taking place in the world? Can you imagine a world without Jesus, Einstein, and Oppenheimer? I can't!

In Dr. Clarke's story about Leland, he told her that watched as cloned humans exited spaceships on the reservation. "THEY LOOK LIKE HUMANS, BUT THEY'RE NOT HUMANS. A FEW YEARS AGO, SIX TO BE EXACT, A CRAFT CAME IN, HOVERED IN THAT FIELD, AND LOWERED A CAR TO THE GROUND." He was told by the aliens that the human-looking beings were being transported to different cities in the United States. Is this the reason for the mayhem and protests taking place throughout the United States now? Sounds incredible but are we dealing with cloned humans who aren't human but doing the bidding of reptilian aliens who want chaos in our major cities worldwide?

Currently, there are beings both humans and aliens who intend to destroy us and Earth. It is time for humanity to awaken from their deep sleep and realize that we are the co-creators of our world. We are faced with the possibility of our own extinction by nuclear weapons in another World War. But Jesus told us, "Where two or more of you are gathered in my Name, there am I also." Jesus said we have the power to move mountains.

A new consciousness change must take place within each of us. You are part of the Galactic Family and have powers you have buried for eons. In the coming years, you will be forced to realize the lies and games that have been played on you. You will discover that certain leaders and military are working with Reptilian aliens and not for the betterment of humankind.

We are visited by beings of other planets that enter and leave Earth's gravitational field without any effort. It is not the gravitational field that keeps us chained to Earth. It's our consciousness!

Together we are on a grand journey to learn the mysteries and wonders of the universe. More and more alien species will find their way to visit Mother Earth, and not all of them are here to watch over us, but there will be those who will have compassion for us and will guide us on our Cosmic Journey. Great wars were fought in ancient times by opposing alien species, according to ancient Indian Vedic records. Will this war be fought again? I have no doubt!

Betsey Lewis

AFTERWORD

Dr. Ardy Sixkiller Clarke

According to reliable sources that I know, Dr. Ardy Sixkiller Clarke had heart surgery in 2019 and other major health complications. We can only pray that she will make a full recovery and return to writing more fascinating books on Indigenous people and their encounters with aliens. My source said that Ardy will probably never write another book, and that is a tragedy for everyone in the ufology field. One YouTube video claims she gave an interview in 2021, but that's doubtful. It appears she has not given an interview since 2017 or 2018.

Oddly, her original book, *Encounters with Star People*, was removed from the bookstores and Amazon. Did someone feel there was too much information revealed in one of her stories? One Native American friend warned Ardy that she should be careful with the information she reveals.

On July 11, 2013, I interviewed Dr. Ardy Clarke on my Rainbow Vision Network about her first book *Encounters with Star People*, and she returned to my show on February 9, 2015, to discuss her *Sky People* book. Dr. Clarke gave two amazing interviews, still available on YouTube. She gave us critical information about the connection between aliens and Indigenous people, and why they are abducted more than other races. Indigenous people have something special in their DNA that aliens want.

It was an honor to have interviewed such a courageous author, Dr. Ardy Sixkiller Clarke, who traveled alone throughout the United States, Central America, and Hawaii to gather true stories of aliens and UFOs from the Indigenous people who normally don't give interviews to strangers. Dr. Clarke showed us that there are benevolent Blue Men who save lives, but the Grays and Reptilians represent a threat to humanity with their dark agenda to change us into controlled hybrids. Many of those people abducted believe a showdown between the dark aliens and humans will take place in the near future. One Native American told Dr. Clarke that humans had superpowers long forgotten through the thousands of years on Earth, and now it is time to reawaken those powers for our survival against malevolent aliens.

The first interview in 2015, received 13,126 views but was removed by YouTube for unknown reasons. Betsey
Encounters interview:
https://www.youtube.com/watch?v=aLfFmjBaFFs
Sky People interview:
https://studio.youtube.com/video/L-dVlncRGkU/edit

The following interview took place between Alex Tsakiris and Dr. Clarke about her *Encounters with Star People* in 2016.

Dr. Ardy Clarke: If you approach it from a perspective that it is part of the universe and that it's nothing to fear, then that's one view. But to be skeptical of it and not believe what you've seen or to deny that it occurs is a totally different worldview. On my way back home I got to thinking, 'Do I want to spend the next five years of my life doing research and evaluation, which is what I've been doing for 30 years at Montana State University? Or do I want to write this book?' Obviously, I chose the latter. I decided to write the book, and not only to write this one but I hope to do two more. One on the Maya and the indigenous people of Central America and Mexico and one on the indigenous people of the South Pacific.

Dr. Ardy Clarke: As I was growing up as a child, my grandmother told me a story that the Star Men came to Earth and they lived with the Sun Women. The Sun Women were the women of Earth. A time came when the Star Men had to leave the Earth and the women of Earth were very upset. So a council was held and it was decided that those who wanted to stay could stay behind and those who wanted to return to the stars could return to the stars.

My grandmother would say to me, "You are a descendant of those Star People and the people of Earth." And that all of us have a special plan for us on this Earth for that reason. So, for me, it was a story that I was told and as I grew older, of course, I put those stories away. They were the stories of my childhood. When I became an adult, it had no impact on my life until I met this individual who told me his personal story. Of course, that brought back all of these stories of my childhood.

Dr. Ardy Clarke: I think that's the thing I was always sensitive to. First, I didn't want to be branded at Montana State University as some psycho professor who was out there advocating belief in UFOs. But at the same time, in the Native community, I wanted to be credible. I think that the key to my success with Native people is that what I did is I just put feelers out.

I didn't go and attempt to coerce anyone into telling their stories. Some of the people, as I revealed in the book, I'd known for 25 years before they ever told me their story. Even though I was part-Native myself, there was that credibility test that I had to pass before the stories came forth. I hope that that shows in the book that the people who confided in me were people who trusted me.

Alex asked about the story of Harrison.

Dr. Ardy Clarke: Well, I think the story that Harrison tells of the craft that crash-landed on his grandfather's ranch in a remote section of the reservation, and the survivors lived there until they were rescued sometime later. He took me to the ranch; he showed me where the event occurred. He told me about how when he was a boy, he had boarded the craft and what he saw and what he felt. His grandfather wanted to remove things from the craft and his grandfather wouldn't allow it because he said it was sacred.

Then the Corps of Engineers came in at a later time and built a dam that literally destroyed any evidence of the craft. His grandfather always believed that as they were excavating the land there, they had discovered the craft and had taken it away. Now this was back in the '40s and obviously, when I talked to him about it, he said there were very few cars on the reservation at that time. He said people would stand beside the road and just watch this equipment go by because they were so enthralled and fascinated just by the size of the equipment and the vehicles that were passing by.

He said they could have removed anything. His grandfather always felt that was what had happened. But his grandfather was also very pleased that he had kept it a secret, that he had somehow protected them from the outside world, and that they had lived there free of observation and free of detection on his land and he was the one who had done that. I had known Harrison for 25 years. I had gone onto the reservation as a consultant, sent there by the university because the school district in the community was attempting to get a bi-lingual education grant funded by the Federal government. They had several children in the school district that did not speak English. They spoke only the Native language.

Harrison resented that. He was a cultural person and the one that everybody turned to, so he resented what he considered university interference. So, it took time to gain his trust. Over the years we became close and became friends but it took him 25 years before he told me this story. And I have no doubt whatsoever that what he told me was true.

Alex Tsakiris: Let's get to that. I think that you have a certain credibility that comes through, not only with Native American tribes but in your work, a longtime, highly regarded academic who is not only familiar with the university but is working with government programs and has the credibility that goes with that. I do think it's interesting in a couple of ways. It sounds like you were the only person who really could have written this book. I mean, it takes a certain tenacity to stay with this thing for that long, but also the kind of trust that's required.

What comes through is that these folks who you collected these stories from don't fit the normal profile of people who are putting forth a UFO story either because it was the most traumatic thing in their life or because they have some other kind of ulterior motive. It sounds like there was a different agenda here in terms of these people. A lot of them have incorporated it into their life just fine and brought it out because you probed, right?

Dr. Ardy Clarke: Right. It was a story that they had shared perhaps with family and friends. Some of them had never told anyone. I think just my presence and when they told me the story, I never tried to interject any personal opinions into what they were telling me. I let them tell the stories without judgment. I'm a social scientist; I'm not in the hard sciences so I wasn't demanding in terms of, "Well, where's your proof? You've got to have some kind of proof." I wasn't looking for that. "You tell me your story. You tell me what happened and I will listen."

Alex Tsakiris: You did something that's much more valuable. You just gathered a lot of these first-person accounts. When we really sort through them and sift through them, we can start looking for the same kinds of patterns that let us know whether they're reliable accounts. I think that's a lot better than tracking down some ticky-tacky photos or little remnants that someone has of it. I don't want to say that, because both can be valuable, and you do have some first-person experience that you had with trace phenomena and all the rest of that. All of it's good.

Dr. Ardy Clarke: I think both approaches are valuable, but I think that hard science often criticizes social scientists. I've had some of that. I didn't set out from the perspective of trying to attack or criticize or delve into motivations or "Where's your proof that this happened," that kind of thing. I just recorded the stories. I think because of that I got some very honest, open accounts of what occurred.

Of course, I think the trust that came along with that was the guarantee that I would not reveal the identities of the individuals. Down the road, if some of them want to come forward and say, "Hey, I'm the person in Dr. Clarke's book," that's fine. But I am committed to anonymity, and I intend to honor that. Many of the people who actually told me the stories have passed now. These stories go back 20 to 25 years.

Alex Tsakiris: What's been the reaction from within the Native American community about the book?

Dr. Ardy Clarke: Nothing. I haven't heard anything from the Native community.

Alex Tsakiris: Anything positive like they want more stories or negative like, "Gee, I wish you wouldn't have brought that out?"

Dr. Ardy Clarke: I haven't heard anything from the Native community. I've had a couple of emails attacking me because I used the term, "American Indians" in the book instead of Native Americans. They were saying, "If you were a Native American you wouldn't call Indians American Indians." Although the book, in the very front of the book, I explain why I used the term "American Indian."

Several years ago, back when I was still in academia, there was a group of us who were Native researchers who decided that we were no longer going to use the term "Native American" in our discussions in general about Native Americans because we based it upon the fact that the term "Native American" was increasingly being claimed by those individuals who were born within the United States, regardless of their ethnicity. When we would say we were Native American, somebody who was not of American Indian heritage would say, "I'm a Native American, too. I was born here."

Alex Tsakiris: I'm six generations Native American.

Dr. Ardy Clarke: So what we decided to do, along with the award-winning journalist Tim Giago, who was the founder and editor of *The Lakota Times* and *Indian Country Today* and *Native Sun News*, we decided that even though Indian is a misnomer, for generic purposes we were going to use the term "American Indian" because any politically-correct thinker who believes "Native American" is the preferred identification tag for any tribe is wrong.

We prefer to be called "Lakota" or "Northern Cheyenne." By our names but if not, "American Indian" is an acceptable term because of the Native American. And I think rightfully so. People who are born here have the right to consider themselves Native Americans. So there have been some attacks along that way toward me but obviously, the people who attacked me hadn't read the book, or at least not my explanation of why I used that term.

Alex Tsakiris: What's been the reaction from within the UFO community?

Dr. Ardy Clarke: If you talk about the UFO community, the people who are in power and the people who you see their names at conferences — total silence. Whitley Strieber has certainly been positive but I'm not sure he's a part of that community as such. My leaders have been just unbelievable. The accolades, reviews, comments, and emails I get have been not one negative one from any of those.

Alex Tsakiris: Where I'd like to go next, I do think that the UFO phenomena, the ET phenomena, is really an important part of what's evolving as our culture, our understanding of who we are. Obviously how we fit into the world, what this thing called consciousness is. So, what I thought was interesting about your book without this even being the purpose of your book, is you shatter some of the paradigms that are most prevalent within that UFO community.

For example, let's start with the whole origin of the ET phenomena. There's this debate. Did the ETs arrive in 1947 with the explosion of the nuclear bomb and then the crash at Roswell? Is this a recent phenomenon? What would your over 1,000 first-person accounts tell us about answering that question? The "when" question in terms of this phenomenon?

Dr. Ardy Clarke: I think for a majority of the people I interviewed; their opinion is they've always been here. That it's not a new phenomenon. They have been visiting Earth for many, many eons. One person said, "Before the beginning of time," when he was telling me some of the ancient stories. He said these stories go back to the beginning of time. They are the old, old stories. Of course, I don't include those in the book but what he was saying to me is that this is nothing new. We've always had interaction with the people from the stars. But I also met other people from different tribes who had no connection or no stories that were related to that. It would appear that, depending upon the tribal group, that also varied. I don't know if you read it but one story, the young man who told me about his grandfather who, when he was a young man, helped bury an alien in the desert. And this was before Roswell.

Alex Tsakiris: I don't remember the story.

Dr. Ardy Clarke: The young man who told me about his grandfather who buried the alien along with some other teenage boys. They found him wandering in the desert and he died, and they just buried him and never told anyone. They considered that Star Person to be a messenger from the Sky Gods. They buried him. It's just a different kind of relationship that we're talking about here.

Alex Tsakiris: Another aspect of the ET/UFO phenomena that we're constantly trying to get our arms around, once you cross the chasm and say, "Okay, there is something here that we need to study and we need to understand," let's jump over there. All the rest is kind of silly to ignore it.

Are we talking about a nuts-and-bolts phenomenon i.e., flying saucers and vehicles and beings? Or are we talking about a consciousness phenomenon? Inter-dimensional, mind control, dream kind of phenomena? Or is it both? What does your research tell you?

Dr. Ardy Clarke: I think it's a combination of both. I've found that to be present, particularly in some of the Maya stories, that traveling back and forth between dimensions. In fact, sometimes I think when I was listening to some of the Mayan elders that probably the Mayans were the first-time travelers because they seemed to have that ability or at least that knowledge of how to travel back and forth. But then Black Hawk also had that ability, the great Sioux medicine man.

I think most of the stories that are recorded in my book were the nuts-and-bolts kind of things. What I find most interesting about them is that they weren't channeling somebody. They weren't under hypnosis. They were telling stories as they remembered them. They were not under some kind of hypnotic spell.

Alex Tsakiris: Let's touch on the potential agenda here, which is speculative and a tricky topic to even approach. I was listening to a presentation the other day by a UFO researcher, Barbara Lamb, who's done regression therapy work with over 1,000 people who claim to have had contact with aliens. She, like many others, has the distinct impression that there's some kind of interbreeding, a hybridization process going on here. Do you have any thoughts on that?

Dr. Ardy Clarke: I had no stories of that among American Indians, but I did encounter it in Mexico and Guatemala, of women who claim to have been abducted and to have borne hybrid children. I had one young woman tell me the story that she had been in the plaza one evening with her boyfriend and her friends. She was sixteen at the time. Her boyfriend was sixteen. They were walking back home and both of them were taken. She told me how they struggled because they were being pulled up into the sky. They kicked and clawed and tried to get away.

The next day, she realizes she's pregnant and she's never had sex. She and her boyfriend decide that it's a Virgin Birth, like the Virgin Mary. They were very strong, devout Catholics. He decides that he has to marry her because if he marries her there will be no one in the village to criticize isolate or shun them. He will marry her to protect her because he knows it's a Virgin Birth. A few weeks later, as the ceremony is being planned, she's abducted again. When she wakes up the next day, she's no longer pregnant.

Alex Tsakiris: Of course, those kinds of accounts directly relate to so many accounts that other UFO researchers, John Mack at Harvard, Budd Hopkins, just many, many very credible UFO researchers have found the same things. It's interesting that you've run across that, as well.

Dr. Ardy Clarke: I ran across more than one case. I had a wonderful guide who knew what I was doing, and he was taking me to these different sites. Back when I was about fifteen years old a librarian handed me this book called, *Incidents of Travel in the Yucatan*. It was by two 19th-century explorers by the name of Stephens and Catherwood.

They had heard rumors of these great cities in the jungles of Mexico and Central America that had been built and they went there in search of them. Of course, the book chronicles their trip. I had promised myself when I was a teenager that one day I was going to follow in their footsteps and go to all these ancient cities.

Then the years passed, making a living and getting my degree took the forefront and my dream of following Catherwood and Stephens through the jungles took a backseat. The day I retired from MSU I was coming home, and I saw a yard sale with a bunch of books stacked up against a garage door. I couldn't pass that up, so I stopped my car and here I found one of these old books by Stephens. I thought, 'You know, this is something I have to do.' I had read the works by Erich von Däniken and different people who talked about the Ancient Astronauts and everything in these cities.

I was interested in following up not only on Stephens and Catherwood but also finding out first-hand the experiences of modern-day Maya with UFOs. Down there, most of them call them the "Sky Gods." So that's what I set out to do and along the way I had some wonderful people helping me. I was taken to this village where six women came forth to tell me their stories. This young woman who was now in her twenties told me the story of what had happened to her. It was quite an interesting night.

It was interesting, too, because of the lack of sophisticated methods of explaining things. Instead of talking about a UFO, two different women described the spacecraft as a gasoline tank that came down from the sky and sat there. I found it extremely interesting to listen to the way they were describing these craft because they didn't have television in their village. They weren't exposed to sci-fi movies and all the information that's out there. They lived on a hillside in Guatemala, away from all that.

Yet when you read UFO literature about the cigar-shaped craft and here they are describing it as a gasoline tank because that's what they've seen in their environment. So that was really interesting.

Alex Tsakiris: Yeah, that is very interesting. It speaks to all the cultural flavoring we imagine goes on in these accounts, especially when we look at the older accounts.

Finally, Ardy, what I want to talk about is spirituality. If we unpack these experiences with American Indians that you're talking about, we assume going in that there's a different spiritual orientation. I mean, you're in your professional career at Montana State University. You have to walk a fine line like we all do. You can't walk around and say,

"Oh, of course, I believe in spirit communication and talking with the dead. Everyone I know just assumes that that's a truth."

We have this kind of cultural barrier in the West regardless of any kind of religious background we may have in terms of talking about and experiencing spirituality. I think we assume — whether this is true or not and maybe you can tell me if it is — that in American Indian cultures, there's a different set of givens. A different orientation regarding the spirit world. What would you say about that? Is that true? Is that a misconception? How might that play into these accounts and someone's receptivity to this kind of experience that they might have?

Dr. Ardy Clarke: Well, I think again you have to separate tribes. There are some tribes where it's forbidden to even speak the name of a dead person. Whereas in other tribes they believe that when someone dies, they stay with them for a year. Their spirit remains with them for a year and then after a year, they hold a ceremony to release that person. They have ceremonies where they can speak with those who have passed on. They have ceremonies where they can speak with the Ancients or where the Ancients come to them and give them knowledge and answer their prayers or their questions.

It depends on the tribal group. It varies greatly throughout the United States and Alaska. So, it's difficult for me to say that is a general rule, that it has a spiritual connection. But definitely, it does with some of the tribes. There's no question about it. Some of the tribes actually talk — and the Maya do this too. They talk about the trip across the Milky Way. That when you die you cross the path of the Milky Way. See, that's what the Maya believe. They talked about going to Xibalba.

You've got a common theme there that the cosmos plays so much a part in the afterlife and death and the ability of the deceased that they never really die. They just move on into another dimension and then they can come back and communicate with the living.

Alex Tsakiris: See, I just think no matter what subtle differences you might have in that worldview, I think that worldview puts you in a completely different place in terms of dealing with the UFO phenomena. I have to tell you...

Dr. Ardy Clarke: I do, too, because Native people on a whole are accepting of it. They aren't skeptical of it. If you approach it from the perspective that it is part of the universe and that it's nothing to fear, then that's one view. But to be skeptical of it and not believe what you've seen or to deny that it occurs is a different worldview.

Alex Tsakiris: Right. I think if you have that worldview that is so prevalent in our society and our culture and when you deconstruct it, which is what this show is about really, not so much deconstructing it from a UFO perspective but from a straight scientific perspective.

Dr. Ardy Clarke: That is what I was going to say. Don't you think that comes from the fact that modern-day society is so controlled by the scientific evidence of everything? Where in the Native community it is not?

Alex Tsakiris: I do think so. But I even think that's somewhat of a misdirect because I think that the best scientific evidence that we have—for the last 100 years all the best scientific evidence and quantum physics has pointed us in the other direction, right? We've just chosen to ignore it...
Dr. Ardy Clarke: We chose to ignore it, right?

Alex Tsakiris: ...because the materialism that is so much a part of capitalism and the thing that we live in that we love and our computers and all that pulls us the other way. So we can't possibly imagine what it would mean to give all that up. So, we hold onto what's familiar. It has all sorts of other implications, as well.

I guess we are coming to that same point, that maybe there is some reality to when people have an orientation where they're free from that baggage they can look at this and go, "I don't know. That happened. It does relate to these other stories I've heard in my past, so it must be true." It isn't as hard to accept. Does that make it easier for them to incorporate it into their life without getting whacked out and thinking…

Dr. Ardy Clarke: Right, traumatized. I believe that's true because I've found very little evidence of trauma among the people that I've interviewed. Certainly, less than 10%. Maybe less than 5%.

I never sat down and took each story and put it in a category, but I think there was one instance I pointed out in the book where the young woman and her cousin had had an encounter and she had witnessed it. Therefore, she had difficulty dealing with it and dropped out of school because she figured if there was something out there that had that much power over you and could do with you at will, then what was the purpose of even trying to do anything? Of course, over time she came to recognize that that was fruitless behavior. But rarely did I encounter that.

Alex Tsakiris: Well, it's a fascinating work and I'm glad to hear that there may be some more down the road.

Dr. Ardy Clarke: Oh, yes. There will be.

Alex Tsakiris: That's fantastic, Dr. Clarke.

Dr. Ardy Clarke: Right now, there's a look at translating it into Japanese, of all things.

Alex Tsakiris: Wow, that's great. So Japanese and probably Spanish has got to be on the table, too, right?

Dr. Ardy Clarke: I don't know. I haven't heard anything, but I certainly have been in contact with some people who are interested in publishing it in Japan. I just referred them to my editor. I think you know him, Patrick.

Alex Tsakiris: At the Anomalous Press. Yeah, great folks over there. They have some great books. Again, the book is *Encounters With Star People: Untold Stories of American Indians*. A fascinating book. Dr. Clarke, it's been great having you on. Thanks so much for joining me on *Skeptiko*.

BIBLIOGRAPHY

Bledsoe, Chris, *UFO of God*, self-published on Amazon 2023.

Clarke, Dr. Ardy "Sixkiller", *Encounters with Star People* (2012, no longer available), *Sky People* (2014, *More Encounters with Star People* (2016) and *Space Age Indians* (2019), Anomalist Books, San Antonio, TX 78209. *More Encounters with Star People* (2016) Anomalist Books, San Antonio, TX.

Dennett, Preston, *Onboard UFO Encounters*, Blue Giant Books, 2020. *The Healing Power of UFOs: 300 True Accounts of People Healed by Extraterrestrials*, Blue Giant Books, 2019.

Druffel, Ann, *The Tujunga Canyon Contacts*, Anomalist Books, 1980.

Felber, Ron, *Mojave Incident: Inspired by a Chilling Story of Alien Abduction*, Fort Lee, NJ: Barricade Books, Inc. 2015.

Fowler, Raymond, *The Watchers*, New York: *Bantam Books*, 1991, *The Watchers II*, Newberg, OR: *Wildflower Press*, 1995.

Fuller, John, *Interrupted Journey: Two lost hours aboard a UFO – the abduction of Betty and Barney Hill*, Vintage reprint May 10, 2022.

Lamb, Barbara, and Lalich, Nadine, *Alien Experiences*, Laguna Woods, CA: Trafford Publishing, 2008.

Paige, Katie, *Letters of Love & Light - Four Decades of UFO Encounters, Experiences & Sightings Shared with Ufologist R. Leo*

Sprinkle Ph.D., Amazon Kindle, 2021.

Strieber, Whitley, *Communion*, Beech Tree Books, *1989* and *The Key Master*.

Walton, Travis, *Fire in the Sky*, DaCapo Press, 1997.

ABOUT THE AUTHOR

Betsey Lewis is an internationally acclaimed psychic and best-selling author with her yearly prophecy books on Amazon. At the age of eight months old, she and her parents had a UFO encounter on a rural road in Northwestern Idaho late one night as they traveled to Southern Idaho. In 1982, renowned MUFON investigator and best-selling author Ann Druffel hypnotized Betsey and her mother and uncovered the missing two hours from their trip — they were abducted by gray extraterrestrials.

At age seven, Betsey witnessed a UFO hovering above her while walking home from elementary school. Shortly after her UFO encounters, and missing time, she began to experience lucid dreams of catastrophic Earth changes. Betsey has investigated alien abductions stories, UFO sightings, ancient archaeological sites in Louisiana, Native American petroglyph sites in the Northwest, and conducted field investigations into the bizarre cattle mutilations throughout the Northwest during the late 1970s, collaborating with Tom

Adams, author of the *Stigmata Report* and renowned cattle mutilation investigator.

Betsey studied indigenous spirituality with Oglala Sioux ceremonial leader Eagle Man and Spiritual Leader of the Western Shoshone Nation, Corbin Harney during the 199os.

Betsey's guest interviews include Coast-to-Coast AM, Ground Zero with Clyde Lewis, KTalk's Fringe Radio, Fade to Black, WGSO AM in New Orleans, and other well-known shows. She was a keynote speaker at the Alamo/Las Vegas UFO Conference in 2013, and a keynote speaker at the UFO Conference in Albuquerque, New Mexico in 2017. She has authored eighteen non-fiction Amazon books and three fictional children's books available on Amazon.

To learn more about Betsey, her books, upcoming events, and her daily Earth News blog visit **www.betseylewis.com**

ABDUCTED

Made in the USA
Monee, IL
09 June 2024

59192240R00157